Bound for Montana

Emigrants Crossing the Plains. *Engraving on steel by H. B. Hall after a painting by F. O. C. Darley from* Picturesque America; or, The Land We Live In, *ed. William Cullen Bryant, 2 vols. (New York, 1874), 2: facing p. 176*

Bound for Montana

DIARIES FROM THE BOZEMAN TRAIL

EDITED BY *Susan Badger Doyle*

MONTANA HISTORICAL SOCIETY PRESS
Helena, Montana

COVER DESIGN BY Diane Gleba Hall

BOOK AND MAP DESIGN BY Arrow Graphics
TYPESET IN Stempel Garamond

PRINTED BY Friesens, Altona, Manitoba

Distributed by the Globe Pequot Press, 246 Goose Lane,
Guilford, Connecticut 06437, (800) 243-0495

Montana Committee for the Humanities

This project is funded in part by a grant from the Montana Committee for
the Humanities, an affiliate of the National Endowment for the Humanities.

04 05 06 07 08 09 10   10 11 9 8 7 6 5 4 3 2 1

ISBN 0-917298-98-5

PRINTED IN CANADA

LIBRARY OF CONGRESS CATALOGING-IN-PUBLICATION DATA

Bound for Montana : diaries from the Bozeman Trail / [edited by] Susan
Badger Doyle.
     p.   cm.
Selected diaries originally published in: Journeys to the land of gold.
c2000.
     Includes bibliographical references (p.   ) and index.
     ISBN 0-917298-98-5 (pbk. : alk. paper)
     1. Bozeman Trail—History—Sources. 2. Pioneers—Bozeman Trail—
Diaries.   3. Immigrants—Bozeman Trail—Diaries.   4. Frontier and
pioneer life—Bozeman Trail—Sources.   5. Overland journeys to the
Pacific—Sources.   6. West (U.S.)—Description and travel—Sources.
7. West (U.S.)—History—1860–1890—Sources. I. Doyle, Susan Badger.
II. Journeys to the land of gold.

F594.B616 2004
978'.02'0922—dc22

                                                    2003022862

For Roger.

CONTENTS

ILLUSTRATIONS

Preface

THESE SEVEN DIARIES are selected from thirty-three diaries and reminiscences published in a two-volume set, *Journeys to the Land of Gold: Emigrant Diaries from the Bozeman Trail, 1863–1866*. The source documents for the full collection were confined to the civilian, as opposed to the later military, Bozeman Trail experience. They included all the known diaries and reminiscences written by Bozeman Trail travelers to enable scholars and enthusiasts to better understand the emigrant period of the trail's history. The diaries in this abridgement are a representative selection from the larger work.

The diaries are presented as they were written, embedded in an introductory and annotated framework. While the entire diaries were presented in the full collection, the sections covering travel on the trails leading to the Bozeman Trail are excerpted in these diaries, but travel on the Bozeman Trail is for the most part uncut. The introductions and annotations expand upon the physical routes of the trails, the travel experience, and the multicultural context of the Bozeman Trail. They provide information about the people, activities, and events recorded in the diaries.

The introductions to the individual documents offer biographical information about the authors, including what became of them after reaching Montana. The annotations within the introductions and the documents enhance the diaries, providing route information and placing them in social and historical context. The documents themselves are presented with as little editorial alteration of the texts as possible, so as to retain their character, style, and especially spontaneity.

For the most part nineteenth-century spelling, punctuation, and writing style have been preserved. There are two exceptions, both regarding the reproduction of the handwriting in the original documents. First, when the author always used a variant capitalized form in place of a lowercase letter, usually an *S* or *E*, those letters have been rendered lowercase throughout. Second, I have substituted the modern *ss* for its nineteenth-century equivalent, double letters that look like *fs*.

Many words in the documents were commonly spelled differently than today, notable examples being the spelling of *to day* and *to night* as two words. Sometimes the misspelling of a word is helpful, such as when it indicates how the word was pronounced. For example, Fort Kearny (usually pronounced Carney) was occasionally spelled *Kerney*, indicating an alternate pronunciation.

A few diarists used a notebook that allowed lengthy entries, but most of the diarists had limited space to write in, resulting in crowded, cramped, and brief entries. In these instances the punctuation was often sparse and functional, and like the commonly used abbreviations, reflects the need to conserve space. To make unpunctuated passages more readable by today's standards, I have followed the convention of inserting several spaces to indicate a period and a few spaces to indicate a comma. Throughout the documents clarifications and modern place names are enclosed in brackets, while all parentheses occurring in the texts were in the original work.

The diary of Theodore A. Bailey appears to have been rewritten later from notes or a diary kept on the trip, which could cause the reader some confusion. As a rewritten version, it falls somewhere in between diaries written contemporaneously with trail travel and reminiscences written later. Since it retains the distinguishing diary characteristics of timeliness and immediacy, it is labeled as diary but is clearly described in the introduction as having been rewritten.

The diarists represent a range of age, gender, and background perspectives. The first two diaries were written in 1864, the next five in 1866. Abram H. Voorhees, a forty-year-old farmer, revealed no apparent reason for traveling to Montana and immediately returned home to Michigan. Richard Owens and Theodore A. Bailey both intended to prospect in Montana, but they differed markedly from each other. Owens, forty, was a coal miner, a Civil War veteran, and was married with a family. He worked in the mines for a while but returned to Pennsylvania two years later. Bailey, twenty-eight, was an unmarried railroad baggage clerk who stayed in Montana and worked in various mines until his death.

Ellen Gordon Fletcher was a twenty-four-year-old bride who accompanied her new husband to Highland, Montana, where he had previously established a butcher shop. They lived in Montana the rest of their lives. Fletcher's diary offers a much-needed female perspective in the predominantly male Bozeman Trail experience. Davis Willson, twenty-five, and Samuel Finley Blythe, twenty-four, are remarkably similar in many respects. They both traveled with close-knit groups of friends, were Civil War veterans, and were unmarried. However, Willson was a store clerk and Blythe was newspaper typesetter, and both continued working in their occupations in Montana. Willson stayed in Montana the rest of his life; Blythe eventually settled in the Pacific Northwest.

The last diarist, Thomas Alfred Creigh, adds a new dimension. Creigh, twenty-five and unmarried, was a Civil War veteran and clerk. He traveled to Montana as the supervisor of a freight train transporting heavy milling machinery to the mines. Although he had much responsibility, he still had time to read voraciously and keep an interesting diary. Taken together, these diaries portray a wide variety of topics, activities, experiences that illuminate civilian travel on the Bozeman Trail.

INTRODUCTION

EACH NEW GOLD DISCOVERY in the West was a magical lure to mid-nineteenth-century Americans, and they rushed by the thousands to the latest mining region over a myriad of overland and water routes. The Bozeman Trail was one of these overland gold rush trails. A short-cut from the Platte River Road to the Montana goldfields, it was relatively short in length—less than five hundred miles; stunningly brief in existence—a mere four years from 1863 to 1866; and strikingly little used—only thirty-five hundred emigrants traveled over it. Yet the Bozeman Trail, opening in the midst of the Civil War and closing just prior to completion of the first transcontinental railroad in 1869, has the enduring distinction of being the last great overland emigrant trail in the American West.

The significance of the Bozeman Trail transcends its seemingly minor role as an emigrant trail. Its opening initiated a series of confrontations between the federal government and the northern Plains Indians that led to more than a decade of warfare. The conflict was not directly caused by the emigrant intrusion, but rather it resulted when the federal government intervened to protect Bozeman Trail emigrants with military force. In the end, rather than providing protection, military presence provoked the Sioux and their allies to all-out war. A major military campaign and army posts established along the trail marked a turning point in relations between the Plains Indians and the United States government and ushered in the final chapter of the national conquest of the northern plains.

In this context, the Bozeman Trail is best known as the cause of Red Cloud's War. Remarkably little, however, has been written about the initial emigrant period of the trail's history. Most historians and writers have focused on the more spectacular events during army occupation of the route between 1866 and 1868. In addition, a number of military works as well as books by soldiers, officers, and wives of officers stationed at the Bozeman Trail forts have shaped the popular image of the "Bloody Bozeman," a perception of the Bozeman Trail as a dangerous trail embroiled in an Indian war. In contrast, the diaries of Bozeman Trail travelers reveal a more complicated and evolving story.

The Montana gold rush was responsible for a dramatic shift in American migration from California, Nevada, and Colorado to the northern Rocky Mountains in the 1860s. Sparked by the discovery of gold at Bannack in the summer of 1862, the rush was fueled by additional gold discoveries in Alder Gulch in 1863 and Last Chance Gulch in 1864. News of the gold strikes spread across the nation, and miners converged on the region from the West Coast, from the declining mining camps of the Colorado gold rush, and from the eastern states. As a result, the population in the goldfields increased dramatically, leading to the creation of Montana Territory on May 26, 1864.

At first, the central overland routes served as the primary trails to the new goldfields. The main central route, the Platte River Road, went up the Platte and Sweetwater rivers and crossed the Continental Divide at South Pass in southwestern Wyoming. The Overland Trail that opened in the early 1860s roughly paralleled the South Pass route some miles to the south and went through Bridger Pass, Wyoming. Miners eager to get to the new gold camps as rapidly as possible prompted the opening of new routes, ultimately resulting in the northern overland route from Minnesota to the upper Missouri River in northern Montana, the northern water route on the Missouri River to Fort Benton, and the Bridger and Bozeman shortcuts from the main Platte road via the Yellowstone Valley to the Gallatin Valley.

Former prospector John Bozeman was a promoter interested in exploiting the demand for more and faster overland routes to what was then designated as Idaho Territory. In spring 1863 Bozeman and his partner John Jacobs, a longtime frontiersman, traveled east and south from the mining camps in the Beaverhead Valley to the overland trail on the North Platte River. There they intended to organize an emigrant train and guide it to the mines over their new shortcut for a substantial fee.

Bozeman and Jacobs had scouted the new route east down the Yellowstone Valley, around the northern end of the Bighorn Mountains, and then south along the base of the mountains to the North Platte River. Their route went through the center of the Powder River Basin, a large plains area bounded by the Black Hills on the east, the North Platte River on the south, the Bighorn Mountains on the west, and the Yellowstone River on the north. The Powder River Basin was in the middle of a larger region that also included the Black Hills and the Yellowstone Valley. The entire area was the last great hunting territory of the northern Plains tribes.

These hunting lands had been guaranteed to the tribes by the Fort Laramie Treaty of 1851. In an attempt to control Indian-white relations, the treaty stipulated tribal boundaries, required the tribes to cease intertribal warfare, provided for punishment and restitution for future offenses committed by whites or Indians, and gave the federal government the right to establish roads and military posts in Indian territories. The intent of the treaty was to provide protection for the overland route along the Platte River, but the Bozeman Trail created complications. The tribes in the Powder River Basin were understandably wary of the American travelers passing through its center. Native peoples were well aware of the consequences of a new road, having already experienced game depletion and habitat deterioration along the main overland routes as seemingly endless lines of wagon trains rumbled along the Platte road.

Bozeman and Jacobs camped at the telegraph station at Deer Creek, a settlement serving as a military and trading post on the North Platte River. Indians at Deer Creek warned Bozeman and Jacobs that tribes north of the North Platte River did not want emigrants crossing their land. Ignoring the warnings, the two men hired guide Rafael Gallegos, a longtime resident familiar with the region and with the Indians living in it, and organized a train of emigrants willing to travel the shortcut to the goldfields, which set out on July 6, 1863.

They traveled about 140 miles without incident, but upon reaching the area of present Buffalo, Wyoming, a large group of Cheyennes and Sioux approached the Bozeman-Jacobs train and threatened to destroy it if they continued across the region. The emigrants conferred and decided to turn around. Retreating about fifty miles, they corralled again on a branch of the Powder River and sent two men and the guide Gallegos back to the military post at Deer Creek to request reinforcements. Refused an army detachment, the messengers returned to the train. At that point Bozeman and nine men left the train and went through the mountains to Montana on horseback, arriving well ahead of the others. Jacobs and the rest of the train returned by a circuitous route through barren land to the main overland road.

Although this first attempt to take an emigrant party over the shortcut was unsuccessful, the encounter with Indians was critical to subsequent events. It was the first confrontation between members of the northern Plains tribes and emigrants in the Powder River Basin. The Indians had made their position clear, but the reason the emigrants turned back was that they did not think they were strong enough to force the issue. If they had received the military support they requested, they would have been strong enough to fight even a large war party, and the Indian wars on the northern plains might have begun in 1863, two years earlier than they actually did. As it was, the events of summer 1863 signaled to the Indians the beginning of an invasion by emigrant wagon trains and warned emigrants that their presence was not welcome.

Undeterred by his confrontation with tribesmen the year before, Bozeman decided to bring an emigrant party over the shortcut in 1864, this time without Jacobs. He succeeded, leading a larger, heavily armed train over the route to Virginia City without incident. Bozeman's was the first train to arrive in Montana, but it was not the first to leave the North Platte in 1864. An extremely large train, made up mostly of prospectors and led by Allen Hurlbut, left Richard's Bridge on June 16, two days before Bozeman's train departed. En route, Bozeman's train passed the Hurlbut train, which had stopped to let some of the men prospect in the Bighorn Mountains. That Bozeman reached Montana first that year is probably the primary reason the trail now bears his name.

With Bozeman and Hurlbut having established the route, others found it practical as well, and two other trains soon followed. Except on the dry, alkaline segment between the North Platte and Powder rivers and another dry, badlands segment between the Bighorn and Yellowstone rivers there was sufficient water, grass, and timber. The few encounters between emigrants and Indians were mostly peaceful. Only one major fight occurred, involving the third train of the season. About fifteen hundred people in four large wagon trains traveled the Bozeman Trail in 1864 in what was considered a successful travel season on the newly opened route.

The first year of successful Bozeman Trail travel forged a new link between the North Platte region and the burgeoning gold camps in the newly created Montana Territory. Those in Montana saw the trail as a boon to commercial interests and anticipated a prosperous season in the coming summer. Events far to the south, however, changed everything. Colonel John Chivington's unprovoked attack on Black Kettle's Southern Cheyennes on Sand Creek in southern Colorado in November 1864 escalated the level of conflict on the Great Plains. In the massacre's aftermath the Southern Cheyennes and Southern Arapahos moved north in early spring 1865 and formed a powerful alliance with the Upper Platte Sioux and the Northern Cheyennes. The tribes congregated in the Powder River Basin and resolved to fight back.

By spring 1865 the fear of Indian attacks along the Bozeman Trail during the coming travel season was so great that the federal government closed the trail to emigrant traffic. It was an unprecedented action, but one that served official purposes. Freed from the prospect of emigrants in the Powder River Basin, the government organized a punitive military campaign intended to end Indian raiding along the trail. Late in the summer, Brigadier General Patrick E. Connor led a four-column expedition into the region of the Powder and Tongue rivers. His intention was to seek out and destroy Indian bands known to have committed acts of aggression, impress those who had not fought, and build at least two permanent posts. Unfortunately, Connor's Powder River Indian Expedition did not discriminate between Indian bands in its two-month campaign. Attacking the first Indian village he found, Connor destroyed a Northern Arapaho village on the Tongue River— a village far removed from the massive Sioux and Cheyenne villages the soldiers sought.

As Connor carried out his campaign, James A. Sawyers unwittingly led a government road-building party into the area. Apparently before anyone realized the potential for disaster, Sawyers's civilian party received authorization to travel through a region that was the focus of a massive military campaign. Though it had a military escort, Sawyers's train was twice forced to form defensive corrals and hold off Indian attacks, first east of the Powder River and later on the Tongue River. Three civilians and three soldiers were killed in the two engagements, as well as an unknown number of Indians. Sawyers eventually reached Virginia City and proclaimed his expedition a success, neglecting to note that no actual road building had been accomplished.

As inconvenient as the Sawyers train was for Connor, it was significant to the history of the Bozeman Trail. As a federally capitalized venture, the Sawyers expedition signifies the substantial governmental involvement that furthered territorial expansion. Equally important, Sawyers's interaction with the Connor campaign tightened the bond between travelers and government protection. Moreover, although Sawyers's expedition did not actually "build" a road as intended, it led to a major change in the route of the trail in the area west of the Bighorn River crossing.

Connor's Indian campaign failed miserably in its intended purpose by engendering the bitter animosity of the Sioux, Cheyennes, and Arapahos. Though Connor built a military post, Fort Reno, on the Powder River, the fort's presence only served to antagonize. The summer of 1865 also marked the shift from Indian raids on tempting emigrant and soldier targets as they passed through the region to armed resistance against an invasion by the United States Army, which now appeared to be a permanent presence. It was the beginning of total war in the Powder River region.

Despite the army's engagement with the Sioux, Cheyennes, and Arapahos, gold-rush emigrants were not deterred from crossing the contested area. In early spring 1866 the first great post–Civil War migration across the plains was about to begin. As a precaution, the United States Army designated which emigrant travel routes soldiers would protect. One of the routes was the Bozeman Trail, chosen partly as a diversion to keep the northern Plains tribes away from the transcontinental railroad, then being built across southern Wyoming. To safeguard travelers, the army issued orders for the construction of three army posts along the Bozeman Trail. During July and August, troops reinforced Fort Reno and built Forts Phil Kearny and C. F. Smith.

Military occupation of the Bozeman Trail in mid-summer sealed Indian resolve to resist the road. Defiant Sioux, Cheyenne, and Arapaho warriors flocked to the camp of Oglala war leader Red Cloud that summer, initiating what has been called Red Cloud's War over possession of the Powder River region. Contrary to its intended purpose, military presence on the Bozeman Trail did not deter Indian aggression or ensure protection for travelers. In fact, military incursion into lands granted to Indians by the Fort Laramie Treaty of 1851 provoked the tribes to armed resistance against all intruders, emigrant and military alike.

In mid-summer conflict along the Bozeman Trail intensified dramatically. During one week in late July several Indian raids, from the North Platte to the Bighorn rivers, left at least twenty-four civilian travelers and soldiers dead and many more wounded. Indian casualties remain unknown but were probably fewer than those they inflicted. A week after they began, the raids suddenly stopped. In their wake, the army required all emigrant and freight trains on the trail to combine into huge trains that were often accompanied by soldiers. In 1866 about two thousand emigrants and freighters in numerous trains traveled the route to Montana, but increased danger from Indian raids made civilian travel impossible after 1866.

For the next two years the Bozeman was used solely as a military road between forts. When the railroad passed Cheyenne in spring 1868, the primary reason for keeping the Bozeman Trail open—protecting railroad construction crews—became moot, and the army was withdrawn that summer. By August 1868 the army had abandoned all three Bozeman Trail forts and left the Indians to believe they had driven the soldiers from their territory. The trail was not used again until 1876, and then as an invasion route during the Great Sioux War.

WHEN THE BOZEMAN TRAIL emigrants proceeded through the Powder River Basin and up the Yellowstone Valley, they did so almost wholly unaware they were entering a region already beset by dynamic, shifting patterns of Indian occupation. In the mid-1860s the predominant tribes in the Powder River Basin were Oglala and Miniconjou Sioux, Northern Cheyennes, and Northern Arapahos. The Crows lived west of the Bighorn River, and the Blackfeet, Piegans, and Bloods ranged in the upper Yellowstone Valley. Although hardly fixed, this distribution was nonetheless the product of two centuries of tribal competition for the expansive hunting territory essential to maintaining northern Plains Indian life.

It was a region of joint use and occupation characterized by dynamic intertribal relations. In this competitive environment, tribes facing outside threats or pressures usually maintained separate identities but enhanced their military strength by forming alliances with other tribes. The Western Sioux, Northern Cheyenne, and Northern Arapaho comprised the most prominent alliance, the so-called Sioux alliance, in the Powder River Basin in the 1860s. Based on impressive success in intertribal warfare, the alliance ultimately focused its aggressive power on resisting American invasion of what its members considered their homelands.

The northern Plains Indians were nomadic hunters. Their primary game animals were bison. Mobility was crucial to these pastoral hunters in their highly competitive intertribal environment and thus required substantial numbers of horses. By the mid-nineteenth century northern Plains tribes supported several horses per person. The nomadic cycle of hunting tribes was linked inextricably to the seasonal migration of bison and the requirements of their horses. In turn, as with bison and horses, Indian movements were tied to the vegetation and water in riverine environments and upper drainages. During fall and winter northern Plains peoples lived in dispersed, politically autonomous bands that ranged widely in search of sheltered locations that offered adequate forage, water, and timber. During spring and summer the bands gathered into a large, organized tribal camp circle in which they conducted traditional, collective sacred ceremonies capped by a communal buffalo hunt. When warfare intensified in the 1860s, however, the forays of far-ranging war parties increasingly consumed the time following the ceremonies.

Plains Indians depended on horses for survival and prosperity. Horses were the basis of wealth, power, and prestige, and the tribes relied on them for hunting, warfare, and transportation. Capture from other tribes was the primary means of obtaining horses, and horse raiding soon escalated into intensive intertribal warfare. Raiding for horses was an opportunistic, small-scale military operation with immediate, limited goals. Horse raids were perceived as "capturing" rather than "stealing" because in Plains Indian belief, seizing an enemy's horses was a means of capturing his power.

The tribes' predominant focus on horse raiding ultimately determined how they responded to emigrants. To incorporate warfare against invading whites into traditional intertribal warfare, warriors viewed the emigrants as another tribe and thus considered them worthy opponents. Consequently, when emigrants left the North Platte River to enter Indian-occupied territory, they became attractive targets for Indian raiding parties, whose members viewed the intruding Americans as alternative tribal opponents. In the Indian perspective, captured emigrant wagons provided useful commodities: oxen were a source of food, and horse and mule herds became prized objectives. The emigrants offered the perfect opportunity for Indian raiding tactics—notably ambush, strike, and retreat—because they moved slowly and loosely guarded their animals, and small groups of men often strayed from the main group.

During the years of the Bozeman Trail, the rapid shrinking of bison numbers and range intensified the endemic intertribal warfare on the northern plains. Decades of subsistence hunting of bison and the Plains tribes' entrance into the market economy left the once-huge bison population seriously depleted. These historical forces were aggravated by a devastating drought in the 1850s and early 1860s at the end of the Neo-Boreal, or Little Ice Age. By mid-nineteenth century the bison range was also being used by more than forty thousand Indians, tens of thousands of their horses, and huge feral horse herds. The bison decline brought hardship, and by the 1860s the northern Plains tribes were on the verge of crisis—just as the Bozeman Trail emigrants entered the scene.

Indian fears about the effects of white emigrants were legitimate, but it should be noted that the Bozeman Trail had a markedly different environmental impact on the lands it traversed than did the Platte River Road on its heavily trodden route. In contrast to the Platte route, the Bozeman Trail was similar to the long-distance Indian and trader trails. Coursing through the Powder River Basin, it crossed streams and moved on rather than remaining in the river valleys like the roads along the Platte. The Bozeman Trail, which skirted the main Indian camping areas located farther down the rivers, merely added another traffic corridor to traditional Indian trails. Although the Bozeman Trail trains comprised a comparable number of people and animals as lived in the larger Indian villages, the emigrants intended to pass through the area, not settle there. Their impact on the land and resources was transient and limited compared to the continual, intense impact of Indian hunting and habitation. Nevertheless, both Plains Indians and whites universally believed that emigrant trails disrupted, and would eventually destroy, the bison habitat. The Indians were determined to prevent the opening of this new road, fearing it would mean starvation for their families.

Thus the Bozeman Trail catalyzed simmering tensions by bringing fundamentally different, culturally determined perspectives into contact. What Americans viewed as "stealing," Indians considered "capturing." What was to the emigrants an "attack," "fight," or "victim" was to the Indians a "raid," "contest," or "target." Because emigrants were oblivious to the nature of intertribal relations in the region, they viewed Indian raids as unprovoked aggressions. Instead of whites seeing themselves as targets of opportunity in an environment of intertribal warfare, they saw themselves as victims of savage and vengeful people and termed the attacks "depredations" and "hostilities" in emigrant accounts, official reports, and newspaper stories.

In spite of their preconceived notions, the emigrants' views of Indians often changed during their journeys. Early in the journey, raids by Pawnee and Sioux tribesmen caused many emigrants to fear Indians. Others merely regarded them as beggars and thieves. When Richard Owens came to a large Sioux village on the Platte River, he wrote, "The people were well clad, but are all inveterate beggars and thiefs. . . . These Indians stole many things from the emigrants."[1] Farther along, emigrants encountered bands of Sioux living at military and trading posts, and many diarists recorded more favorable impressions. Nellie Fletcher described at length the colorful clothing, jewelry, and hair ornaments of the Sioux Indians camped around Fort Laramie, concluding, "They were dressed in style, I tell you."[2] To Davis Willson, the Sioux he encountered near Scotts Bluff "seemed very friendly." He recorded, "The Chief was the handsomest & most honest looking Indian that I have seen."[3] On the Bozeman Trail in 1866, prior to the July series of raids by allied tribes, emigrants traded with Arapahos, obtained trail information, and received assistance at river crossings.

Concern about Indian danger, expressed in many Bozeman Trail emigrant diaries in 1864, is often exaggerated in modern interpretations

1. Owens diary, June 11, 1864.
2. Fletcher diary, June 9, 1866.
3. Willson diary, July 7, 1866.

of the emigrant experience. That the Indians meant to resist the road appears to have been common knowledge, and travelers' concerns were based on that belief. As Richard Owens approached the Bozeman Trail, he wrote: "The Indians are very wicked. Stealing horses and mules. Yesterday they killed a man right on the road near where we are now encamped. . . . Travelling is very dangerous now on the plains *on account of the Sioux Indians, who are bent on murder and theft.*" Two weeks later, other emigrants in Owens's train, also concerned about Indian danger on the Bozeman Trail, met to discuss their options prior to departing. Owens summarized their anxieties: "This day there was a motion put forward and carried in the morning for the indiscriminate slaughter of all Indians, but was reconsidered and acted upon in the evening and resulted in favour of letting them alone so long as they did not intrude on us."[4]

IF RELATIONS with Indians provoked much emigrant discussion, the predominant focus of overland travelers was logistics. Both men and women busied themselves with preparations, wanting to ensure they had adequate supplies for the journey as well as goods to begin their mining efforts. They also needed to plan how and with whom they would travel, and then they decided which route they would take.

The mode of travel, and how to obtain it, was the first key decision. Emigrants used all kinds of wagons, including farm wagons, freight wagons, and ox carts. Many started from home with a wagon, while others bought wagons in outfitting towns, where thriving businesses sold wagons, equipment, and provisions for the overland journey. Emigrant wagons were almost always covered with canvas or other heavyweight, durable cloth, stretched over shaped wooden bows. Emigrants often carried extra wagon bows in their wagons. Made of hickory, they were hard to come by on the trip.

The majority of emigrant wagons were drawn by oxen, although by the 1860s emigrants and especially freighters increasingly used mules. A few emigrants used horses to pull light wagons or carriages, but most horses were brought along for riding. Oxen and mules, the two main choices for overland travel, were both developed to work specifically as draft animals. Oxen are castrated adult male bovines called steers that have been trained to work. Those used to pull wagons were normally at

---

4. Owens diary, July 1, July 14, 1864.

least four years old. As trail animals, oxen were slower but had several
advantages over horses. They possessed greater pulling power through
obstacles, performed better in rough uneven terrain, and were less sus-
ceptible to disease. In addition, they required less training, needed sim-
pler equipment, and generally did better in any situation requiring
endurance and patience rather than speed. At least two-thirds of all
overland emigrants used oxen to pull their wagons.

Mules were the primary competitors of oxen on the western trails.
A mule is the hybrid offspring of a male ass (a genus that includes the
donkey) and a mare, or female horse. Mules were faster than oxen but
not as strong. Thus, because more of them were required to pull the
same load, they were more expensive to use, and unlike oxen, which
eat only grass, mules require additional kinds of feed. Some emigrants
used mules to pull light wagons or buggies, and some of the Bozeman
Trail freight trains were mule trains.

Regardless of the beast of burden used, traveling by wagon train
could be expensive. John Campbell's widely used guidebook, *Idaho:
or Six Weeks in the New Gold-Diggings*, recommended a nine-month
outfit for wagon travel. For four persons, the guide estimated that three
yokes of oxen, a farm wagon and cover, food, and equipment would
cost $600. This compares to the average price of $150 that individuals
were charged for passage with a wagon owner. In addition to the initial
outlay, there would be expenses along the route for ferries, services,
and purchases. It was a considerable expenditure. An option for men
without money was to hire on as a driver, herder, or teamster.

An adequate food supply for the journey was critical. Supplies necessary for the three-month trip from the Missouri River to Montana
included flour, beans, rice, bacon, coffee, sugar, crackers, and a wide
variety of condiments. Nellie Fletcher listed "sixteen quarts of tomato
catsup" and "a little keg of Golden Syrup" among her provisions.[5] Most
travelers also packed dried fruits, dried vegetables, and canned goods.
Many emigrants also took a barrel of whiskey, which several diarists
mention when commenting on celebrations of special occasions such
as the Fourth of July or the accomplishment of a difficult task. Whiskey was also commonly thought to be a treatment for snakebites. In
addition to food supplies, cooking and eating equipment, from dishes
and kettles to frying pans and churns, were necessary. Some emigrants
even carried sheet iron cook stoves.

---

5. Fletcher diary, May 23, 1866.

Also essential were tools—axes, saws, and devices for repairing wagons—and such spare wagon parts as axles and wheels, all of which would be difficult if not impossible to repair or replace on the trail. Knowing the distance traveled was important to many emigrants. Some estimated the number of miles traveled each day while others tracked their mileage using an odometer attached to one of their wagon wheels. An odometer, sometimes called a roadometer, was a device attached to a wheel of known circumference, and each turn of the wheel acted on sets of cogs that recorded the mileage with a high degree of accuracy. Odometers were developed in the United States in the mid-1830s to be used on carriages. By the 1860s they had been improved significantly and were widely available commercially, although many were home-made affairs.

Candles were another necessity. Experienced travelers preferred candles made from sperm whale oil rather than tallow, because oil candles were less likely to melt and run together in the heat of the trip. Many emigrants packed their clothes in bags rather than trunks because the pliable bags took up less space in the wagon. Blankets, quilts, pillows, mattresses, and other bedding articles were packed. Nellie Fletcher listed "a straw bed and feather bed and pillows, one sheet and two blankets" for her bedding.[6] Some emigrants slept in their wagons, others in tents, and some made their beds under their wagons. No one slept out in the open for fear of an oxen stampede.

Emigrant guidebooks were popular throughout the western emigrant trails era. The only published guide that included the Bozeman Trail was commonly known as Campbell's guidebook. In summer 1863 John Lyle Campbell, a reporter for the *Chicago Tribune*, traveled overland to the gold camps in newly designated Idaho Territory. He toured the region gathering information about placer gold mining, and while he was in Virginia City he talked with John Bozeman, who gave him a table of distance for the route he reportedly surveyed earlier that year. Campbell returned to Chicago in late fall, and his book, *Idaho: or Six Weeks in the New Gold-Diggings*, was published by the Tribune Book and Job Office, Chicago, in 1864. It was also published later in the year in New York and again in Chicago in 1866.

In addition to describing the placer mines in Idaho, Campbell's book was intended as a guidebook for travelers. He provides information about outfitting and itineraries for the major overland routes to the

---

6. Fletcher diary, May 18, 1866.

gold mines. While his information is mostly accurate for the main routes, his distances for the Bozeman Trail are woefully inadequate because Bozeman, his sole source of information, never actually traveled the exact route of the Bozeman Trail when he and Jacobs scouted it in spring 1863. As a result, virtually every diarist who used Campbell's guidebook complains about its lack of accurate information about the Bozeman Trail. Nonetheless, it was the only guidebook available at the time that included the Bozeman Trail and was considered necessary for travelers contemplating taking the route.

Beyond practical arrangements and equipment, national events and rapid changes in transportation and communications defined the Bozeman Trail's character and shaped the emigrant experience in ways that distinguished it from that of earlier overland travelers. The Civil War in particular set the context for the Bozeman Trail. Because gold was needed to support the war effort, the Union government in Washington promoted migration to the gold regions in the West. Consequently, tens of thousands of Americans, both Northern and Southern, migrated west. They came mostly from the rural Midwest, having chosen not to participate in the war for a variety of personal reasons. The emigrants brought their loyalties with them, but their accounts offer little evidence that the war caused excessive tension on the trail or shaped the makeup of the trains.

Regardless of their sentiments, emigrants were fascinated with war news, to which they had access via telegraph. Completed in 1861, the telegraph line ran along the central overland trail that followed the Platte River, the route that Bozeman travelers took to the Bozeman Trail turn-off. Thus, as long as they traveled along the Platte road, they remained in contact with current news reports. After the war the telegraph continued to connect the 1866 travelers to events farther east.

Improvements in mail service also affected the overland emigrant experience in the 1860s. As long as they traveled the main Platte route, emigrants could pick up or send mail at numerous road ranches, military posts, and telegraph stations. Virtually all diarists carefully recorded every letter sent and received, indicating the value they placed on maintaining communication with those left behind. Emigrants often hungered for national news, and many diarists recorded seeing newspapers and magazines at post offices and hearing news reports at telegraph stations.

Intensified relations between emigrants and soldiers distinguished Bozeman Trail emigrant experiences from those of earlier overland travelers. To the emigrants, the soldiers were the visible representatives of the federal government's presence along the overland trails. Some emigrants took the soldiers for granted and paid them little notice, while others gratefully made use of their services. Still others looked down upon the soldiers and wrote critically of them. Soldiers sometimes expressed an equal dislike for emigrants, viewing the travelers as unruly and demanding nuisances. As friction from overcrowding, exacting travel conditions, and interpersonal strife increased on the trail, tension mounted between the army, the provider of a service, and the emigrants, the users of that service. As a result, each side harbored a growing disrespect for the other.

THE EMIGRANT HISTORY of the Bozeman Trail is embedded in the complexity of western migration. From 1841 to 1869 overland migration to the Rocky Mountains and Pacific Northwest occurred in waves, with the gold rushes representing the crests. Each decade of the emigrant trails era exhibited distinct characteristics as the three gold rush migrations—California, Colorado, and Idaho-Montana—meshed with agricultural migration. One attribute that varied with the type of migration was the percentages of male and female travelers. At least 50 percent of agricultural emigrants went as members of extended family groups. Adult women comprised at least 15 percent of all emigrants, and children about 20 percent.

The gold rushes were markedly different. During the peak years of the California gold rush, 1849–52, the composition of the migration shifted from families to an overwhelming proportion of men—at least 80 percent and at times 95 percent. Similar disruption in the agricultural migration pattern occurred in the next two major gold rushes: the Colorado gold rush, 1859–62, and the Idaho-Montana gold rush, 1863–66. Overall, for the three crests of mining migration, the emigrants were predominantly male—probably at least 80 percent men and about 20 percent women and children.

During gold rushes, men left their families at home if they intended to return after they accumulated a sizable amount of gold. Only those who planned to settle in the new territory took their families along. Women and children thus almost always traveled with family members. Although they shared many of the concerns and responses of the men in their trains, women experienced the overland journey differently. This was primarily because trail life reflected the realities of mid-nineteenth-century gender relations, which were characterized by an ideology of the private, domestic sphere of women in contrast to the public, business-political sphere of men.

As the gold rushes gained momentum, more of the travelers were freighters and merchants, many of whom already had business connections in the region. In fact, one of the most important factors in settlement of a mining region was that a significant number of travelers already had some form of personal connection to their destination. This was certainly true for Nellie Fletcher and her husband Billy, who traveled to Virginia City in 1866. Billy Fletcher had gone there in 1863 and established a business. In 1865 he returned to New York and married Nellie, and in 1866 he returned to Montana with her and two other former Montana associates.

Like overland emigrants of earlier years, Bozeman diarists offer personal views of an experience that was both challenging and rewarding. Their narratives vividly describe not only the journey's hardships, dangers, obstacles, and uncertainties but also its enjoyments and enthusiasms, as well as an appreciation for traveling companions and the landscape. What they wrote reflects the whole range of human experience on the overland trails as well as the ideas, expressions, and themes common to Victorian America. Many diarists' colorful terms and phrases convey the era's American English in such expressions as "first rate," "started in good season," "concluded to," "the order of the day," and "on my own hook."

The diaries included here reflect themes common to mid-nineteenth-century American life. Although men, women, and children wrote differently about the travel experience, they shared similar cultural perspectives and so wrote about similar things—the people they traveled with, why they made the trip, what they saw and did, and their expectations and feelings. Concerned always about their progress, men and women alike recorded distances and told of landmarks and trail conditions.

Travelers wrote of their feelings about Sunday observance on the trail. Religion was an important aspect of mid-nineteenth-century American life, and its observance provided a sense of continuity with the familiar customs of home. But Sunday travel conflicted with religious observance, and thus whether to travel was a major emigrant concern throughout the overland trails period.

Patriotic holidays were important, and many of the Bozeman diarists recorded celebrating the Fourth of July on the trail. Wrote Theodore Bailey in 1866, "we fired a <u>National Salute</u> with guns & pistols this evening & had very good music from a band of 2 violins, bass viol & brass horn."[7]

---

7. Bailey diary, July 4, 1866.

Other diarists mention special foods and beverages served during Independence Day celebrations, including pudding, oyster stew, canned or fresh peaches, lemonade, and milk punch. Milk punch, a sweetened alcoholic beverage, was often concocted for such occasions.

Another shared overland experience, camp activities, served as a recurrent diary topic. Not unlike they did at home, people worked and socialized. But the context was different. Conditions were new, and the community was mobile rather than stationary. The days a train "laid by" in camp provided travelers with the opportunity to do domestic chores, hunt, play games, and relax. Men as well as women did mending and washing. Nellie Fletcher recorded, "I mended Billie's pants for him, put patches of antelope skin on the knees." Though both men and women noted washing clothing, only the men mentioned swimming and bathing in the rivers. While camped on the Platte River in eastern Nebraska one evening, Abram Voorhees wrote, "the boys had a good wash in its waters & after supper they sung songs untill it was time to retire."[8] While in camp on the Bighorn River that July, Voorhees described another typical day: "all is quiet to day   some are out hunting while others are enjoying themselves playing games   trying tricks walking to a pole blindfolded &c." A few weeks later, however, frustrated with having to lay by longer than he wanted to, Voorhees wrote, "our usual work is to lay around camp   some fish   some play cards some are going to & from the camp that is in the canyon just above us & are trying to kill time."[9]

Evening music was a frequent source of enjoyment in the camps. Many of the diarists or others in their trains had musical instruments with them. Davis Willson, for example, played his violin frequently during his 1866 journey. One evening, he "Got out violin. Played some   Charlie R[ich] sang 'What's the old man thinking'. Hopkins [Taylor] sang with him and I played, accompanying him with violin. Mr. Buck ... shed tears."[10] Dances were also popular at evening gatherings in camp. When few women were in the train, the dances were stag dances.

Trail narratives also reflect the group dynamics of a mobile situation—how the trains functioned as communities, the processes of decision-making, assignment of authority, sharing and allocation of resources, and other cooperative behaviors necessary to maintaining social cohesion during what were long, sometimes difficult, and dangerous passages.

---

8. Fletcher diary, June 12, 1866; Voorhees diary, May 4, 1864.
9. Voorhees diary, July 6, July 31, 1864.
10. Willson diary, June 18, 1866.

Each traveling party reflected a unique set of social relations, but the authors in this collection shared a common heritage that recognized hierarchical group structure, sustained deference to authority figures or elected leaders, followed instructions, and operated in an atmosphere of consensus.

Most people traveled to Montana in the parties they began the trip with. A few, not making final travel arrangements until they were ready to depart from one of the Missouri River outfitting towns, joined strangers who were also beginning their journeys across the plains. All of them had become part of larger wagon trains by the time they turned onto the Bozeman Trail. Considering the contingent nature of forming the large trains, interpersonal relations in most were relatively smooth. In some trains, however, members experienced problems getting along with each other and broke up and reformed into new configurations along the trail.

Trains commonly broke apart because the various kinds of teams pulling the wagons traveled at different speeds, causing slower teams to fall behind. But personality clashes were a constant threat to harmonious relations on the trail, especially when a leader in a train was the offender. William Phillips, captain of Davis Willson's 1866 train, was so obnoxious that two diarists noted it. Willson reported Phillips's bad behavior several times, writing finally in exasperation, "Phillips is the meanest man I ever knew." At the Bighorn crossing, when Phillips learned that one of the men in his train was planning to leave and join another train, Willson reported, "he played mean with him by not letting him cross when his turn came, but commenced putting his own teams across." Writing of the same incident, diarist Samuel Blythe said, "One train made a 'flank movement' on the others, and were the first to the ferry."[11]

On rare occasions the leader of a wagon train so irritated other emigrants that they either left his train or elected a new captain. Abram Voorhees experienced both consequences. Voorhees kept a common journal for his company and recorded the increasing dissatisfaction among the men in the train when Hurlbut failed to live up to his extravagant promises to lead them to gold mines. When the men in the train finally became so disgusted with Hurlbut's leadership that they refused to stay with him, Hurlbut left the train in disgrace, and Voorhees was elected captain in his place.[12]

---

11. Willson diary, August 14, August 16, 1866; Blythe diary, August 16, 1866.
12. Voorhees diary, July 5, July 19, 1864.

Bozeman Trail narratives are also filled with reports of dissension over the conditions of traveling. Offensive behavior ran the gamut from quarreling to assault. Resentment and disagreements were most likely to occur at times of difficulty or hardship. A notable example, occurring early in the 1866 travel season, came at the last in a series of difficult river crossings. Theodore Bailey recorded what his party decided to do about some repeat offenders: "our train has dwindled down from sixty five to fourteen wagons, as every ferry has made a good opportunity for men to show their dispositions. some of them as soon as they got over would leave the train. we passed a resolution not to let them back or help them in the least."[13]

Dissension occasionally erupted from the volatile mix of social classes, backgrounds, and occupations thrown together on the trails. Diarists noted problems in both their own and in other groups. In recording a troubling incident in 1866, Nellie Fletcher revealed one way order could be maintained on the trail. One day the train was halted when Mr. Smith hit his wife with the butt of his whip, stunning her. His fellow emigrants, particularly the train's captain, acted swiftly to contain him by compelling him to travel in the middle of the train, where he could be watched, and threatening him with a beating if he hit her again.[14]

OVERLAND MIGRATION was a defining nineteenth-century American experience. The Bozeman Trail diarists graphically convey what it was like to travel over the trail during its brief existence and allow future generations to preserve and understand the emigrant experience long after the trails are gone. The Bozeman Trail era was marked by change—for both the route itself and the character of the emigrant experience. Notably, those who most influenced the routes and character of the trail were the people and forces in place long before John Bozeman attempted his first passage: the Indians, mountain men, and traders in the Rocky Mountains and northern plains. Bozeman pioneered very little of the trail. For most of the route, he was guided by local traders or followed other trains. Yet in our mythic perspective of the past, he has come to symbolize the trail. Focusing on a captivating individual to characterize the frontier experience, the Bozeman Trail typifies the American tendency to reduce complex realities to singular, spectacular concepts and dramatic events.

---

13. Bailey diary, July 12, 1866.
14. Fletcher diary, June 25, 1866.

In contrast to this mythic view, which often simplifies and even misleads, these diaries offer a more complicated, richer story. As carriers of their cultural heritage, these Bozeman Trail authors provide an illuminating glimpse into the larger society and express the expectations, hopes, and preconceptions of mid-nineteenth-century middle-class Americans. Theirs are the stories of men and women seeking opportunity in the American West. Their narratives elucidate, as only primary sources can, the emigrant experience on a gold rush trail, the journey of a lifetime to a new and beckoning horizon.

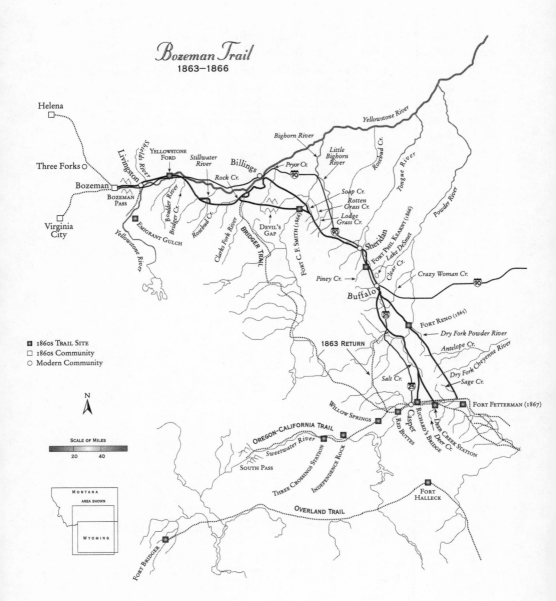

Bozeman Trail
1863–1866

Abram H. Voorhees

DIARY, 1864

ABRAM H. VOORHEES traveled to the Montana goldfields in Captain Allen Hurlbut's wagon train, the first train in 1864 to leave the North Platte at Richard's Bridge and take the Bozeman Trail. Voorhees was forty years old when he started out from his prosperous farm near Mendon, Michigan, leaving at home his wife Sophia, thirty-nine, and daughters Maria L., eighteen, and Ellen S., ten.[1] Voorhees and five other men from St. Joseph County had formed a company to travel to Montana. The other members of the company were James S. Barnebee, thirty-eight and married with three children; Thomas H. Crumbaker, thirty years old and married; F. Columbus Marantette, twenty-two and unmarried; Thomas H. Jacobs, twenty-five and unmarried; and Charles Uptegrove, about whom no other information was found.[2] All six partners in the company were farmers or sons of farmers, comprising a typical cross-section of mid-nineteenth-century rural America.

The members of the company shared duties and expenses, each contributing at least three hundred dollars to the company fund, out of which they purchased draft animals and all supplies for the trip. The partners chose Voorhees—perhaps because he was the oldest and the most prosperous—to keep the records of the company. These included the financial accounts, a daily journal, and copies of three letters he wrote on behalf of the company to the St. Joseph County newspaper. Voorhees

SOURCE DOCUMENT: Abram H. Voorhees, Diary, 1864, original, WA MS S-926, Beinecke Rare Book and Manuscript Library, Yale University, New Haven, Connecticut.

1. The 1860 Michigan census, St. Joseph County, Mendon, p. 37, lists Abram Voorhees as a farmer, with real estate valued at $6,000 and personal property at $950. Abram and Sophia were born in New York, and their daughters were born in Michigan.

2. The 1860 Michigan census, St. Joseph County, Mendon, lists James Barnebe[e] and family (p. 43); Thomas Crumbaker and wife (p. 55); and F. Columbus Marantette in the household of his father Patric[k] Marantette (p. 61). Thomas H. Jacobs appears in St. Joseph County, Sturgis (p. 241). Charles Uptegrove is not listed in the St. Joseph County censuses.

Abram H. Voorhees.

recorded the company records in a ruled composition book, which he titled, on its first page, "Company Book."

Voorhees proved a meticulous record keeper. Throughout the portion of the trip where commodities could be purchased, he noted the varying prices paid, both in the journal and in a ledger in the back of the book. He was also a shrewd buyer. At Council Bluffs he went several miles out of town to pay a lower price for hay, but during the rest of the trip, he had no such opportunity to comparison shop and had to be content with merely noting the fluctuations in prices. The appended ledger is an informative record of expenses for an overland journey. It also includes copies of the three lengthy letters he wrote to his county newspaper describing the trip. If he had not written the diary, the letters alone would have served as an excellent account of this important wagon train. But since they are repetitious and add little to the diary, they are not reproduced here.[3]

Voorhees's diary is significant because it is the only known account of Allen Hurlbut's wagon train. It also adds important information about John Bozeman's 1864 train (which followed Hurlbut's), about which little is known. Voorhees's diary reveals that his company joined Captain Hurlbut's train on May 19, soon after crossing Skunk Creek, 280 miles west of Omaha. Hurlbut evidently impressed the Michigan men with his knowledge of potentially rich goldfields on the Tongue and Bighorn rivers.

More emigrants joined the Hurlbut train as it traveled along the north-side route. When the train arrived at Richard's Bridge on June 11, it had grown to 274 men, two women, and one child. While the Hurlbut train camped at the bridge to organize, John Bozeman was also forming his train there. There is no evidence, however, of communication between the two trains. While the members of Hurlbut's train waited and collected more wagons, Hurlbut went north and explored the proposed route. When his train left on June 16, it was the first to leave Richard's Bridge and travel over the cutoff. Voorhees does not mention hiring any guides at the bridge, so it appears that Hurlbut himself pioneered the new route. Two days later Bozeman's train left Richard's Bridge and followed Hurlbut's track.

Voorhees's diary provides considerable detail about the experience and composition of the large Hurlbut train. It consisted primarily of men who were anxious to get to the nearest gold mines, and reflecting this gold-rush composition, there were 418 men in the train and only ten women and ten children. In his letter of July 17, Voorhees listed the officers of the train: [Allen] Hurlbut of Illinois, captain; A. H. Voorhees, himself, marshall; John Ferguson of Iowa and S. F. Ward of Wisconsin, guard masters; and Samuel Ferris of Illinois, in charge of corrals. Voorhees also gives an interesting fact not usually noted in the diaries, that there were twenty dogs in the train.

---

3. The letters were written at the Bighorn River on July 17, at the Yellowstone River on August 3, and at Virginia City on August 10 to an unspecified newspaper. The tone and nature of the content of the letters suggest that they were written to a local newspaper for publication.

For the first few weeks of the trip, relations between Hurlbut and the Michigan men were apparently mutually respectful. On July 17 at the Bighorn River crossing, in the first of the letters he wrote to his local newspaper, Voorhees wrote glowingly, "Hurlbut is a man of considerable experience as an explorer & ex-prospector having been several times over the Mountains & being familiar with . . . the gold region." But Hurlbut did not live up to his promises that he would lead them to rich goldfields. After several unsatisfactory stops so that some of the men could prospect in the mountain streams, relations between Hurlbut and the emigrants rapidly disintegrated as they neared the Bighorn River. In contrast to his letter, in his diary entry for the same day, Voorhees wrote, "there is not much good feeling towards the captain at this time."

By the time Voorhees wrote his second letter, at the Yellowstone River, the train had acrimoniously split up, and Voorhees had been elected captain. Voorhees wrote that Hurlbut was nearby, "but his conduct towards the company has been in the highest degree censureable & he has few if any friends among those who at first so readily listened to & so imperfectly believed his extravagant stories & golden promises [that] he will probably never lead another train through the Mountains."

In contrast to Hurlbut, Voorhees and the men in his company were respected and looked up to by the others in the train. As Voorhees's diary indicates, they had good teams, used sound judgment, and were well organized. Voorhees, in particular, seems to have won the admiration and respect of the men in the train at large. He must have had an authoritative, decisive personality, as he easily assumed a position of leadership in a time of dissension. His central role in the events of the trip makes his diary all the more meaningful.

Like the members of the other 1864 trains, Voorhees was at least moderately concerned with the possible Indian threat, and he wrote that his train had 2,092 gun and pistol shots available. Nevertheless, the only time they needed their guns was during a dawn raid on their horse and mule herd on July 20, thirty-two miles northwest of the Bighorn River crossing. The unguarded herd was quite a distance from camp, and when the raiders struck, the emigrants were eating breakfast and could not react quickly. The Indians easily got away with twelve horses and mules, leaving the emigrants without enough stock to pull all of their wagons, one of which had to be abandoned. They placed extra guards on the herds after that, and there were no more Indian incidents.

Voorhees's motives for traveling to Montana are unclear. Nowhere in his diary or letters does he state why he went. He seems to have left a comfortable life for an adventure in the gold rush. Consequently, he behaved like a nineteenth-century tourist and traveling correspondent rather than a prospective miner or settler. His diary reflects his desire to keep a detailed record of the experience, and his letters are typical of the kind overland travelers wrote to local newspapers.

It is also a mystery why Voorhees chose to take the Bozeman Trail. He obviously felt that Hurlbut's claims of rich goldfields on the new cutoff were believable and that the danger from Indians was negligible. But once they arrived in the purported mining regions, Voorhees did not go on any of the prospecting expeditions. Nevertheless, he evaluated the circumstances and concluded that Hurlbut had misled them, which he dutifully reported in his letters. And bolstering the notion that he took the trip as a tourist, he and his company avidly hunted the abundant game they found.

Voorhees arrived in Virginia City on August 10. Finding prospects in the mines extremely poor, he and his company decided on the day they arrived to divide up everything in their outfit and go their separate ways. Voorhees noted the high prices of merchandise in the booming town and the correspondingly low price of oxen, which were "coming in by the hundreds every day." They were so anxious to leave that they sold their oxen for the dismal price of $15.00 per yoke, about one-tenth of their value.

Voorhees and James Barnebee stayed in Virginia City only long enough to settle their affairs. On August 15, only four days after they arrived, they hired their passage back to Michigan with Charles Uptegrove, who bought a four-mule team and wagon; they left the same day. They took the Lander Road to the Platte Road, crossed the North Platte at the upper or Guinard's Bridge at Platte Bridge Station (later named Fort Caspar), and continued on the south-side road to Fort Kearny, where they forded to the north side. At Omaha they bought tickets and went by stage to Grinnell, Iowa; from there they traveled by railroad to Chicago. They continued on the railroad to Sturgis, Michigan, and stayed overnight with Hiram and Phoebe Jacobs, the parents of their original traveling companion, Thomas Jacobs, who stayed in Montana with two of the others to try mining.

The next day, October 10, Voorhees arrived at his home near Mendon and wrote, "find the folks all well & ourselves well pleased." His lengthy trip to Montana and abrupt turnabout for home seem inexplicable, except for the fact of his age. Today we might infer that, at age forty, Voorhees had experienced a midlife crisis. This is mere speculation, however, since little is known about his subsequent life. He is listed, with his wife Sophia and daughter Ellen in the 1870 Michigan census for Mendon, as a farmer with real estate valued at $6,600 and personal estate at $1,730. He is also listed as the justice of the peace in Mendon in the 1885 *Michigan State Gazetteer and Business Directory*. Abram Voorhees died at age sixty-eight in Mendon.[4]

Eventually Voorhees's diary and photograph were acquired by the Frederick William and Carrie Sperry Beinecke Western Americana Collection, in the Beinecke Library at Yale University. The diary was written in ink in a legible script. It is a meticulous and detailed record of the expenses and events of the company, enhanced with his personal observations. Voorhees's letters written to the local newspaper, which he copied in the back of his diary, particularly reflect the contemporary practice of travelers corresponding with those in their home communities and providing useful information about such a journey. The letters also reveal how Voorhees's attitudes changed when his expectations were not realized. In his last letter he wrote, "the expenses toil & privations incident to a trip to the mining region are not justified by the real condition of things here." He concluded, "not one miner of a thousand [gets] rich" while only "the trader & speculator & those who have money to work upon profit by the excitement."

Voorhees's writing style in both the diary and the letters is typical of the mid-nineteenth century. Since he rarely punctuated his sentences, I have inserted spaces for reading clarity. His capitalization was erratic, and he seldom capitalized the beginning of sentences. Though his spelling deviates from today's standards, it reflects accepted usage at the time. For instance, he spelled "to day" and "to night" as two words; he wrote "stoped" and "untill"; and he generally used the *fs* variant of *ss*, which was common at the time. In spite of these features, Abram Voorhees's remarkable diary is a coherent and detailed document that reflects the assurance and confidence of its author.

---

4. Abram H. Voorhees, Mendon, age 68, is listed among the recently deceased in the "Memorial Report-St. Joseph County," *Michigan Pioneer and Historical Collections*, 21 (1892), 261.

ABRAM H. VOORHEES DIARY

COMPANY BOOK

This book belongs to a company from Mendon St
Joseph County State of Michigan & their names are as
follows Thomas Crumbaker Charles Uptegrove James
Barnebee Columbus Marantette & Abram H Voorhees,
who on or about the first of March [1864] formed
themselves in a company for the purpose of going to
Idaho & the above named persons did agree with one
another that they would furnish money one as much as
the other & not less than three hundred dollars apiece
that they would stand to & abide by & work for the best
interest of the company share & share alike in all the
profits of the company untill such time as they shall by
mutual consent agree to dissolve their copartnership &
not be bound one to the other any more, & as long we
are a company we do agree one with the other that in all
cases the majority shall rule, and we do further agree that
if one or more of us do wilfully wrong or attempt to
wrong either one of us or the company that he or they
shall forfeit all further claims from the company[5]

    [signed]   Chas. W. Uptegrove

                 Abram H Voorhees

                 T.[homas] H. Crumbaker

                 F. C.[olumbus] Marantette Esq

                 James S Barnebee

                 T[homas] H Jacobs

*[Voorhees and Barnebee started from home on April 4.
They traveled by railroad from Sturgis, Michigan, to
Marshalltown, Iowa, where they met the others, who had
gone ahead to purchase wagons, provisions, and cattle. From
Marshalltown, the company traveled by wagon across Iowa
to Council Bluffs at the Missouri River.]*

5. This written, signed agreement is a rare extant example of a partnership contract for an overland company. The term "company" was loosely used by emigrants to describe a range of informal to contractual arrangements. In this case company refers to a joint-stock organization or partnership.

Wednesday [April] 27th we drove in town [Council Bluffs] & pitched our tent in a ravine in the midst of a lot of others that had camped there   bought some hay & corn for 75 cts per 100 [pounds] & bus[hel]   fed our teams then strolled around town the most of the day the most of [us] got letters from home to day   A. J. VanNess having went ahead of the rest of us the day before to Omaha & came back with the letters for us about noon

Thursday [April] 28th hay has advanced to $1.00 per 100 lbs in town & we thought best to go out in the country to buy   & did so & bought for 60 cts & had it brought in for us   & we bought some corn for 70 cts we have been looking around town to find things that we want to take with us.

Friday [April] 29th to day we bought our flour & some other things that we want to take with us   Abram [Voorhees] went over the river to Omaha to day

Saturday [April] 30th we loaded our flour, meat & some other things we had bought & made preperations to start on Monday   some Centreville boys took dinner with us to day[6]

May 1st 1864, it being Sunday to day we stayed in camp most of the time & wrote letters & fixed ourselves for a start on the morrow   in the afternoon we had a severe storm of wind & towards night it grew cold & remained so all the night   but on Monday May the 2nd it was pleasant & after we loaded in over nine hundred pounds of meat & some few things we had bought we started for the plains   we crossed the muddy Misoura [Missouri River] whose waters were low at the time between ten & eleven oclock   & drove in the city of Omaha where we bought our shovels & picks   & when all was ready our company bought the beer for the boys that were with us   then we left the city & drove five miles & camped for the night on a small stream [Cole

6. The men were from Centerville, Michigan, nine miles from Voorhees's hometown, Mendon.

Creek] that ran through the pararie without any timber
here   we paid two dollars per 100 for hay & $1.00 for
corn here   we cooked our supper with cattle chips

*[The company traveled on the Omaha to Fort Kearny
Road. The road came to the Platte River twenty-five miles
west of Omaha and followed the north bank of the river to
Fort Kearny. When they came to the Platte, Voorhees wrote,
"the boys had a good wash in its waters & after supper they
sung songs untill it was time to retire." The transcontinental
telegraph line was built alongside the road, and the uninsulated
iron wires were a dangerous hazard in lightning storms.
Voorhees noted that they passed a place "where the lightning had killed 5 oxen while passing under the telegraph
wire." At the Loup River crossing, he recorded, "we saw a
man get hurt on the ferry boat" and "saw three boys try to
ride their horses across the river & came near drowning."]*

Thursday [May] 12th was warm & pleasant   country
well setled   passed 3 saw mills one drove [powered] by
wind 2 with water   to day we drove 24 miles & camped
at night on wood creek [Wood River] for the night
found the grass very poor none at noon   Platt river is 6
miles south of here   we saw men marking corn ground
saw one woman planting corn & a negro making fence

Friday [May] 13th the country is still level & good
land   we saw men planting corn in several places   had a
thunder shower in the afternoon & at night we stoped
opposite ft kearny at a ranche it being the last house this
side of Larimie [Fort Laramie] on the north side of the
[Platte] river[7] about 6 miles back we passed a ~~still~~
Brewery[8] but not untill the crowd drank a few gallons
of Beer at 75 cts per gallon   the Telegraph wire crosses
the river here

Saturday [May] 14th we got an early start   but
before we had traveled far & hardly out of sight of the
old flag that floats over Ft kearny [Fort Kearny] we
overtook a train of several wagons that were waiting for

7. The Miller &
Company road ranch
was opposite Fort
Kearny. The proprietor
may have been Lorin
Miller, an early settler in
the area. His son Dr.
George L. Miller was a
prominent physician in
Omaha and the sutler at
Fort Kearny from 1861
to 1864.

8. James E. Boyd
operated a road ranch,
stables, brewery, and
blacksmith shop at
Nebraska Center Post
Office on the emigrant
road on the north side of
the Platte River, ten miles
east of the Miller ranch,
one mile west of present
Gibbon, Nebraska.

more to come up   they had been told there was 2000
Indians camped 5 miles ahead & were prepared for war
we thought best to stop a short time & wait for more to
come & after dinner we made a start with others that had
come along train being about one hundred   we drove
about ten miles & camped on the bank of the Platt river
for the night   we saw no Indians nor anything that
looked like them   but we passed a large village of pararie
dogs   we also saw a number of wagons on the opposite
bank of the river   the grass is still very short & thin

Sunday [May] 15th was warm & pleasant & we
stayed in camp all day   we being in company with a
large train of men with their families bound for
Calafornia   some of our boys went over the Bluffs &
killed two Deer. they saw a number of buffalo tracks
there was a number of wagons passed us to day. we saw
several trains on the opposite side of the river   near here
is grave of a child   Fred Engle gave the crowd a
temperance lecture in the evening

Monday [May] 16th we got an early start & drove
two or three miles & came to a grave of a man that had
been murdered the day before by his comrad   there was
three others with him   there had been some difficulty
between them & the man & his wife started back & had
got over two miles when they saw the 4 men after them
the man leaped from his wagon & ran towards a camp
but the boys that were after him unhitched his mules &
overtook him & shot one shot at him with a rifle the ball
passing through the groin   he then threw down his
pistol & begged for [his] life but his comrad picked up
his pistol & fired two balls through him before anyone
could get there to inte[r]fere   they made no attempt to
escape but after burying the body the crowd that were
camped near[by] took them & kept a guard over them &
sent a man to fort kearny & the officer of the fort came
with some soldiers & took them & the woman to the fort

9. Three days later, on
May 19, Lucretia
Epperson camped near
here on Elm Creek and
wrote: "A few days ago, a
gentleman from Indiana
was murdered near where
we were encamped. He
was murdered by four
men whom he was
bringing to California.

they took the evidence of those that were there that saw
it & heard the quarrel   & the man that first came up to
them after they were done shooting went back at night
they having sent for him from the fort. they detained him
one day & then let him have a government horse to ride
to fort Laramie & overtake his company[9]

[*Soon after Voorhees's party crossed Skunk Creek on
May 19, they overtook Captain Allen Hurlbut's large train
and joined them. The combined train of thirty-six wagons
then passed the junction of the North and South Platte rivers
and continued traveling up the North Platte.*]

Friday [May] 20th we left our camp with the
[Hurlbut] train   our wagons [are] numbers 15 & 16
whole [train] number[s] 36 & after driving a mile or two
we came to a large spring of good water   filled our
things with water & traveled over sandy roads untill near
noon we stoped on the bank of the river [North Platte
River] for our dinner & while we was there an old man
64 years old Died   he was sick but 36 hours   he was
carried along untill night   then he was buried on the
banks of [North] Platte w[h]ere we camped for the night
[at Black Mud Creek][10]

[*Voorhees recorded that the train now included 111 men,
202 head of cattle, and eleven head of horses and mules.*]

Sunday [May] 22nd we had a splendid rain last night
& was raining in the morning but it soon cleared away &
the day was fair & warm wind blowing gently from the
west which made it very good for us to dry our blankets
& some other things that had got wet by the severe
storm of yesterday   & while we are thus doing &
preparing for a start in the morning our cattle seem to
enjoy themselves for they [are] quietly feeding in the
valley above us   on the bank of the [North Platte] river
whose waters are flowing rapidly by   in the evening
Fred Engle gave us a lecture while some were list[e]ning,
others were enjoying themselves in some other way.

The men told his wife
that if she let it be
known, they would put
her out of the way too.
They took possession of
his stock, and proceeded
on their way as if nothing
had occurred. His wife
made it known before
going far, a man returned
to the fort, procured an
officer, and had them
detained before night.
They were made to
unearth the remains of
the murdered man, which
were removed to Fort
Kearney, where the
murderers will be held
for trial. I saw the
ground where the
remains were taken
from." Lucretia Lawson
Epperson, "A Journal of
Our Trip, 1864," in
Covered Wagon Women,
ed. and comp. Kenneth
L. Holmes (Spokane,
Wash.: Arthur H. Clark
Co., 1989), 8:169.

In a letter on May 24,
Jonathan Blanchard also
wrote about the men who
were taken to Fort Kearny:
"Five Missourians are in the
fort opposite here, who
conspired and killed a man
on the road, to get away his
handsome wife. The
soldiers say they are to be
hung." Robert H. Keller Jr.,
ed., "The 1864 Overland
Trail: Five Letters from
Jonathan Blanchard,"
Nebraska History, 63
(Spring 1982), 73.

10. The deceased man
was T. Foster, age sixty-
four, from Ohio, who
was buried at the Black
Mud Creek crossing.
Richard Owens noted
the grave on June 9,
although he recorded the
date of death as May 24.

Monday [May] 23rd we started from camp in good
spirits & drove but a short distance when we were joined
by a party of 15 men with 5 wagons & 38 head of cattle
which makes us 126 men 40 wagons & 240 cattle 8
horses & 3 mules   there is two women in the train & has
been for sometime   their husbands are with them   one
of them has a child 6 months old   they are from Green
County, Ill. to day we passed the first Sioux Indian
camp we have seen also some heavy sand hills & some
low ground   grass is midling good   two large trains of
horses passed us to day   two men from our train went
out to find some game & did not get in untill near twelve
oclock at night   they gave the camp a little fears of their
safety   they brought in an antelope

Tuesday [May] 24th we passed a number of small
streams of clear water runing from the bluffs to the
[North Platte] river   at noon we stoped to dine on the
[North] Platt not far from a camp of Sioux   they came to
our tents & wanted to buy flour & meat   one of them was
dressed in military suit & carried a sabre with him   some
of us gave them something to eat   some bought moccasins
of them   they had money both silver & Greenbacks   in
the afternoon it was very warm & some sandy roads   the
bluffs are near the [North Platte] river here for some
distance   at night we camped on camp creek [Camp
Creek] & shortly after we stoped there was two men got
in a quarrel about their work   their weapons were drawn
but the women ran between them & other men
inte[r]fered & it was soon stoped   the feed on this creek
[Camp Creek] is good

*[As the train continued up the North Platte, Voorhees
commented on well-known emigrant landmarks, several
graves, and another group of men from a town near his
hometown.]*

Tuesday [May] 31st we started at four oclock & we
drove 14 miles & stoped for noon a little above Scotts

Bluffs   we passed two men that were living with the Indians   they kept cattle to trade to Emigrants that had lame ones & such as were likely to give out   they had a lot of ponies also.[11]   at night we camped in the bend of the [North Platte] river   the grass is very good

Wednesday June 1st   it was raining when we awoke but it soon held up & we made a start but had not drove far before it commenced again & continued through the day   we drove untill noon   then we camped & kept inside our tents the rest of the day   it was cool through the night   this is the first rainy day we have had since we left Omaha   we have had some storms of wind hail & rain but they were short   no guard out to night

Thursday June 2nd   it has been raining all night but it has now held up & we started. George Dodge & myself left the train on horseback for Larimie [Fort Laramie] a distance of 34 miles after our letters & for them that may be there for the rest of the boys   the roads were bad most of the way   near Larimie it was very sandy   we got our letters & recrossed the [North Platte] river at sundown   we rode back 3 or 4 miles & stoped for the night with the colon [Colon, Michigan] boys   there is no feed here or near here on the road   the colon boys are comeing in our train when it comes up   we found Ft Laramie to be quite a town   some 500 soldiers there some good buildings of wood & some of stone

Friday [June] 3rd   this morning the colon boys are prepared to come in our train[12]   & while we were a writing some letters home there came a train of horse teams along & after some enquiries from our train I found they had not started when they came along   some of the cattle were gone   I then saddled our horse & started for the train   went about three miles & met the captain [Allen Hurlbut]   the cattle had been found   our flag hoisted for the first time   the train set in motion & the captain went forward to reconoitre   I turned around

11. Throughout the emigration years, Indian traders and proprietors of road ranches along the overland trails operated profitable businesses exchanging worn-out emigrant stock for those that had been previously traded and fattened up.

12. The men from Colon, Michigan, included brothers Victor E. and Frank Cline, who became prosperous farmers in Montana. James U. Sanders, ed., *Society of Montana Pioneers, Register* (Akron, Ohio: The Werner Co., 1899), 98; Michael A. Leeson, ed., *History of Montana, 1739–1885* (Chicago: Warner, Beers & Co., 1885), 1111.

we went back to where I had stayed the night before &
waited untill the train came up   which was near noon
our cattle was then turned out on the poorest feed they
have had for some days   after dinner we had several
horse & mules teams join us & we drove a short distance
beyond the fort when we were obliged to stop on
account of a storm of rain   & it did rain to[o] for an
hour as though it meant it   no feed here   there is a ferry
here[13] [and] some Indian tents or rather white mans tents
with Squaws for wives

13. A ferry had operated
on the North Platte
River at varying
locations opposite Fort
Laramie since 1847.

Saturday [June] 4th   our cattle were turned loose &
drove to the bluffs w[h]ere they found very little feed
there was a lot of the boys that went to the fort [Fort
Laramie] & took the letters that had been written the night
before   our boys bought 2 buffalo robes of some traders
[on] this side of the river   our cattle were brought up
between 9 & 10 oclock and we hitched up & drove 10 miles
& camped near the [North Platte] river on some bottom
land[14]   the feed is short   there is a lot of other teams here
that have been waiting for our train to come   the road from
the fort is rough & hilly & will be for some ways for we are
near the black hills & in sight of Laramie Peak   last night
our cattle were put inside of the carrell for the first time &
to night they are again   the horses are hitched to the hind
wheels of the wagons or picketed close by

14. Historians have
named the route on the
north side of the river
from Fort Laramie to
present Casper,
Wyoming, the Child's
Cutoff, while emigrants
usually called this
segment the Emigrant
Road or the Mormon
Road. The train was
camped at the popular
north-side route camping
place about eight miles
west of Fort Laramie,
where the road left the
river and took a
circuitous route through
the hills north of present
Guernsey before coming
back to the river.

Sunday [June] 5th   we are now in camp all day to rest
& refresh ourselves as we have usually done since we
have been on the road   but our peace was disturbed. 10
oclock in forenoon a man that was keeping a ranche a
couple of miles from us came to our camp & told us
there was some Indians shooting his stock & [he] wanted
some of our men to go with him   our captain & some
men went with him, while the rest of us kept a good
lookout for our cattle & horses   those that went with
him followed the Indians some ways but did not come
across them   Jud Peak lost an ox   he was sick but a short

time   we are camped on a bottom nearly ten miles from
Laramie   the feed is short   the day is fair   our boys have
been washing their clothes   there has been some more
teams joined our train to day   it now numbers 274 men
& two women & one child

Monday [June] 6th   we got an early start & drove
near 15 miles among the black hills & at night we were
obliged to camp among them   no water near   some had
water in their kegs   some had not   the roads were very
rough & hilly[15]   there were some Indians that shot at
two men the day before where we stoped at noon   it was
where the road came to the [North Platte] river   the ball
passed between them & hit an ox in the hind   at night
there was 40 men that stood guard   20 at a time   I saw a
man that came near strangling by the side of the road

*[Voorhees's train continued traveling west on the hilly,
sandy Child's Cutoff on the north side of the river. One evening
they camped opposite Deer Creek Station, and some soldiers
came across the river and took letters from the emigrants to
send to Fort Laramie to be mailed from there. At another
campground, thirty Masons held a meeting.]*

Monday [June] 13th   we got an early start & drove
over but little good road   it being rough & hilly & most
of the way   was sandy   one place the bluffs came near
the river & it was a narrow place to pass through   it was
said there was a four mule team & wagon that fell in the
river & all was lost   the bank gave way under the wagon
[and] the driver leaped on shore   it happened on
Saturday June the 11th   there is a freight train of 30
wagons on the south side of the river opposite to us
they are bound for Bannock [Bannack]   two men in our
train was out on a hunt   they killed one antelope &
found two good mules some 5 or 6 miles from the road
at night we camped near the river just below the first
bridge across the Platt river [Richard's Bridge]   it is
owned by individuals[16]   there is another one 5 miles

15. They went through
Rocky Pass, crossed over
Emigrant Hill, and came
back to the North Platte
River at the mouth of
Broom Creek at noon. In
the afternoon they left
the river and traveled into
the hills again.

16. John Richard and his
business associates built
the first or lower bridge
just north of present
Evansville, Wyoming.
Richard operated a
trading post on the south
side of the bridge.

17. Guinard's Bridge, six miles upstream from Richard's Bridge, was garrisoned by a detachment of Company G, Eleventh Ohio Cavalry, commanded by Lieutenant Henry Clay Bretney. The post was called Platte Bridge Station until it was renamed Fort Caspar following the death of Lieutenant Caspar Collins in July 1865.

18. Hurlbut's train was the first emigrant train to go north from Richard's Bridge. Hurlbut had no local guides and relied solely on his own experience and information to find a route. Thus he scouted ahead for a wagon route that would have adequate water and feed for the animals.

19. The men went across to the south side of the North Platte to hunt on what is now called Casper Mountain.

20. Several saline springs are located at the head of Sand Spring Creek, near the route they traveled.

above this   there is a Telegraph office there & 20 soldiers stationed there to guard it[17]

Tuesday June 14th was warm & pleasant & we lay in camp all day the captain [Allen Hurlbut] took another man & went out to recoinoitre [they] came in late at night after having traveled all day without finding water[18] his object was to find a feasible route from this place north towards the big horn mountains some of our boys went over the river to hunt for game but found none[19] they went up to the snow that still lies in some of the ravines they found some small stream of good water also some timber that was near 18 inches through there was a freight train of 30 wagons passed us on the other [south] side of the river they were bound for Bannock [Bannack] some boys in our train bought some shovels of them & paid $16 apiece for them

Wednesday [June] 15th we have orders to be ready at noon to start which order was recalled & we stayed in camp all day   in afternoon there was a man came to claim the mules that had been found by two of our boys found on Monday but could not describe them   they were left with the train   there has a number joined our train to day

Thursday June 16th our cattle were yoked without being turned out of the carrelle to feed & we drove near 1/2 mile & then left the main road for the Powder river & big horn mountains [Bighorn Mountains]   the first few miles was sand hills & after crossing them we stoped & let our cattle feed a short time we then drove a due north course the rest of the day. we passed over a low piece of low land about two miles wide—covered with low brush that had some resemblance of spruce afterward the country was rolling   at night we camped on the bank of a ravine that had a few holes of bad tasteing water & it was the first water we have come to since leaving the Platt a distance of 12 miles[20] by diging about 3 feet we found plenty of water for the horses but it had a bad taste   we at first thought it was alkali but soon found it was not   most of them called it salt petre [saltpeter]²¹ the grass was good   there was one horse Died here soon after we stoped. when we left the main road we numbered 124 wagons 112 horses 68 mules 392 oxen 70 cows 418 men 10 women 10 children 2092 gun & pistol shots & 20 dogs   dis[tance] 12 miles

Friday June 17th we got an early start & drove untill near ten oclock   then found water for our teams in a ravine called spring canion [Sand Spring Canyon] among bare sand hills   it had the same brackish [salty] taste that it had the night before   at noon we stoped on a small pararie surrounded by hills & inhabited by pararie dogs the road in forenoon was sandy & hilly   we passed by some large hills of bare sand no vegetation whatever   in afternoon our road was good & through a very good looking country some rolling. at night we came to a large ravine called the dry branch of powder river [Salt Creek]²² there was water enough for our teams but it had the same taste of that we had before   our cattle drank it freely but it did not appear to satisfy them there was plenty of grass & we found wood to do our cooking   there was a few green trees here   the first we have seen on this route   when our cattle came in the carelle there was a number of them sick but we gave them lard & vinegar & the most of them were well in the morning   we drove about 18 or 20 miles

Saturday June 18th we were off in good time   drove all day down the [Salt Creek] ravine we came in the night before   sometimes we were out of it for a short time but were obliged to get in it again on account of the high & rugged hills on either side of it   our road was sandy all day & very crooked   some very hard pulling. at noon we stoped on a bottom that overflows in time of high water it was covered with sage brush   the banks was near 100 ft

21. Saltpeter or saltpetre is a naturally occurring sodium or potassium nitrate. Potassium nitrate is used in the manufacture of fireworks and gunpowder. Saltpeter is poisonous to cattle. The primary treatment for saltpeter poisoning is the administration of anti-inflammatory protective agents such as fat meat or lard.

22. Here they intersected John Bozeman's 1863 route that went northwest from Deer Creek. In 1864 Bozeman left the North Platte at Richard's Bridge two days after Hurlbut and followed his track.

high. in afternoon our road was rougher than it has been
before   at night we camped on a piece of table land in
sight of the snow mountains [Bighorn Mountains]   we
are all feeling first rate to think we are out of the dry
branch of powder river [Salt Creek] & in sight of snow
thinking we will soon have good water   we have drove
about 16 miles

Sunday [June] 19th having laid by two days last week
we thought best to travel & it was necessary that we
should to find good water   but we did not find it for we
did not drive far before we were obliged to enter the [Salt
Creek] ravine we left last night & were in it all day   at
noon we stoped on a bottom where there had been some
Indians camped but a short time before there were a few
trees here   rough roads in afternoon   high bluffs on
both sides   at night we camped on a bottom that was
covered with sage brush   water as bad as ever   a number
of cattle are hard up   we drove about 14 or 15 miles

Monday [June] 20th we started in good season but
find ourselves in the same [Salt Creek] ravine we have
followed & is as crooked as ever   rather more water than
before but it is in holes   no running stream yet   at noon
we stoped in a grove of small trees   some were poplar
water the same   feed rather poor   saw signs of Indians
found an Indian dog blindfolded   he had been left by the
Indians to starve to death   some of our train shot him
thinking him to be some wild animal as he had a piece of
buffalo skin tied over his head   before noon an ox gave
out & was left to Die & towards night another gave out
he was ~~lame~~ left near w[h]ere we camped   3 miles this side
[south side] of powder river   we drove 14 or 15 miles

Tuesday [June] 21st all of us were ready & willing
[to] start for we were to leave the dry creek [Salt Creek]
we had followed since friday last & to get to powder
river   & after about 3 miles drive we came to it   & were 1
1/4 hours crossing the stream [Powder River]   it was 5 or

6 rods wide water hub deep   our teams were refreshed &
we traveled up the [Powder] river a few miles & stoped on
its bank for dinner[23]   there is plenty of cottonwood
timber along this stream as far as we followed it   the
Indians had cut down large quantity of it to browse their
ponies the winter before   in the afternoon we passed over
a rough and hilly country[24] & at night we camped on N
fork of powder river [North Fork Powder River]   very
little wood on this stream   we drove near 12 or 13 miles
NW course

Wednesday [June] 22nd Mr Washburn left one ox
this morning he was sick & gave out   we were off in
good season & drove a few miles & then we left the
stream [North Fork Powder River] we camped on the
night before but not untill our teams were watered &
kegs filled   we then drove untill near noon when wagon
no [number] 20 had one wheel give out   the train was
stoped & they having some spokes with them it was
soon repaired   while we were waiting we cooked our
dinner with buffalo chips as there was neither wood nor
water here. I bought 1/4 antelope for $1.75. in the
afternoon we traveled over a rolling country & good
roads   no timber or water but at night we camped on a
small stream [South Fork Crazy Woman Creek] of good
water   & we found wood to cook with   there was
several antelope killed to day   one ran through the train
& was shot at by a number but was not hurt   we drove
near 18 miles to day

[*The next day the train camped at the base of the Bighorn Mountains. While many of the men went prospecting
in the canyon of Middle Fork Crazy Woman Creek,
Voorhees and others stayed in the camp. He recorded that
those who stayed behind busied themselves hunting, fishing, tending the stock, "lounging around the camp." When
the prospectors returned three days later, he noted that tensions had mounted between those who wanted to prospect*

23. They traveled up the
north bank of Powder
River six or seven miles
and stopped for noon
camp.

24. They went through a
narrow draw in an area
where the bluffs
extended to the river.
Three weeks later,
Captain Townsend—
seeking to avoid a
potential Indian ambush
in the narrow passage—
turned from the road to
cross his train to the
south side of the Powder
River before entering the
draw. In spite of his
caution, the train was
attacked and besieged for
several hours on the
north bank of the
Powder at the place they
planned to cross it. Four
emigrant men and an
unknown number of
Indians were killed in the
engagement.

and those who wanted to keep traveling to their destination, but "the captain [Allen Hurlbut] was called for just a[t] evening & an explanation was given all things were made right & we are to move on in the morning our rules & regulations were read & a unanimous vote was given for them then three cheers were given for the captain."]

Monday June 27th we were a little late in starting this morning some of our cattle had made a start to go back & had got some 3 miles before they were caught those that went after them saw another train comeing some 8 miles behind us & through the day we found it to be Bozeman with a train of 83 wagons & Edwards of fort Wayne behind him with 25 more[25] our roads to day were not very rough but hilly at noon we crossed a small stream [North Fork Crazy Woman Creek] the bed of it was very stony & slow crossing it we stoped on its bank for dinner its name was willow creek[26] there was fish in it in afternoon our roads were ~~straighter~~ some smoother than in forenoon & at night we came to a large dry creek [Bull Creek] & camped for the night there was a good spring of water in it but none for our cattle[27] as they being dry they started for water & went near 4 miles before they were surrounded & it was dark before they were carelled. we drove 18 miles to day we had for our breakfast a fine dish of fish we took hard tack & tea for dinner [at noon] & for supper we ate very hearty of mountain sheep

Tuesday [June] 28th hitched our cattle up & were off in good season & drove for 2 or 3 miles then came to Rose bud river [Clear Creek][28] found it some 5 to 7 rods wide its water was about 2 feet deep & ran very swift but we were soon crossing it in 3 different places & in an hours time we were on the opposite side we then drove a few miles & came to a small stream [Rock Creek] & after driving a short distance down it we stoped for dinner in a small but beautiful grove there

25. This was John Bozeman's train. It left the North Platte at Richard's Bridge on June 18, two days after Hurlbut's train had departed. When he reached the Powder River, Bozeman waited two days for another small train to come up before following Hurlbut's route. This is the only known reference to the size of Bozeman's train.

26. Willow Creek was the North Platte traders' name for the North Fork Powder River. The emigrants evidently had been told they would cross Willow Creek, but they did not know which stream it actually was.

27. The spring, now known as Big Spring, is located at the Cross H ranch, five miles south of present Buffalo, Wyoming.

28. The Clear Creek crossing was on the eastern edge of present Buffalo, Wyoming.

was plenty of grass   the hills were high on both sides of
us & it is said that this is the place where the Indians
stoped a train of 40 wagons last season & turned them
back   there has been a wagon track for us after the
second day we left the Platt river but in some places it
was rather dim & here it stoped[29]   it was here that I shot
at an antelope   in afternoon we traveled up the creek a
few miles then left it and drove over a high & rolling
country   passed a lake [Lake De Smet] some 2 or 3 miles
long & near one wide   from the road it was beautiful
this evening we camped on a small stream [Shell Creek]
after driving about 16 miles to day   we have seen more
antelope than any day previous   Wash Embly & Cub
went out & came in with one   there were two buffalo
killed   one after we camped for the night

Wednesday [June] 29th   in the morning was cool &
cloudy   but it soon became warm   we drove a few miles
then crossed a small stream [Little Piney Creek] & about
one mile further we came to what was called little horn
river [Piney Creek][30]   & there we stoped near 6 hours
waiting for the captain to find a suitable road on the
other side[31]   & while waiting there was an occurrance
happened that might have proved fatal   there were some
men that came across a grizly bear   one man shot him
then went in some brush   the bear pitched in for a fight
bit the man in the arm   & while he was fighting another
man shot him   the bear then turned on him & came near
killing him before the bear was killed   the man was
brought in on [a] blanket   the bear drawed in camp with
a rope   we had small piece of him   there was 3 Elk killed
near here   we had all we wanted of them   there is some
timber on this stream & some of it is small pine[32]   there
was goose berries   wild currrants & strawberries along
this river   they were the first we have seen on the route
in afternoon we had a hilly road   one very steep [Lodge
Trail Ridge]   at night we camped in a small valley on a

29. The wagon track they
followed was John
Bozeman's route from
Deer Creek the year
before, which Voorhees's
party intersected two
days north of Richard's
Bridge. This camping
place was four miles
north of Clear Creek on
Rock Creek, where in
1863, Bozeman's train
was stopped by Indians
and persuaded to turn
back to the North Platte.

30. They were at the site
of Fort Phil Kearny,
established in July 1866
on a bench between the
forks of Piney Creek.

31. The train waited at
Piney Creek while
Hurlbut looked for a
route over the ridges on
the other side. After
scouting ahead, Hurlbut
chose a route over Lodge
Trail and Fetterman
ridges that became the
Bozeman Trail.

32. After Fort Phil
Kearny was established, a
logging camp about five
miles upstream furnished
the timber used to build
the fort.

small stream [Jenks Creek][33] with high & rough hills on every side   while we were carelling another bear was killed   he was a large one but poor   I got the skin from the upper part of the fore leg for to cover our saddle with Mr Barrett & James [Barnebee] brought in an antelope to day we drove some 8 or 10 miles

Thursday [June] 30th   we had Elk meat for our breakfast   the first I had tasted of   it was first rate   we left our camp at 6 oclock & drove over some high rolling country for near 8 miles   about two miles from camp we crossed a small stream [Prairie Dog Creek] of cool water at noon we stopped on another [Prairie Dog Creek] & in afternoon we traveled down it some 8 or 9 miles[34]   high bluffs on right of us   in forenoon we saw wild barley & flax   some timothy [grass]   in afternoon we had a storm of rain & some hail   there is considerable small timber on this small stream [Prairie Dog Creek]   but there was a large quantity killed by fire   drove near 16 to 18 miles

Friday July 1st   we drove near 4 miles & then came to pass river [Goose Creek] just below the junction of Stinking river[35]   its currant is swift   its water near 3 ft deep   the stream from 6 to 8 rods wide   the captain crossed [and] went ahead some ways   then came back & went up the stream   I went with him   we crossed the two streams & went about two miles ahead   then he concluded to cross where the teams were [waiting]   then go below in a small valley   followed it untill we came to a small stream [Soldier Creek]   crossed it & soon stopped for dinner[36]   the captain now tells us that the mountains on our left are the big horn mountains & we will go to them   & after dinner we go for them & drive near 5 miles & camp for the night [at South Dry Creek].   soon the cry of grizly is heard & men are after him   but he is in the brush that grows along the stream a few rods wide & no one wants to go in   the dogs dont drive him out   by & by a man on a horse rides in & the bear is

killed   he is large & fat   there is but few antelope killed
to day we drove som[e] 12 to 14 miles

Saturday July 2nd   our trains were hitched up
without being turned out to feed   & as soon as our
breakfast was over we drove down in a valley [Wolf
Creek] & followed up it near 5 miles & camped some 5
miles from the mountains   it is a nice place   plenty of
grass some dry wood & a beautiful stream of water
running throug[h] it[37]   we intend to stay here a few days
& look for gold in the mountains that lie to our left
they are a snowy range & we suppose them to belong to
the big horn mountains but some say they do not[38]
there is lots of game here in sight to day   deer &
antelope are runing in every direction   number of
buffalo have been in sight   one ran near camp & there
was some big shooting done but the buffalo was not
killed   some 50 head of cattle undertook to run off after
them but were stoped nearly 2 miles from camp   James
Barnebee & Columbus Marantette shot 3 antelope apiece
& I could not tell how many have been killed within
sight of our camp   Bozemans train came within 6 miles
of us & passed by[39]   good many are wanting to go on &
others want to stay & prospect

Sunday July 3rd   to day has been spent in hunting by
a large number of our men   antelope are killed in sight
one not 20 rods from our camp   some buffalo came in
sight but are driven off to keep them from our cattle   the
day is fair and warm   near 50 Masons meet to day on a
hill from which can be seen another valley & a stream of
water [Tongue River] runing through it   there is a
number of men fixing to go in the mountains to morrow
some excitement prevails in camp   a number of men are
not satisfied to stop here & wants to go to the big horn
river some 30 miles distant   the captain [Allen Hurlbut]
told a number of us that he knew where there was plenty
of gold   but small parties could not get it   but 200 men

37. They were on Wolf
Creek, which runs
northeast to Tongue
River. They camped five
miles up the creek from
the road, closer to the
mountains.

38. These are the Bighorn
Mountains, northwest of
present Sheridan,
Wyoming.

39. This is where
Bozeman's train passed
Hurlbut's and as a result
was the first to arrive in
Virginia City in 1864.
Because of this, Bozeman
became known as the first
person to take a train over
the Bozeman Trail.

were safe to go any where after it & he wanted to get them to go with him   he made no charge to show them he has an interest in two wagons & we have followed him here in company with the number that I have before written   & two more teams have joined us since   & now we begin to think he has fooled us some   & there are a number that will leave the train two morrow morning without doubt[40]

Monday 4th of July Idaho [Territory][41] this morning there were 27 teams that are hitched up to leave   those that were a going out to prospect do not want to go unless the train will wait for them one week & they want a vote from the crowd   the captain [Allen Hurlbut] refuses to have one taken   but the guard master & myself go inside the carelle & call out the men   a vote is taken   the whole crowd say they will wait untill next Monday for them   then the captain & some 60 others start for the mountains   the train is left in charge of the guard master & myself   & all those that were hitched up soon left leaving us 99 wagons in carelle[42]   towards night we made a new carelle & all is quiet again   but little game is seen to day

Tuesday July 5th all is quiet untill near noon when a party of men came in that had been sent out to prospect some 10 days ago   they found no gold & one of the party named Hatch undertook to raise a row in camp by circulating a paper through it requesting the crowd to arrest the captain [Allen Hurlbut] & have him tried if he does not find or show us the mines as he represented[43] but the crowd did not think much of him or his project & he soon see it & his team soon pulled out & left   8 others left with him & leaves us with 91 wagons   the guard master left with him   after they left we found he had an idea of breaking up our train [and] form one out of those that would follow him & he [Hatch] would be captain   but he did not succeed   there was two many

40. By this time the members of Hurlbut's train were strongly divided between those who believed his claims that there were good places to prospect in the region and those who did not and wanted to keep moving.

41. They were actually in Montana Territory. Unknown to Voorhees, Montana Territory had been created out of Idaho Territory on May 26, 1864.

42. Here the train split into two trains. Abram Voorhees was in charge of the train that remained in the corral.

43. Hurlbut told them at the outset about the supposedly rich mines in the region of the Tongue and Bighorn rivers, but none had been found.

that had pledged their word to wait for those that had
gone in the mountains   there is considerable game killed
to day James [Barnebee] killed 3 antelope & Thomas
Jacobs one   one man shot at & wounded a bear   the bear
made for him but he sprang in a tree that was near   the
bear kept him there near two hours   he would have shot
him while in the tree but in loading his gun he droped his
cap box & was obliged to sit & wait untill he left
towards night we had a storm of wind which took down
some of our tents   an ox that had been sick a few days
Died to day

Wednesday [July] 6th all is quiet to day   some are
out hunting while others are enjoying themselves playing
games trying tricks walking to a pole blindfolded &c
soon after noon a large buffalo was seen comeing
towards camp   the men got their guns [and] form in line
some of the dogs see him & go for him & the men begin
to fire   he runs the guantlet well   some think they hit
him while others shoot in the hill above him   soon after
a doe antelope ran near by her fawn close to her   she
was allowed to pass unmolested   three teams have been
out after game   one brought an Elk another two
another 5 antelope   our boys are drying a fine lot of
antelope meat & so are a number of others in camp
towards night some of the boys come in [from
prospecting]   find no gold

Thursday July 7th we are all anxious to have the rest
of the boys come as we are all satisfied there is no gold
here. near night some come in with a line from captain
[Hurlbut] requesting me to move the train in another
valley [Tongue River] some 5 or 6 miles[44] & at night all
came in but 9 men & it was thought by some that they
were lost after night guns were fired & a fire built on
high hill for their benefit. they that came in say they had
good time   lots of game   on 4th of July they had game
of snow ball in the mountains   they say there is plenty

44. This was the Tongue
River Valley, the next
valley to the north over
the divide. To reach it
they would have to go
back down Wolf Creek
and follow Bozeman's
trail over the divide.

of timber brush in some places very thick   some very
nice streams of water   no fresh signs of Indians

Friday [July] 8th we are all ready to start but are
waiting to make arrangements for some few teams with
men & provisions for those that are not in   finally it is
arranged & we start at half past 8 oclock & it was
understood by most of the train that we should follow
the road that Bozemans train had made untill we should
arrive at the big horn river or to some mining point
beyond   & in case the captain [Allen Hurlbut] would
follow the road & move along we would follow him & if
not our teams should go ahead & the most of the crowd
would follow us   we drove near 4 miles when the word
came back that the captain said stop the train   there was
a large drove of buffalo some ways ahead of us   we
thought at first we were stoped to have them pass by
before we came up. while we were waiting word came
that the captain was looking for another road   James
Barnebee was driving our head team   I was driving our
other   the rest of the boys from our town [Mendon,
Michigan] was next to us   James told the man that was
driving the captains team to drive on or he would go by
he did not start his team & James & myself drove by   as
soon as the man that was driving the head team saw we
were going by he started his team & kept them close to
the team that I was driving & kept the rest of the train
behind him   we drove untill near noon then stoped in a
valley on stream of water [Twin Creek] grass was first
rate   we then found the captain had not sent any word
back whatever   but we were allowed to drive ahead & at
night while carelling the rest of the Mendon boys came
in ahead & took their places next to us   the whole crowd
are pleased with the change as we have good teams &
they know they will make good time   the captain finds
no fault with it   we have had hilly roads but not very
rough   saw lots of game to day   we saw the first large

drove of buffalo   it was thought there was from 3 to 5
hundred in it   at night we camped on small stream [Pass
Creek]   some of the boys called it grizzly creek   those
that stood guard at night heard one growling near by
drove 15 miles[45]

Saturday [July] 9th   our teams lead off over a rough
& hilly road   move up then down all day & have crossed
a number of small streams   two quite prominent ones
the first was thought to be Salmon river [Little Bighorn
River] some 5 or 6 rods wide   water 18 inchs deep   some
cottonwood timber on its bank   the other [Lodge Grass
Creek] was thought to be clarks fork[46] not as large as the
other & less timber on its bank   we have seen several
large droves of buffalo & a number of small ones   one
single one came within 50 rods of our head team then
stoped to fight the dogs that were bothering him   we
stoped a few minutes for fear he would scare our oxen
but men were soon there & shooting at him   he ran
across the road some way then turned his course & ran
for nearly a mile along the train within gun shot then
turned & ran towards the train & came near it then ran
towards the front end of it for some way before he was
made to fall   he was an old setler & was fired at by
nearly two hundred men   near night there was 3 bear
killed & 4 others wounded   number of antelope were
killed   Jud Peak & Thomas Crumbaker killed one   they
went out to kill buffalo calf but could not get [a] shot at
one   the old ones kept them inside   we camped at night
on the bank of stream [Rotten Grass Creek] nearly two
rods wide   some high bushes & small trees   small valley
high hills on every side   drove 18 miles

July 10th Sunday   our train is moving to day as we
are all anxious to get to the big horn river & we have
found the hilliest road to day we have had on the trip   in
forenoon Jud Peak & myself went out from the train to
hunt   found some very nice berries but no game   at

45. During this day
Voorhees's train traveled
some distance behind
Hurlbut's train to Pass
Creek. Both trains
followed the trail
Bozeman had pioneered a
few days earlier.

46. The emigrants had
very little accurate
information. The Salmon
River is in Idaho, and the
Clarks Fork is about
seventy-five miles
northwest of here in
Montana.

noon we stoped in small valley surrounded by high hills
a nice stream of water [Soap Creek] runing through it   at
night we camped on a small stream [West Soap Creek]
near the mountain & in sight of the big horn river   it is a
pretty place so near the mountain & on the edge of the
valley of the big horn river   the grass is good   some
small trees   water first rate   the captain [Allen Hurlbut]
& Reeves had some words   drove 18 miles

Monday [July] 11th   we are off in good season &
drove down [to] the valley of the big horn some 6 miles
& carelle our wagons on the bank of the river & then
look for a better place to cross than the one that had
been used by the teams that crossed a few days before
but could not   the river at this place is divided into 5
different streams & the water runs very rapid[47]   the
deepest one is near 4 ft deep & was fun to see some teams
cross. we raised our wagon beds & got all ready to cross
the river in the morning. through the day there were
some first rate prospects found but it was fine gold &
will not pay without proper tools & it may not then   but
the most of our crowd want to try it a few days.

Tuesday [July] 12th   our teams are hitched up at three
oclock & as soon as we eat our breakfast we made a start
for the other side of the river   our teams ahead James
[Barnebee] driving the front team & I was the other
James went across all right   but when I was just nicely in
the third channel the bolster gave away & let the front
end of our box down[48]   there was a [sand]bar near by &
I drove on that & rigged it up again   a number of teams
had all they could do to make the riffle & some came out
several rods below. there were some 3 or 4 small
accidents that happened while crossing but nothing
serious   after crossing I received a note from our guard
master   he having left our train a few days before, that
the party he was with found a portion of the remains of
those 8 men that were killed by the Indians   also an axe

47. They followed
Bozeman's track down
Soap Creek Hill to the
Bighorn River, about
eight miles below the
opening of Bighorn
Canyon. The trail
crossed at an old Indian-
trader ford now known
as Spotted Rabbit
Crossing.

48. Bolsters are
horizontal supports
between the wagon bed
and the front and rear
axletrees. In this instance,
the front bolster broke
and the front end of the
wagon collapsed onto
the axletree.

pick & pack saddle   there is no doubt but that 8 men were killed near here last July[49]   as soon as we were all across & carelled near by which was done before 10 oclock the captain [Allen Hurlbut] proposed to drive some 5 miles up the river to a bottom where there was plenty of feed for our teams, (we having crossed the stream some 8 miles below where it comes out of the mountains [at the mouth of Bighorn Canyon]) & there stop a few days & prospect the mountains   & 69 wagons and 232 men did so   while we were stoping Charles Uptegrove proposed to leave us & we gave him [his] share of what we had & he left with Jud Peak for some other mines[50]   there were 21 teams left us when we started up the river

Wednesday [July] 13th   we are in camp near 3 miles from where the river comes out of the mountain[51]   a number of men are out prospecting   others are fishing the others are laying in the shade & there is need of shade for the captains [Hurlbut's] thermometer stands 135 in sunshine & 102 in the shade   I gathered a dish of wild currants here & Cub caught a mess of fish   we had good swim in big horn [Bighorn River] to day

Thursday July 14th   all quiet in camp   more men go out prospecting   captain [Hurlbut] goes with them Thomas [Crumbaker] & myself goes up to where the river comes through the mountains   find it to be very deep canyon [Bighorn Canyon][52]   rocks & hills hundreds of feet above the water & looking at it in any way you can it looks as though it was not more than 50 feet wide but standing on the top of the rocks that looks to be perpendicular you make a good throw to throw a stone to the water & the water must be very deep for it runs through that chasm for miles without a riffle below the mountains a short distance is the first falls we see   it falls about 2 feet & several more between it & where we crossed. the cattle are doing first rate here   no

49. In May 1863 Crow Indians attacked James Stuart's prospecting party of fifteen men on the west side of the Bighorn River, in this vicinity, and three (not eight as Voorhees states) of the prospectors were killed. James Stuart, "The Yellowstone Expedition of 1863," *Contributions to the Historical Society of Montana*, 1 (1876), 149–233.

50. These men presumably followed Bozeman's trail, and some of them are known to have caught up with his train.

51. They camped on the west side of the Bighorn River, near the 1866 ford and ferry site below the mouth of Bighorn Canyon.

52. Today Yellowtail Dam is at the mouth of the Bighorn Canyon, and the waters of the Bighorn Canyon National Recreation Area fill the canyon behind the dam.

game   no signs of Indians being here this summer   a few
signs of white men being here within a month or two as
there was a pick found here without rust on it. a rope
was found also that was sound[53]

53. The prospectors may
have been members of
Bozeman's train.

Friday [July] 15th it is as warm as ever & men are
laying around the camp playing diferent games or
snoozing in their tents   this morning an Indian dog came
to our camp & was caught by James Mann & is kept with
us   our cattle are doing first rate   Fred Engle killed an
antelope to day. some of the men came in that were out
on prospecting & report about the same prospect up the
river as here & that a party will go on still farther &
return on Sunday

Saturday [July] 16th finds us still in camp 3 miles
below the foot of the mountains from where the river
comes out of them & are passing off our time as
agreeably as posible   some of our boys are out to find
some berries   some are fishing others are looking after
the cattle   there was some of them that went down the
river & word came they were crossing it   we soon had
men after them & they were brought back   they did not
cross as was supposed   the guard that were out in
forenoon had neglected them   at night the boys had gay
time at a dance also trying tricks

Sunday July 17th was some cloudy most of the day
& of course it is more pleasant to lay around than when
the sun shines so very hot as it has since we have been
here & we are waiting patiently for the boys to come in
at last they come   they say they think there is gold on
[the] head waters of this river but we are on the wrong
side of the mountain   they went up the river some 40 or
50 miles & find it to be the same deep chasm as it is here
but could see a large valley [Bighorn Basin] beyond
where they were & beyond that another range of snowy
mountains & they think the fine gold we find here came
from there   but we cannot go across to it from here[54]

54. The only way through
the high cliffs along the
river was on an Indian
trail marked with
prehistoric rock cairns
that went through what is
known as Bad Pass.

we will now make a break for the Yellow Stone river in the morning   there is not much good feeling towards the captain [Allen Hurlbut] at this time   he has deceived us to[o] much   our cattle have been some trouble to us to day   they were bound to go down the river   one of ours is sick & stays in   there has been a letter written for our county [news]paper to day[55]

Monday July 18th   we make a start from the big horn river at 5 oclock & travel down it some 5 miles to the road we left last tuesday[56] & soon are out of sight of the big horn [Bighorn River] we have heard so much of. this river has been prospected before to the sorrow of some parties for near here where we are camped were found a part of the remains of 8 men that were killed last July by the Indians   they were found by a party from our train that crossed the river 3 days before we came to it   they found a pack saddle   an axe & a few other things that were left   some of our party found a pick & rope   also a 3 quart bason [basin] that had been shot through with an arrow[57]   after leaving the river we drove over some hills for a mile or two then came to some table land that looked very well for a few miles   at noon we found a small stream [Beauvais Creek] & camped for dinner there were 3 different kinds of wild currants here & were very nice   in the afternoon we had the poorest country we have passed over for 1/2 day at a time since we were on the trip   being very hilly   the hills covered with stone & sage brush & a number of what was called soap wells they being deep deposits of a soft substance resembling soft soap[58]   no grass or water untill night then found good grass   the water [Little Woody Creek] stood in small puddles but had no bad taste   no game of any kind we drove 16 miles from the river

Tuesday [July] 19th   our men not being satisfied with the prospecting done on the river proposed to get up a party & make their way through a gap to the other side

55. Voorhees copied the letter that he wrote to his local newspaper in the back of his diary. The letter is a lengthy, detailed description of the country and the train's progress to the Bighorn River.

56. They went back down the Bighorn River to where they had crossed, and from there they followed Bozeman's trail northwest to the Yellowstone.

57. These were probably articles left after the attack on James Stuart's prospecting party in May 1863.

58. The deposits were bentonite, a soft, light-colored, porous, pliable clay formed from the decomposition of volcanic ash. Bentonite is also known as mineral soap because of its ability to absorb water up to fifteen times its own volume and to become the consistency of soft soap. It covers every basin in Wyoming and is extensively mined today. It is used as a sealant and binder in the manufacture of paper, adhesives, automobile polish, detergent, paint, insecticides, insect repellents, toothpaste, and facial cosmetics.

59. The prospecting party proposed going through the Pryor Mountains to the Bighorn Basin. From there they would either have to go south to the South Pass road or turn around and come back on the Bridger Trail.

60. Voorhees reported in the second letter he wrote to his county newspaper on August 3 that he was elected captain of the train to replace Hurlbut.

61. Their route had crossed Beauvais Creek and Little and Big Woody creeks, and they camped at Pryor Creek, then called Nez Perce Creek or River.

62. The early morning raid was a classic example of the Plains Indian horse raid. The unguarded emigrant horse and mule herd grazing some distance from the corral presented the perfect opportunity. The raiding party struck at sunrise, while the emigrants were eating breakfast, and escaped with the captured horses and mules before the emigrant men could mount up to chase them. In a letter Voorhees later identifies the raiders as twenty Cheyennes. But since they were deep in Crow country, it was more likely a party of Crows or Arapahos, though small Sioux and Cheyenne raiding parties occasionally ranged west of the Bighorn.

of the mountains[59]   & give it another try & make then their way to Virginia City on the opposite side from where the train was moving   & while getting ready the captain [Hurlbut] started his team & 5 others follow him leaving 62 wagons & 205 men in the carelle   as soon as he started the men came together and elected another captain & their under officers & were soon under motion[60]   our road was rough   at noon we found a good spring of cool water   good grass for our stock   at night we camped on a bottom that borders on small stream thought to be nez perces [Pryor Creek][61] there is some small timber along it but of no account   the stream runs through a rough country as far as we can see for both ways   we drove some 16 to 18 miles   good grass & water

Wednesday [July] 20th   we were up at three oclock & our stock turned loose & guard went out with the cattle but the horses had no guard with them & were on opposite side of carelle from the cattle   & here the horsemen were careless & had been before & while the cattle had guards with them the horses were looked after from their tents if looked after at all   & just as we were eating our breakfast the Indians   about 20 or 25 of them were seen among the horses that were a mile away from the camp   men with their rifles were after them   horses running in every direction trying to get to camp & some were lucky enough to reach it   one mule came in with an arrow sticking in its side   while 6 horses & 6 mules were driven off by them before our men could [get] near to them   there were a good many shots fired at them but none were killed   but we think there were two wounded as soon as horses could be caught men were on them & followed them untill near noon but could not overtake them   we lay by to day to arrange it so as to take those men & their affects with us for there are 3 wagons without a horse or mule   one with two   one with one   we leave one old wagon   at night we have a double guard[62]

Thursday morning [July 21] 4 Indian dogs came to our camp but we see no Indians our stock was well guarded we start at six oclock & drive near 10 miles & reach the Yellow Stone at noon after crossing over some crooked & hilly roads in some places hardly room for a wagon to pass on top [of a ridge] with out sliding down for some ways below[63] at noon we were detained to have an axle put in a wagon there is some timber at this place [on the bank of the Yellowstone River] & first rate feed for our teams there is plenty signs of Indians here they were here but a short time since in afternoon we traveled up the river a few miles then left it & drove untill after dark then camped without wood water or grass[64] we have been following Bozemans road & here he took a wrong course & went out of the way for nearly 15 miles over the worst kind of roads drove 20 miles[65]

Friday [July] 22nd we started as soon as it was light & drove down a long hill which was steep & stony into a deep ravine [Duck Creek] for two miles then came to a river [Yellowstone River] supposed to be Clarks fork[66] we then carrelle & get our breakfast stop here 2 & 1/2 hours to let our cattle feed then drive up the [Yellowstone] river 5 or 6 miles & cross it & drive 2 or 3 miles & stop for dinner[67] we saw fresh signs of Indians & it was the rule from then on that men should stay by their wagons afternoon we made a long drive & camped after night on its bank again but we were away from it from noon untill night[68] near night we came to where Bozeman had missed his way & was obliged to turn back there was a notice left for us not to climb the hill but turn to the left[69] good grass here some timber drove 20 miles

Saturday [July] 23rd we got an early start & drove but a short distance then came to captain Bridgers road that leaves the Platt river at the red Buttes for Virginia

63. They descended the bluffs lining the south bank of the Yellowstone River to the river, opposite present Billings, Montana.

64. After their noon stop, they went up the south bank of the Yellowstone River about two miles to where the bluffs meet the river and block passage along the bank. Here, just after crossing Blue Creek, Bozeman's Trail turned south, climbed back onto the bluffs, and wound back toward the Yellowstone a few miles upstream. Voorhees's train did not make it back to the Yellowstone and was forced to camp in the highlands.

65. After succeeding trains developed the route, this segment over the bluffs and back to the Yellowstone was about nine miles.

66. They came back to the Yellowstone River at the mouth of Duck Creek.

67. They went up the south side of the Yellowstone River five miles to the mouth of Clarks Fork, crossed it, and continued westward about three miles on the narrow stretch of land between the Clarks Fork and Yellowstone rivers. Here the Clarks Fork makes a sharp bend to the south, and Bozeman's trail also swung south and went up the Clarks Fork's west side.

68. During the afternoon they traveled up the west side of Clarks Fork. They may have been on higher ground, away from the

river, and so Voorhees did not realize when they intersected Rock Creek. They camped in the evening on Rock Creek and not on Clarks Fork, as Voorhees assumes.

69. This is another indication that Bozeman struggled to find a route in this area. Voorhees probably found the note from Bozeman's train on the divide between Clarks Fork and Rock Creek. Most likely, Bozeman had unsuccessfully sought a route that would continue up the Yellowstone River.

70. They intersected the Bridger Trail where it crossed Rock Creek one mile below (or northeast of) present Joliet, Montana. Bridger pioneered his route through the Bighorn Basin with a large wagon train that left Red Buttes on May 20 and arrived at Virginia City on July 8. From here Bozeman generally followed Bridger's trail to the Gallatin Valley.

71. From the Bridger Trail crossing, the trail went up the west side of Rock Creek for one mile, crossed back to the east side, went up the east side for five miles, and recrossed to the west side just above the mouth of Red Lodge Creek.

72. Snake is the name other tribes, and especially whites, used for Shoshone Indians in the nineteenth century. The name Snake

[City] & follow it[70]   we soon cross stony creek [Rock Creek] & have to recross before we leave it[71]   its currant is very swift but not very deep   at the last crossing one wagon gave way & had to be repaired   while fixing it we turned out our teams   got our dinner   in afternoon we followed up a small stream [Red Lodge Creek] & camped on its bank for the night   we met two of the snake tribe of Indians[72]   they had good ponies & they could talk a little english language   we have rather poor feed to night but lots of wild currants   drove near 18 miles

Sunday [July] 24th we left the small stream [Red Lodge Creek] & drove over a rough & hilly road   the weather is very warm & the hills to our left has been burnt over & there is some fire burning now near the mountain   at noon we stoped on creek [Beaver Creek] that was near dry   any quantity of currants here   in [the] afternoon we went down a long crooked & sideling hill it was steep a[nd] rocky & the worst one to go down we have found[73]   after driving about two miles on the bottom we came to a stream [East Rosebud Creek] supposed to be tongue river & crossed it   drove two or three miles & camped on little rose bud [West Rosebud Creek] drove 15 miles

Monday July 25th we started early crossing the stream [West Rosebud Creek] water near 3 ft deep currant swift bottom stony the road is still rough & hilly just before noon we crossed big rose bud river [Stillwater River] it was bad crossing it was very rocky & the ford was crooked after crossing we stoped for dinner while stoping here captain Bridger [Jim Bridger] came along in a buggy drawn by two mules he is a tough looking old chap there were a number of wagons both freight and returning emigrants with him[74] we saw them coming & thought it was a chance to send some letters home we pitched in & wrote a few & some of his party carried them off with them they tell a mournful tale of the mines & that men are leaving for home as fast as they come   that stock is low & everything else   but we are going on & drive a few miles & camp for the night by a beautiful spring   we find good grass & plenty of water   drove 14 miles   Bridger tells me to be sure & take the right hand road that he made to day when we leave the spring as it will save 5 miles & a deep canyon [Bridger Canyon][75]

Tuesday July 26th we started before 5 oclock & took the road that Capt Bridger told us to & found it a very good one untill we came to the valley of the Yellow Stone   we had a very bad hill to get down[76]   we then drove up the valley untill we cam[e] to the [Yellowstone] river which was near three miles & camped for the balance of the day as well as for the night for it was 3 oclock before we stoped   the Yellow Stone river at this place is something like the Platte or Misoura   it being muddy but not as much so as the above named   & its currant is more rapid   the valley is narrow & very stony for some ways along here and above there is some timber here & like that on other streams most all cottonwood   we drove 17 or 18 miles to get here to day

Wednesday [July] 27th we started 1/2 past 5 & drove until 1/2 past 11   then stoped in the edge of some timber that grew on the banks of stream [Boulder River] some 5 or 6 rods wide   bottom very stony   & the road has been stony all forenoon but level   being on bottom of yellowstone river   after crossing this stream we traveled over a rough country for a few miles   then came in the valley of Yellow Stone   we passed some men that were building a boat to go down the Yellow Stone river homeward bound   camped at night on its bank   we had first rate grass for our stock   we drove 20 miles

Thursday [July] 28th we started at 20 minutes before six & drove near 3 miles then came to the [Yellowstone] ford   the water was about 3 ft deep   swift currant   a long

originated in the eighteenth century as a misinterpretation of Indian sign language. The sign for "grass weavers," the Shoshone name for themselves, is very close to the sign for "snake," which also means "enemy" to some Plains tribes.

73. Many diarists commented on this steep descent to the Rosebud Valley, six miles south of present Absarokee, Montana.

74. Almost immediately after arriving in Virginia City, Jim Bridger started back to Fort Laramie, guiding a group of freighters and emigrants eastward over his route. He arrived at Fort Laramie in early August and was rehired as post guide. But he did not stay long, and on September 18 he left Red Buttes with a small train on his second trip of the season over his road.

75. Bridger directed Voorhees to a new road to the Yellowstone across the top of a divide, now called Stockade Hill, that avoided the treacherous descent down Bridger Canyon made by his earlier train (and probably the route Bozeman's train had taken). The spring Voorhees mentions was seven miles north of the Stillwater River crossing.

76. They came off the highland down a steep descent on the east side of Bridger Canyon, about a half mile above the mouth of Bridger Creek.

77. The Yellowstone ford was three miles below or east of present Springdale, Montana. The ford went diagonally upstream.

78. The mineral hot spring known as Hunters Hot Springs was four miles northwest of the Yellowstone River crossing. Jim Bridger visited the hot spring in the 1830s, and the trail to Montana that he opened in 1864 passed by the spring. In 1864 Andrew Jackson Hunter, a physician from Missouri, traveled the Bozeman Trail with his wife and three children in the small train that accompanied Bozeman's train. Dr. Hunter was impressed with the hot spring and returned with his family and settled there in 1870. He built a log cabin, dammed the spring, and opened Hunters Hot Springs. In 1873 he built bathhouses, then a hotel, and by the end of the decade his resort was well known throughout the territory. Hunters Hot Springs burned in the mid-twentieth century, and today only the foundations of the hotel, a few of the buildings, and the remnants of the hot spring plunge remain at the site, which is privately owned.

ford & slow crossing having to go 2/3 of the way across the stream then go up it for near 100 rods   the bank is very steep coming out[77]   after crossing we drove couple of miles & came to a beautiful little stream [Hunters Creek] but those that undertook to drink from it found themselves fooled for its waters were nearly hot   one [man] that was near the spring burned his lips to a blister it came from a spring [Hunters Hot Springs] just above the road[78]   at noon we stoped at a spring of cool water but very little grass but plenty of water from spring for cattle   we have left the bottom land & are on the hills again [Sheep Mountain] & drive untill near night   then come to the bottom land of the Yellowstone river & drove some 3 miles & camp near [where] 4 wagons are stoping   we soon learn they have a sick man & are waiting for him to Die   we have drove near 15 miles

Friday [July] 29th we do not start untill near noon we want to help bury the man   he Died this morning near 5 oclock & was buried at ten   there were 5 wagons that could not wait to help bury the man & pulled out of the train   the 4 joined us   we were nicely started when we met Mr Ward from Wisconsin that left us on big horn river & he told us they had a very good prospect up the [Yellowstone] river & wished us to go up there that the horse teams that left us on big horn river were most of them there   so we made up our mind to go there   we soon turned off the road & were on our way for another prospect   we camped just below an Indian camp that was on opposite side of the river from us   soon after we camped there were three came to our tents   one of them was the son of the chief of the Crows   he appeared to be very friendly & a good natured fellow   they had good ponies   in fact they were the best we had seen on the trip soon after there were 4 more come 2 were squaws   we gave them some bread & meat   the first three with ponies went off   the 4 stayed all night   just at night we

had a heavy shower of rain very sharp lightning & heavy
thunder we drove 10 miles

Saturday [July] 30th the rain of last night has made
the ground soft & very sticky & we do not hurry to be
off but after a late breakfast we hitch up our teams &
drive near 4 miles & make a stop nearly half the men go
out to prospect & all go in the same direction & that is
towards the gulch that the excitement is about we hear
all kinds of stories one that an Indian is piloting a party
to where it is but he takes them to the same place
another is [that] 80 miles above here is a lake
[Yellowstone Lake] & it is there the rich digings are a
party of 30 men go there will be gone 15 days some of
them that stay in camp is ketching some very nice fish
there is plenty of them in this stream a good portion of
them are trout drove 4 miles

Sunday [July] 31st we hitch up our teams & drive up
the [Yellowstone] river near two miles & camp on its
bank just where it comes out of the mountains[79] our
carelle now numbers 50 wagons[80] our usual work is to
lay around camp some fish some play cards some are
going to & from the camp that is in the canyon just
above us & are trying to kill time

Monday august 1st we hear both good & bad reports
from the mines above but nothing deffinite they are
building a sluice & will have it running to morrow if it
dont pay they will abandon the river at this place we will
know by wednesday great curiosity is felt in regard to it

Tuesday August 2nd some of the boys come in to day
says it wont pay to work that they find but small prospects
& that is very light they are working the sluice to day &
will report to morrow what it does. two wagons leave to
day & more will to morrow pay or no pay they are bound
for Virginia City good many talk of going home

Wednesday [August] 3rd nearly all the men are down
from where they have been for the last 10 days & say it

79. They were two miles
south of present
Livingston, Montana,
where the Yellowstone
River passes between two
high bluffs. This is the first
of four canyons on the
Yellowstone, known to
emigrants as the Lower
Yellowstone Canyon. The
fourth or upper canyon is
the Grand Canyon of the
Yellowstone in Yellowstone
National Park.

80. This was slightly more
than one-third of the
original 124 wagons that
left Richard's Bridge on
June 16.

81. The men were working the mining area some miles upstream that became known as Emigrant Gulch later in the season.

will not pay to work there[81]   the sluice is a failure & teams are leaving from camp above a few from ours & we will go to morrow

Thursday [August] 4th we get started soon after six the camp above us leave without letting their teams feed. we drove 10 miles & stop for dinner near a small stream of very nice water good grass here   wood plenty for us in afternoon we crossed quite a number of small streams & some bad hills one very stony[82] we have seen &

82. They went over Bozeman Pass and descended Kelly Canyon to the Gallatin Valley.

passed more timber to day than any one day yet   it was mostly pine & were small trees & standing very thick   it was on the mountains & to our left   at night we camped on small stream [East Gallatin River] near where those were that started before us without letting their teams feed   I shot a sage hen with revolver   drove 18 miles

83. This was the site of Bozeman, Montana, where a month earlier, on July 7, D. E. Rouse and W. J. Beall located adjoining claims of 160 acres each and a third one for John Bozeman nearby. Rouse and Beall immediately began constructing the first house, which was a tent made out of a wagon cover on top of a log foundation. This was the ranch that Voorhees saw, and it was probably Rouse and Beall whom he met. Four days later, on August 9, the meeting was held there, at which the town was established and named Bozeman.

Friday [August] 5th we got an early start & drove but a short distance then came to a ranche that had just been taken but a short time ago[83] it was on a small stream [Bozeman Creek] & a very good place for one small valley with good grass & plenty of wood   they were cutting hay expect to feed it to pony express company stock as we learn there is one to be established on this route (meaning Bozeman & Jacobs) (we met the men yesterday that were establishing the stations.)   soon after leaving this ranche we crossed East Gallatin [Bozeman Creek] a small stream & runs through a very fine valley timber on the mountains near by   Bozeman had just commenced to build a cabin at the crossing from here to the west Galatin [Gallatin River] was 12 miles over a beautiful valley well watered by small streams but most of it will have to be irrigated to produce crops   there is considerable timber on this river as far as we can see both up & down it   after comeing to the river which was where Bridgers road came to it (we having traveled on Jacobs road from the Yellow Stone)[84] we traveled down it [Gallatin River] for 2 miles to what

84. Voorhees went through Bozeman Pass to the Gallatin Valley, which was the route John Jacobs took his train on earlier in the season. At about the same time, Jim Bridger took his train through a pass a few miles to the north known as Bridger Pass.

is called the lower ford then camped for the night   there
was first rate grass wood & water   just after we stoped
some of our boys that went out on prospect tour 18 days
ago came in & before sundown they all came in but three
& those left the crowd last saturday morning & they
have failed to report   we had a good wash in the river   it
is divided in 5 different branches but they are narrow
except the main one & that is about 15 rods wide
between these two rivers at this point the valley is about
12 to 15 miles wide & it extends far below   on East
Galatin [Bozeman Creek] there is a number of farms &
they are raising fine crops of wheat & very fine
vegetables   this river runs near the mountains & the best
farms are at the foot of them   on Saturday [August] the
6th we lay over to have some boys go over to where
there were some men were at work prospecting   they
found them but they were not finding anything & were
going to leave   some of our train stoped here to locate a
farm   we saw cattle that had been here two year[s] that
have not eat any hay since they were here   there being no
snow in the valley in winter   while in the mountains it is
very cold & snow falls very deep   game of all kinds
come in the valley to winter[85]

    Sunday [August] the 7th   our teams are hitched up in
good season   our kegs filled for we are to go 12 miles
without water & we are off over a very dusty but not a
bad road   at noon we get to water but it is in small
quantities   but we have good grass   no timber. after dinner
we drove about 11 miles then came to Madison river
found it to be a very nice looking stream of water   its
bottom is very stony   no timber on its banks as far as we
can see   the mountains are high   & very stony on its bank
its waters about 3 ft deep   it is about 20 rods wide where
we crossed it[86]   after crossing it we drove about 2 miles &
camped on its bank in a small valley   but it is so stony it
can never be used for anything but to stop on over night

85. This is an excellent
description of the
Gallatin Valley, a
sheltered mountain valley
in which stock and game
can graze through the
winter.

86. They crossed the
Madison River a few
miles below or north of
the mouth of Hot Springs
Creek. After the crossing,
the road went up the west
side of the river for four
miles and then went
southwest over the hills
to Hot Springs Creek and
turned and went up it.

shortly after we stoped another train came up & camped near us that was apart of a train of 152 wagons that had some difficulty with the Indians near powder river & had 4 men killed[87]   they say the Indians came to their carelle in the morning & were fed by the train & when they left they appeared to be friendly   but before the train started they were fired into by the red skins   they having some good rifles   but the men from the train soon dispersed them   at night there was 4 head of oxen came to our camp & were stoped & drove back to virginia city   we drove 18 miles

Monday [August] 8th   we had a very sandy stony hilly & sideling road for a few miles & before noon we passed a boiling spring   its water is so hot that you cannot hold your hand in it[88]   for some rods below & a short distance above is a good spring of cold water   near here we passed the first house since leaving the Platt   it was built of small logs or poles   covered with the same and dirt thrown on the poles   they were puting up hay at this ranche   at noon we stoped on willow creek   in afternoon we passed several ranches & at night we camped on meadow brook near Newmans ranche   it is the first time we heard the sound of a reaper   here they were cutting hay with one   this ranche is near 20 miles from the city [Virginia City] & there is a number of acres fenced in   has very good garden   some corn & potatoes there is several more ranches on this stream above this place   this stream empties in the Madison river a short distance below   no timber on this stream in sight   we drove about 16 miles to day   we made a new road for a few miles

Tuesday [August] 9th   we started about 7 oclock & drove 10 miles up the Madison over a very good road then left the river & went two miles & stoped for dinner on the smallest stream we have seen. hardly water enough to water our cattle   no grass   in afternoon we climed the longest hill we have seen & camped on the top

87. This was the Townsend train, the third train of the 1864 season to traverse the Bozeman Trail.

88. Norris Hot Springs are on Hot Springs Creek, at present Norris, Montana. These frequently mentioned hot springs are thirty miles northeast of Virginia City on the road from Bozeman to Virginia City. Natural mineral water flows out of these artesian springs at 128 degrees. Today Bear Trap Hot Springs, a small RV park and soaking pool, is located here.

of it   found very little grass   no water   wind blowing
very cold   hills covered with rock

Wednesday [August] 10th we hitched up our teams at
day light & left the summit   drove some 3 or 4 miles then
stoped on small streams[89]   got some breakfast watered
our cattle   then drove to Virginia City   found its streets
filled with men & teams & everything seemed lively   we
drove through the town & stuck our tent near by   drove
our cattle in town & sold them for $15.00 per yoke   that
was the best price paid that day & now we are in Virginia
City after a long journey & where we did not expect to go
when leaving the Platt   but not finding that for which we
sought on the way we have kept looking up to here & find
the prospect rather small here[90] & we have made up our
minds to divide our things for Thomas [Jacobs] wants to
go to Norwegian gulch[91] with two others that are going
there to try it & [stay] on

Thursday [August 11th]   we divided up satisfactory
to all and Thomas [Jacobs] left us & James [Barnebee] &
myself with most of the boys from Mendon [and] with
many others from our train having made up our minds
that if nothing showed itself better than what we had
found we would make a break for home & the rest of
the week and Sunday we were around among the miners
that were at work & found plenty of claims to buy &
also found some of the boys [including Charles
Uptegrove and Jud Peak] that left our train at the big
horn river [Bighorn River] that had bought [and] paid
[out] all they had & now had forsaken their claims &
were looking for work   our young men thought they
would stay & try it [and] if they did not find any thing
here they would try it somewhere else & James
[Barnebee] & myself let the boys have what they wanted
of our things sold the balance to others & made
preperations for going home   the prices of diferent
articles of food seemed high to those that had never been

89. The road descended
from the summit down
Daylight Gulch, north of
the present highway.

90. Voorhees and his
companions intended to go
with Captain Hurlbut to
mines in the Bighorn River
region when they left the
North Platte in his train,
but they did not find any
there and continued on the
Virginia City without him.
Voorhees's appraisal of the
poor mining opportunities
in Alder Gulch substanti-
ates reports they had heard
on the trail.

91. Norwegian Gulch was
seven miles northeast of
present Norris in the Hot
Springs mining district. A
gold strike in 1864 brought
three hundred miners to
the gulch by that summer,
and mining continued in
the gulch for ten years.

92. The value of currency, or greenbacks, in Virginia City during the first few months after the gold strike was usually 50 percent of face value. The value of currency rose during the next years, and in 1867 most businesses began accepting greenbacks at par. Larry Barsness, *Gold Camp: Alder Gulch and Virginia City, Montana* (New York: Hastings House, 1962), 174–75, 177.

in a mining town before   flour was selling from 18$ to 20 in gold or double that in green backs[92]   bacon 35 to 40cts dried apples 35cts per pound   beans 35cts   sugar 50cts butter 80cts per pound or double that if paid in green backs   clothing was selling for gold about the same as in the states for paper [money]   horses & mules were in very good demand & were selling very well   cows & good wagons were selling well   oxen were comeing down & were comeing in by the hundreds every day   on Sunday [August 14] the streets were crowded with stock of all kinds to sell & everything was lively

Monday Morning [August 15]   we get ready to start for home   we hire our passage with Charles Uptegrove he having bought a four mule team & wagon   & seven of us go with him consisting [of] Mr Barrett, Dodge, [Jud] Peak, Van Ness   James [Barnebee] & myself & a man by the name of John Ferguson from Iowa   we with several other wagons leave Virginia City in afternoon & drive out about 10 miles & camp on stinking water river

Richard Owens

DIARY, 1864

RICHARD OWENS was a member of Cyrus C. Coffinbury's train, the third train to travel the Bozeman Trail in 1864. Owens left Huntingdon and Fayette counties, Pennsylvania, in David B. Weaver's company. Weaver's company consisted of Weaver, Owens, David Shorthill, Alexander Norris, George Travis, brothers John and William Hackney, and Melus Clark. Their company joined the Coffinbury train at Richard's Bridge and traveled in the second division of the train, under the direction of Captain John A. Kramer. Made up of acquaintances, friends, and relatives from a particular region (in this case, Pennsylvania), the Weaver party typified a gold rush company. Many of its members were already miners, having worked in the Pennsylvania coal mines or participated in an earlier gold rush. Their overland experience reveals the primary advantages of traveling in a company: mutual support and sharing of resources.

Richard Owens was born in Wales around 1824. It is not known when he came to this country, but it was probably in the early 1850s, since his wife Jane was also born in Wales and their daughter Mary was born in Maryland in 1855. Sometime after that, the family moved to Pennsylvania, where Owens worked as a coal miner (which was very likely his occupation in Wales).[1] On August 12, 1862, he enlisted as a private in the 125th Pennsylvania Volunteers, Company F. Another member of the Weaver party, David R. Shorthill, was a private in the same company. Owens was captured at the battle of Chancellorsville, Virginia,

---

SOURCE DOCUMENT: Richard Owen[s], Diary, 1864, typed transcripts of two versions, Small Collection 613, Richard Owen[s] Diaries, 1864–1866, Montana Historical Society Archives, Helena (hereafter SC 613, MHSA).

1. The 1860 Pennsylvania census, Huntingdon County, Huntingdon, p. 86, lists Richard Owens, 36, his wife Jane, 28, both born in Wales, and daughter Mary A., 5, born in Maryland. Also in the household were Edward Owens, 23, and David Lewis, 23, who were both born in Wales and were likely related to Richard Owens and his wife.

Richard Owens.

PHOTOGRAPHED BY KRUGER, HOUTZDALE, PENNSYLVANIA.
MONTANA HISTORICAL SOCIETY PHOTOGRAPH ARCHIVES, HELENA

on May 3, 1863, and taken to Libby Prison. Paroled on May 15, he was sent back to Pennsylvania, where he was mustered out on May 18.[2]

Older than his traveling companions, Owens was forty years old in 1864. He left his wife and daughter at home in Pennsylvania. He was also the first member of Weaver's traveling group to depart from Montana; he returned to Pennsylvania in a fleet of forty boats that left the boat-launching site south of present Livingston on September 16, 1866. He died at Brisbin, Clearfield County, Pennsylvania, in 1896.[3]

David B. Weaver transcribed Richard Owens's diary and John Hackney's diaries. The whereabouts of the original diaries are unknown. Some confusion exists over Owens's diary. There are two transcribed versions in the Montana Historical Society, and the exact history of how or when they were made is unclear. A reconstruction of the sequence from the notes on the manuscripts indicates that Weaver transcribed the original diary for Professor Milburn L. Wilson, a professor at the College of Agriculture and Mechanic Arts (Montana State University since 1965) at Bozeman. Wilson then retyped a second version from Weaver's transcription. No dates, however, are indicated on either version.

Weaver's version is titled "Crossing the Plains in 1864." Inexplicably, it begins on June 21, a month after Owens had departed from Omaha. Across the top is written "Copied from Richard Owens Diary for the use of Prof. M. L. Wilson, Agricultural College, Bozeman, Mont." It appears to be a close transcription, with little punctuation and capitalization. In contrast, Wilson's version has been edited and is punctuated, capitalized, and formatted in paragraphs. It is titled "Diary of the Travels of Richard Owen[s], From Omaha Nebraska to the Gold Regions of Idaho," and it begins on May 21, the day the party left Omaha. Because it is more complete, Wilson's version is the primary document presented here. I have inserted—in italics—excerpts from the transcription prepared by Weaver from the original diary where they add information or clarity.[4]

Richard Owens was designated to keep the communal diary for the Weaver traveling company, making his account significant beyond the

2. Military service records for Richard Owens, National Archives, Washington, D.C.; *History of the One Hundred and Twenty-fifth Regiment Pennsylvania Volunteers, 1862–1863* (Philadelphia: J. B. Lippincott, 1906), 312.

3. Information about Richard Owens's death is in a handwritten note in David B. Weaver, "Crossing the Plains in 1864, Copied from Richard Owens Diary," TS, p. 22, SC 613, MHSA.

4. M. L. Wilson died November 22, 1969, in Chevy Chase, Maryland. His wife donated his papers, including Owens's diary, to the Montana Historical Society the following year. Because Wilson wrote Richard's surname as Owen rather than Owens, the Society's records list him that way as well.

personal level. Keeping a communal record was not uncommon in closely-knit parties, and as such, his diary compares to the record Abram Voorhees kept for his company. Since Owens kept track of activities and incidents for the others, his record keeping exempted him from the evening duties and chores, such as milking cows and getting wood and water. And because Owens's diary was a communal record, the other members of the company always had complete access to it.[5]

According to David Weaver, Owens wrote his diary in a blank book, that is, one without the dates printed in it. Sometimes he used a whole page for one day's entry, so that he was able to write more than John Hackney, who was confined to a limited space. But since the dates were not printed in his book, Owens sometimes made mistakes, and Weaver then took Hackney's dates (which were pre-printed) to be the most accurate. Weaver also noted that Owens wrote with pen and ink, making his diary more legible than Hackney's, which was written in pencil.

Owens's entries are observant, meticulous, and detailed. He is serious and reveals no humor or lightness. His is the diary of a mature family man. His background as a coal miner is evident in his prolific interest in geology and natural resources. A frequent letter writer, he recorded all the letters he wrote and received during the trip. Ultimately he was a typical miner, and he prospected for gold at every opportunity along the way. His diary provides an informative and interesting glimpse into the experience of a gold rush company.

---

5. David B. Weaver, "Pioneer Reminiscences and Tales of the Early Sixties," transcribed by M. L. Wilson, pp. 13–14, 23, Small Collection 969, David B. Weaver Papers, 1865, 1907–1918, MHSA.

RICHARD OWENS DIARY

DIARY OF THE TRAVELS OF RICHARD OWENS
FROM OMAHA NEBRASKA TO THE GOLD REGIONS OF IDAHO

May 21, 1864. We commenced our march from
Omaha and traveled about eight miles and encamped
early in the evening on a small stream of water called
Coal [Cole] Creek.[6] We had a beautifull day. We had to
cook our sup[p]er and bake our bread with cattle chips
in the absence of wood.

May 22. After traveling 2 miles we came to the Little
Papillion. Three miles farther we came on to the Big
Papillion, a small stream of pure water, thence to
Elkhorn City[7] Distance to Omaha 22 miles. We traveled
one mile out of the way to a good camping ground on
the river. Here a Pawnee Indian came to us, armed with
bow and arrow.

May 23. Moved out and left the town called Elkhorn.
One mile farther we crossed the Elkhorn river at a place
called Bridgeport then we travelled all day across the Raw
Hide Flat, a place noted for its electricity [lightning
strikes]. Nearly all the telegraph poles have been struck by
it. In wet weather this must be a bad country to travel, but
happily for us the roads were dry and in good order so we
came to a small town called Fremont very near the Platte
River, then we came on about 2 miles farther and
encamped for the night on the Platte River.[8] Just now an
Indian came to visit us. Distance from Omaha 37 miles.
The Indian lay by our fire and slept all night.

May 24. We had to lay in camp untill noon, a waggon
belonging to the party being repaired, yet we travelled 14
miles. The roads are very dusty.

May 25. A fine morning, all the men are in good
health and spirits. About one mile in travel we struck the

6. The Cole Creek
crossing was seven miles
from Omaha. Today the
location of the crossing is
at the southern edge of
Benson Park in northwest
Omaha. In 1866 Nellie
Fletcher called this creek
Mud Creek. Fletcher
diary, May 15, 1866.

7. Elkhorn City was a
settlement on the road
from Omaha to Fort
Kearny, twenty-two
miles west of Omaha. It
was one mile east of the
Elkhorn River crossing.
Today the town is named
Elkhorn and has a
population of approxi-
mately 1,400.

8. The settlement of
Bridgeport was situated
twenty-three miles west
of Omaha, on the east
bank of the Elkhorn
River at the crossing of
the emigrant road. A
military bridge across the
Elkhorn River was
located at Bridgeport.
Today the course of the
Elkhorn River is west of
its location in the 1860s,
and the site of Bridge-
port, which no longer
exists, is now in a field.
After crossing the
Elkhorn River, the
emigrant road continued
northwest across the
Rawhide Creek Bottoms,
heading to the Platte
River.

9. The road from Omaha came to the Platte River on the north side of a great bend, at present North Bend, Nebraska.

10. The settlement of Buchanan, Nebraska, was established in 1856 on the east bank of Shell Creek. Abram Voorhees noted the ranch of one of the town's founders, Isaac Albertson. Voorhees diary, May 5, 1864.

11. Columbus was established in 1856 on the east side of the Loup River, about three miles above its junction with the Platte River, by a town company from Columbus, Ohio. The founders built a sawmill, gristmill, and ferry at the Loup River crossing of the newly surveyed Omaha to Fort Kearny Military Road. In 1864 Columbus resident George Francis Train announced that the town was the geographic center of the United States and was therefore the proper place for the national capital. While his suggestion was not seriously considered, Columbus continued developing as a strategic location on the north-side road between Omaha and Fort Kearny. Today Columbus, forty-seven miles west of Fremont on U.S. 30, has a population of nearly twenty thousand.

12. A giant, lone cottonwood tree stood on the north bank of the Platte River, 131 miles from Omaha. The tree

North Bend of the Platte River.[9] Three Pawnees came to us begging. Plenty of water all day travelling along the Platte. Passed the Buchannon House at Shell Creek.[10] Good camping ground. Encamped on a lake full of fish. We all enjoyed ourselves in the evening, fishing and bathing. Travelled this day about 15 miles. A fine school for children here.

May 26. All the men are well. We here met an Englishman, a Mormon from Utah. He has settled on a fine ranche near the river. Encamped for the night on the Loup Fork. Many [Pawnee] Indians visited us during our stay here. There is a small town here, called Columbus.[11] Here I saw a Welchman by the name of Rees Davies. Distance from Omaha 85 miles.

May 27. We crossed the [Loup Fork] ferry, a miserable poor one, then went on about 15 miles and encamped on a stream with much fish in it. This night was very cold.

May 28. We started early in the morning through a beautifull country. The valley from bluff to bluff must be about 40 miles wide. The river is about 4 miles wide. We are now encamped on a ranche by the edge of the river. Alkali in these mud pools. We had to get wood from an island to cook with, about a hundred yards off in the river.

May 29. We lay encamped on the bank of the Platte. A fine, warm day. All of us enjoying ourselves in bathing and cooking and washing and mending our clothes. Dave M. Caver is hunting on the Grand Island. We are getting anxious about him. If we should lose him it would be a great loss to us for he is indeed a good fellow. Dave came in. We encamped for the night.

May 30. All in good health. We started early in the morning and at noon came to Lone Tree Ranche. Dined here and put my name on the tree as many emigrants do.[12] Here the boys fired several times at a large pelican, but all missed it. The valley is very wide here. The eye cannot penetrate as far as the bluffs on the right, but on the south side the bluffs are not far distant. Many teams are on the other side [south side] of the river. The Platte is high. We are now encamped on the ranche called Shoemakers Point.[13] A beautifull day, but very dusty.

May 31. We were rather delayed, our cattle having strayed on an island. We all of us nearly had to cross before we could get them. It was far advanced in the day before we started. We came through a populous settlement, halted near that place to dinner at a farm house. We picked up a man and woman. About 4 o'clock we halted at a house and [black]smith shop, the owner is a Dane, both him and his wife work in the shop. We took two wheels off our waggon to cut their tiers [tires]. Traveled about 16 miles.

June 1. We traveled about five miles and came to Wood River. Two saw mills near the crossing. A fine country. Antelope numerous. We came on about 9 miles and encamped on this stream. Plenty fish here. Mosquitoes kept us awake near all night. The Platte is distant from us about 7 miles.

June 2. We started early in the morning, arrived at Nebraska Center Post Office in three miles.[14] We then moved forward and arrived oposite Ft. Kearney in the evening. We passed a [prairie] dog town a few miles from the Ft.[15] Encamped on the Platte this night. Distance to Omaha 195 [miles].

[Owens's party continued up the north side of the Platte and North Platte to Fort Laramie. He commented on several graves, emigrant landmarks, and Sioux Indians. When they came to a Sioux village on June 11, he wrote, "The people were well clad, but are all inveterate beggars and thiefs. . . . These Indians stole many things from the emigrants."]

June 25. We came up to oposite the fort [Fort Laramie] and halted there a few minutes. Some of the

was a landmark for north-side road travelers and could be seen for many miles in every direction on the otherwise treeless prairie. In 1858 the Lone Tree Ranch was established nearby. The ranch served as a stage station and eventually became present Central City, Nebraska. The great tree died after hundreds of passing travelers carved their initials or names on its massive trunk, and it was finally destroyed in a storm in 1865.

13. Jesse Shoemaker's ranch was at Shoemaker's Point on the north-side Platte road, twelve miles west of Lone Tree Ranch, and fifteen miles west of present Central City, Nebraska. Shoemaker's Point is listed in contemporary guidebooks as having good accommodations.

14. James E. Boyd operated a trading post, stables, brewery, and blacksmith shop at Nebraska Center Post Office on the north-side Platte road, ten miles east of the Miller & Company Ranch, one mile west of present Gibbon, Nebraska.

15. There were many large prairie dog towns along the Platte in this area. Had Owens crossed to the south side of the river at this point, he would have passed through Valley City, also known as Dogtown for the large prairie dog town in the vicinity, eight miles east of Fort Phil Kearny.

men went over to the P[ost] Office for letters, but failed
to get any so we moved on and halted to [eat] dinner
about 3 miles above, then we moved again and came over
bluffs and deep gullys about 4 miles, and then halted for
the night close by a cmpy [company] of soldiers. Pretty
good grass, plenty of wood and water. The soldiers are
the 11th Ohio Cav.[alry]

June 26. this being Sunday we lay in camp to rest our
cattle, and wash our clothes and having a talk with the
soldiers, who seem to be a fine set of fellows.

June 27. We started early in the morning and came about
five miles when we struck a good spring of cool water on
the right of the road among some cottonwood. *We have a
small pamphlet called Campell's Guide to Idaho which has
been of use to us in finding camping places, but now we find
the Guide book unreliable and as likely wrong as right.*
Here Campbell's guide is wrong. About 4 miles we came
through a very mountainous country.[16] The rocks are
formed of flint, lime, and red sand stone. We then came to
the [North Platte] river and encamped for the night. No
grass. Distance to Omaha 540.

*[They traveled west from Fort Laramie on what is now
known as Child's Cutoff on the north side of the river.]*

July 1. We this day joined *our three wagons to a* large
train. Many waggons. We had to join them for our
protection. *now we are in a train of 13 wagons* The
Indians are very wicked. Stealing horses and mules.
Yesterday they killed a man right on the road near where
we are now encamped. We travelled about 15 miles today
over a poor and barren country. Hardly any grass.
Travelling is very dangerous now on the plains *on
account of the Sioux Indians, who are bent on murder
and theft.* During the day the sun is very hot and the
nights cold. Distance from Omaha 586.

*[Owens's party did not stop to celebrate the Fourth of
July as most travelers did. The country was barren, so they*

16. They went through
Rocky Pass and crossed
over Emigrant Hill north
of present Guernsey,
Wyoming.

kept going to find feed for the cattle. They finally camped
when they came to the bottom on the North Platte, where
there was adequate grass, wood, and water. The camp-
ground was opposite Deer Creek Station on the other side
of the river.]

July 6. This day we made an early start. Travelled
over a good road for five miles, then dined in plenty of
grass. Moved out again into the bluffs. A very sandy
road untill we came down to a bridge [Richard's Bridge]
over the [North] Platte. A ranche on the South side of
the river, held by a frenchman [John Richard]. Crossed
the river and came [southeast] about five miles to
encamp. Indian fires in the mountains. Good water and
grass and wood. Distance to Omaha about 650.

July 7. We have stopt here all this day, awaiting trains
[to come] in so that we may get a large comp[an]y to go
the Bozeman route. We have now in camp about one
hundred [men and] 50 waggons and we are going to lay
here till Monday. *Myself and [Dave] Shorthill took our*
guns and struck for the mountains at the foot of which we
are camped. Near the top of the mountains I run into a
herd of Mule Deer, they were a sight to see with their
monstrous big ears. These were the first of this kind I
ever saw, they got away before I got a shot at them but
Shorthill was more fortunate. Dave shot a fine deer
today. Snow on the mountains.

July 8. Here we lay in our camp. Place the same. A
meeting this day to know the minds of the men with
regard to the best route.

July 9. We encamped on the same place. The boys
shot two deer in the Black hills.

July 10. We are here still. A comp[an]y of 30 waggons
have just come in. They ask of us to stay over tomorrow
and they will go with us so we agreed. *quite a warm*
discussion is indulged as to [the] *best of the two routes* [to
Virginia City].

July 11. They moved out and left us *and took the
Bridger route.* We felt insulted, and the following
morning

July 12. We moved over the bridge, crossing the
[North] Platte river, bidding our old comforter adieu. *Mr
Richard did not charge us toll for crossing either way as
he is interested in getting the travel over the Bozeman
route* We at once struck the sandy bluffs on the North
side of the Platte and moved Northeast into the interior
across these sand hills for about 3 miles. Road very
heavy. *the women in our train are making trouble fearing
that we will be massacreed by the Indians* One poor
woman crying and did not wish to come along with us,
finaly she consented. The next 9 miles is a good road. We
encamped in the evening by some mud holes [Sand
Spring Creek]. Water very bad indeed.

July 13. Our captain [C. C. Coffinbury] staid behind
at the bridge to try to induce other teams to come along
with us. We lay in camp till noon, and then determined
among ourselves to move out, for our cattle will soon die
for the want of water. Plenty grass here, no wood, and
little water. We sunk a good well in the morning and put
a barrell into it about 2 miles up stream from the old
mud holes. Distance to the Salt water from the Platte
river 12 miles.

We started out in the evening. Travelled over a very
sandy, bad road for 6 miles and a half [miles]. Arrived at
a small stream of water [Sand Spring Creek] strongly
impregnated with coperas, or some other mineral *salts.*
Substance injurious to both man and beast. Here we
encamped for the night. Sage *brush* for cooking use.

July 14. Here we lay all day, awaiting other teams up
to join us, which came up in the afternoon, 17 in number.
This day there was a motion put forward and carried in
the morning for the indiscriminate slaughter of all
Indians, but was reconsidered and acted upon in the

17. Owens's statement
reveals a critical turning
point in relations between
emigrants and the northern
Plains tribes. The 1864
emigrants were aware
that their intrusion into
Indian territory was not
welcome, although they
probably had not

evening and resulted in favour of letting them alone so long as they did not intrude on us.[17]

July 15. We are laying still, awaiting another train [coming] up. All this range of country is barren and bluffs. We could not sleep last night with the prairie wolves, who were howling around our corral nearly all night.

July 16. We turned out early this morning and after travelling 2 miles and a half, very sandy ground, we at length came out on the open prairie. Good hard road for about 10 miles. Plenty of splendid iron ore. It lay along the plain in abundance. Called by some, liver ore.[18] Came to Dry Creek [Salt Creek] and encamped. Plenty of water by digging about two feet in the bed of the stream. Tolerable good grass and plenty wood. Distance to Platte about 30 miles. My favorite [dog?], Fleet Fan, was run over this day. I had to shoot her.

July 17. We started this morning down the bed of a creek [Salt Creek] called by emigrants Dry Creek. By noon we had travelled 8 miles up and down through a very rugged defile or kanyon. In the evening we came about four miles. Arrived into a basin surrounded with rocky precipieces. Two outlets from the interior of the basin. I have examined carefully these rocks and find them to contain plenty of iron stone of excellent quality. I have found five stratas of ore within the height of 60 feet. Small seams of coal. Plenty rattlesnakes in this basin, wood plenty and grass, but very bad watter. Here we encamped for the night. Distance to the Platte 42.

July 18. As usual we started early, but owing to some delay we went slowly through the same river bed [Salt Creek]. The bed of the river is all white with salt and saleratus.[19] We came on about 14 miles and encamped on the creek. One of our oxen has been alkalied [poisoned by alkali] and is not able to work. Distance to Platte 56 miles.

July 19. At eight this morning we moved out. The sun

heard about the attack on the Townsend train on July 7. Their discussions reflect their concern for the risk of traveling this route and their ambivalence about how to respond should they encounter native peoples. Other accounts indicate that the discussions were quite heated, but fortunately the majority arrived at a reasonable attitude of accommodation.

18. The iron ore was called liver ore for its dark reddish color resembling the color of liver.

19. Saleratus is sodium or potassium bicarbonate, a white chalky substance that was an early form of baking soda, a leavening agent to make bread and cakes rise. The name is from the Latin *sal aeratus* meaning, "aerated salt." Saleratus became commercially available in 1840 and was packaged in paper envelopes. For it to work properly, the saleratus was mixed with an acid food or chemical such as cream of tartar, just as baking soda is today. Saleratus worked best when added to dough that was baked rapidly at a high temperature, and thus it was ideally suited to baking in cast iron utensils over the intense heat of an outdoor fire. Occasionally overland travelers supplemented their supply of commercial saleratus from natural soda springs or the crusts of alkali deposits, but those who used natural saleratus often found it imparted a bitter taste to the bread or cake.

very hot and the men all covered with dust. I saw some splendid veins of coal and also very large beds of good free stone. One of our party shot a fine deer. Our ox is sick today. Borrowed another yoke from a friend and travelled through the same river bed. Found an Indian skull on the plain. No water fit to drink, only in the wells. Cottonwood begins to be plenty. Travelled about 13 miles. Distance to Platte 69.

July 20. Last night the rains fell and raised the creek [Salt Creek], making it impassable. It is a stream of mud. We lay here all day, digging wells and busying ourselves generaly.

July 21. We moved out early this morning and travelled down the stream [Salt Creek] and crossed it 15 times in 7 miles, then arrived on the Powder River, a small muddy stream like the other but a little larger. Crossed it. The coal formations are to be seen to the river. After crossing we came about 6 miles and struck the North Fork of the Powder River, a fine stream of pure water.[20] We enjoy it heartily. We are now encamped on this stream [Powder River]. Plenty wood and grass and water. Just now a white man's scalp is exhibited, found in a pine tree. Killed lately.[21] Distance to Platte 81 miles.

July 22. We moved out at 8 this morning and some of our advanced guard came on the body of the man killed. He had been buried by his friends, but the wolves had taken him out and devoured much of his body. We buried him again. His name is Frank Hudelmeyer. Also we found the grave of A Warren, of Missouri, killed by Indians on the 9th [8th] inst.[ant] [the present month] but the former on the 7th.[22] We travelled on the North Fork about 13 miles.[23] In the evening came up to Clear Creek [South Fork of Crazy Woman Creek] about 9 o'clock.[24] That night encamped there. During the night the wolves howled awful. We could not sleep. We are

20. They came to where the South Fork of the Powder branches off to the south, or to their left. However, the emigrants assumed the South Fork was the main branch and that they were turning onto the North Fork. In actuality, they were continuing up the main branch, and the North Fork of the Powder branches off a few miles farther west of this point.

21. This was the scalp of the man named Mills in the Townsend train who went back to look for his stray cow on July 7, the morning of the Indian attack.

22. Both men were killed in the Townsend train fight on July 7. Frank Hudelmyer was buried that evening; A. Warren died about 2:00 a.m. and was buried near him the next morning.

23. They continued up the Powder River five miles, crossing it twice, to the North Fork Powder River. They turned and went northwest up the North Fork six miles to where the stream makes a bend to the west.

24. From the bend in the North Fork Powder River, they crossed over the hills fifteen miles to South Fork Crazy Woman Creek.

now near the foot of the Big Horn Mountain, the tops are covered with snow. Had a fine antelope this day. Plenty of grass and water. We are now in the Snakes and Crows country.[25] Cunning and cruel people. Distance to the Platte 102.

July 23. Our cattle are very tired, consequently we have to lay here this day. Our men went into the mountains to prospect, but were unsuccessfull. Many antelopes were killed today, also a very large cinamon bear was killed in a thicket at the foot of the mountains by two of the boys. After he was wounded he made a rush on one man, but a revolver soon terminated the struggle. During the night the wolves howled awfull. We killed one of them.

July 24. We set out at 7 o'clock this morning and travelled over a good road for about 3 miles and came to a creek [Middle Fork Crazy Woman Creek] of good water not mentioned in our guide,[26] then came on about 4 miles farther and struck another stream [Poison Creek] of good water, with much fish in it. This I believe to be Tongue River.[27] Watered our stock and moved on 3 or 4 miles and came on another stream [Muddy Creek] of good water. Encamped on this for the night. Some of the men have gone after buffalo. We are now at the foot of the Snowy Range [Bighorn Mountains], but it is delightfull and pleasant in the valley. Boys and men fishing and the women milking the cows. Plenty of grass and water, but the beavers keep the stream muddy. Distance to the Platte 116.

July 25. We moved out all right this morning and travelled over a good road all day, excepting in crossing the dry bed of a creek [Bull Creek] which is sandy. Two men [John Boyer and Rafael Gallegos], french guides formerly of Capt. Townsend's Train, who were on their way to the Platte river *are with us tonight.* They took several letters with them belonging to our men,

25. Owens may have read about the Crow and Snake tribes, but his information was not correct. The Powder River Basin was formerly Crow territory, but by 1860 they had been pushed west of the Bighorn River by the Sioux and their allies. The traditional territory of the Snakes (Shoshones) was west of the Bighorn Mountains.

26. Campbell's guidebook was totally inaccurate for the Bozeman Trail. Few streams they crossed were listed in it.

27. The Tongue River was one of the few streams in present Wyoming listed in Campbell's guidebook, although it was many miles north of this stream.

[charging] fifty cents each for conveying them. We crossed several dry streams during the day. Encamped on a splendid place on Lodge Pole River [Clear Creek], a fine stream of water as clear as crystal, which descends from the Snowy Range. Plenty of grass and wood and game. Coal in abundance.[28] Distance to the Platte 130.

July 26. This day it was agreed among the comp[an]y to halt here one day for the purpose of ascending the mountains to prospect for gold. I was one of the party detailed to go and about 14 other men. We travelled about 14 miles up into a kanyon and did our duty well, but failed to find gold in the mountains. Berrys of different kinds are here in abundance. Bears and buffalo and elk are numerous in these mountains. Many white men have lost their lives in these kanyons.[29]

July 27. We moved out this morning and crossed the creek [Rock Creek] five times in the course of three miles. We then left the stream and came to a dividing ridge. Crossed it and came in view of a fine lake [Lake De Smet] surrounded by burnt hills, as red as brick.[30] All been once in a great conflagration and the lake in the middle of it, very large masses of lava are lying on the border of the lake.[31] The lake on examination is surely a deadly body of water for it has a very stinking sulphurous smell.[32] At the lower end of it a seam of coal has been exposed for several acres in extent by a flood of water and on its surface are very large petrified trees. Some parts of them has turned into iron, while others are turned into rock. Game, grass water and wood abundant. Road good for travelling. Distance to the Platte 143.

July 28. This morning is cloudy and colder than usual. We moved out early, after travelling about 3 miles we came on a good stream of water [Shell Creek], then came on 2 miles. Came on another fine large stream of excellent water [Little Piney Creek], then about two

28. They were traveling through the western part of the Powder River Coal Basin, which contains some of the world's thickest coal seams.

29. Although a few white men had been killed in the Bighorn canyons, this statement that many white men had lost their lives in the canyons is an exaggeration based on rumor.

30. This region is known for the striking beds of bright red scoria or clinker formed when exposed coal beds were ignited, such as by lightning. The coal beds burned slowly, baking the surrounding shales and sandstones into a red slag, in the same process as when clays are baked to form brick.

31. Here Owens is mistaken, since scoria is sedimentary and not volcanic in origin.

32. Lake De Smet was a small saline lake in the Bozeman Trail era. In the twentieth century dams at both ends and water diverted into it changed it into a much larger freshwater lake.

miles farther came on another good stream [Big Piney].
Thence we took the mountains. Very steep descent, but
not so bad in ascending them.[33] [H]ere the boys shot a
fine buffalo, abundance of meat for all the members of
the train. Many antelopes and deer has been shot today.
We came on a small stream [Jenks Creek] again and
halted for one hour. Moved out again in the evening and
arrived on another small creek [Prairie Dog Creek] and
encamped here for the night. Grass, wood and water
abundant. Distance to the Platte 160.

July 29. We started at 7 in the morning and travelled
about 4 miles, when Tomlinson's waggon broke,
consequently we had to halt. We turned the cattle out
and at 2 p.m. we again started down the same stream bed
[Prairie Dog Creek] for five miles. This river bed [valley]
we followed 15 miles, then crossed out of it and took to a
mountain road [divide], which we travelled along for
three miles, and arrived at Tongue river [Goose Creek],
as they call it.[34] A fine stream of good water. Passed coal
formations all this day and on the right of the road the
burnt hills [scoria] are very numerous. Some Indians
were seen visible, but very shy. In the dead of the night
our cattle stampeded and created a great confusion in
camp. We expected it [was] a night attack by Indians, but
were happily deceived. Distance to the Platte 172.

July 30. At eight this morning we broke camp.
During the day we crossed three small streams of
watter.[35] Fine coal formations on the way. Seams croping
out of the bluff sides. Buffalo abundant. The men shot
many of them, then leaving them to rot on the plains,
which I think is a sin.[36] We arrived in the evening on a
fine stream or river [Tongue River]. Splendid water, grass
two feet deep, wood plenty. They are bringing an elk
into camp now. Distance to the Platte, 187.

July 31. This morning we started at 8 and after
travelling about 8 miles came to a small creek [South

33. They climbed Lodge
Trail Ridge, descended to
Fetterman Ridge, and
went down the back of
Fetterman Ridge to
another sharp descent.

34. During this day they
traveled down the east side
of Prairie Dog Creek,
crossed it, and went west
over the divide to Goose
Creek at present Sheridan,
Wyoming.

35. They crossed Soldier
Creek, South Dry Fork,
and Wolf Creek as they
traveled northwest from
Goose Creek to Tongue
River.

36. Here Owens goes
beyond the usual diarist's
comment that the wanton
killing of bison is wasteful,
characterizing the
slaughter as sinful.

Fork], but it is now nearly dry. Moved forward again 3 miles and then struck another stream [Twin Creek]. A little water here. We watered our cattle here and then moved forward about 3 miles and a half and then struck a good stream of pure water [East Pass Creek]. Encamped here for the night. Buffalo along the plains in all directions. The men are killing them in large numbers. I feel sorry to see such destruction. They leave tons of good meat every day to be devoured by the wolves at night. Distance to the Platte 201 miles.

August 1. We crossed the creek this morning at 8 o'clock and after we travelled half a mile we crossed another small creek [West Pass Creek], then about 4 miles farther we crossed another creek, called Rose Bud [Little Bighorn River]. Then after travelling 7 1/2 miles came to another creek [Lodge Grass Creek]. Game is abundant on this stream. Bear, buffalo, elk, antelope and deer. Many are killed this evening by our men. Beaver are also plenty. Several Indians were seen on this stream, but when they heard the reports of firearms by our hunters they left. This stream is called Little Horn [Lodge Grass Creek]. We encamped on this river for the night. Wood, water and grass abundant. Distance from the Platte 213.

August 2. Two of our men are very sick. The train is not permitted to leave. The men are hunting buffalo and curing the meat.

August 3. This day we started about 8 a.m. and crossed two or three dry river beds; about 4 miles we came to a creek [Rotten Grass Creek]. The water muddy. Many beaver dams above. Then came on about 6 miles. A splendid stream of water [Soap Creek]. Tastes very pleasant and sweet. Then moved forward again about 4 miles. Struck a small stream [Deer Creek]. Encamped on this for the night. Plenty wood, water and grass. Distance to the Platte 226.

August 4. We started at 8 a.m.. Crossed two dry creek

beds then came on a fine stream of water [Soap Creek].
Soon we descended a steep hill and came to the Big Horn
river, which is muddy. Supposed to be so from a number
of miners at work upon the stream. Immediately we
commenced to prospect and found a good discovery of
fine gold. Plenty fish here. Wood and grass in abundance.
Distance to the Platte 234 miles.

August 5. Forty men has been detailed to ascend the
river to prospect it, while the ballance of us lay about
fishing and enjoying ourselves hunting and other
exercises, awaiting the result of the expedition. The river
is now low and not easy [easily] fordable. It is about 150
yards wide. Wood is here in abundance.

August 6. We lay here about midnight, three of the
men belonging to the expedition returned, having lost
the others.

August 7. In the same place. The men all returned,
having failed to cross a large kanyon [Bighorn Canyon]
in the mountains.

August 8. We commenced preparing our waggons for
fording the river.[37] We raised the waggon beds about one
foot and then started the crossing. All went well
excepting one horse, which we lost. We were all over by
noon on the other side [west side] of the river. The Major
[C. C. Coffinbury] and six men went up into the
mountains this morning. We prospected this evening,
found some gold. Encamped here this night.

August 9. This day we moved out at an early hour.
Came on a fine spring of water on the left of the road,
about five miles from the river. Then about half a mile
farther we came on another spring on the right side of
the road. Then about 6 1/2 miles we came on a muddy
stream of bad water [Beauvais Creek]. Encamped on this
stream for the night. Not much grass or watter. This day
Dave [Shorthill] and I nearly fell into a hornet's nest. We
brought an Indian into camp.

37. They forded the
Bighorn River eight miles
below the opening of the
Bighorn Canyon at
Spotted Rabbit Crossing.

August 10. This day we started early over a dry
barren country. About noon we came to a dry creek bed,
but found no water. We might have sunk a well here and
found water, but we travelled forward yet 12 miles and
then the night had set in and the roads steep and
dangerous for travell. Also very much exposed to Indian
atacks, who are very numerous on this road but seem to
be friendly, many of them riding their ponys along all
day and slept within the corral all night. Therefore we
were compelled to form our corral on a dividing ridge on
the plain without water or wood. During the night a wild
beast came into the corral and took away a dog with him.
The poor dog howled mournfully as he was carried away
into the thicket. Distance travelled this day 22 miles.

Aug. 11. This morning we started at break of day.
Drove about 4 and a half miles and arrived on a stream
called Nez Perses [Pryor Creek]. Water good. Plenty cat
fish in it. Encamped here for the remained of the day and
night. Plenty grass and wood and goosberrys and
currants and all kind of game in abundance. Distance to
the Big Horn 38 miles and a half.

Aug. 12. We lay in camp all day. Several Indians
around us. They apear to be friendly. The people
gathered berrys and dried them in the sun for packing to
be used in the winter. Also plenty of hops as large and as
good as they are in the States.

Aug. 13. The men returned to camp today after
travelling about 50 miles in the Big Horn mountains,
reporting that they could not cross the deep kanyons and
were compelled to return.

Aug. 14. We moved out today and crossed a very
hilly country. Very dangerous to travell. Arrived about
noon on Clark's Fork [Yellowstone River].³⁸ A fine large
stream of water. Plenty fish in it and also much fine gold
in it which will be worked by some partys ere long. Our
opinion is that many are now at work on this river up in

38. They came to the
Yellowstone River
opposite present
Billings, Montana.

39. While traveling in
the hills south of the
Yellowstone, a dog in
the train caused a
stampede that severely
damaged wagons and
oxen. Captain
Coffinbury suggested
killing all the dogs in the
train, but the emigrants
refused and split into
two trains. Coffinbury's
train of about twenty-
five wagons took all the
dogs. Calling themselves
the dog train, they
referred to the other
train as the anti-dog
train. Owens's party

the mountains and have no doubt but it pays well. Plenty grass, wood and water. Distance from Nez Perses [Pryor Creek] to the Yellowstone about 11 miles. No water on the road today.

August 15. We left camp early this morning. Came about 3 miles on the [Yellowstone] river bottom and then struck the bluffs for 10 miles. Descended a steep declivity to the river again. Encamped here for the night. Grass, wood and water plenty here. The train divided [over the dog question].[39] Travelled this day 13 miles.

Aug. 16. We started early this morning and travelled on the level plain near the [Yellowstone] river about five miles, then the road led into the bluffs for about 2 miles then descended the plain and came in sight of a river called by some the Clark's fork. Crossed this without trouble, then went over a ridge to the Yellowstone River.[40] Halted for dinner on its bank, then came on again across another hill to this river [Clarks Fork] again. Halted here for the night.[41] This is a fine stream [Rock Creek], plenty trout in it. Flows from the Snowy Range. Travelled this day 21 miles. Plenty wood on this river and grass.

August 17. We moved out early in the morning and after we travelled about 2 miles we came on Bridgers Road. Here many trains has passed on this road. We then came on several miles on a very good road and crossed the Fork [Rock Creek].[42] We then, after traveling a few miles, came on another small stream of water [Red Lodge Creek], followed it up a while and then encamped on it for the night.[43] Wood, water and grass. Three white men passed down Clarks fork [Rock Creek] today in a canoe. We did not speak to them. Also this evening David Shorthill was struck down in a thicket by a bear. He was not hurt. The bear left and Dave was glad. Travelled this day 16 miles.

Aug. 18. We started at 6 a.m. and travelled along the

stayed in Coffinbury's dog train. More humorously than belligerently, the two trains competed to get ahead of each other for the rest of the trip.

40. In the morning they traveled five miles up the south bank of the Yellowstone River to the mouth of Clarks Fork. Instead of crossing as the previous trains had, they turned southwest and went over the bluffs for three miles to Clarks Fork and forded three miles above its mouth. Then they went north over the divide about a mile to the Yellowstone River where they stopped for noon.

41. During the afternoon they traveled south over the hills on the west side of Clarks Fork, passed the mouth of Rock Creek, and camped on Rock Creek. Owens did not realize they had turned up Rock Creek and thought they were camped on Clarks Fork.

42. They intersected the Bridger Trail where it crossed Rock Creek a mile below present Joliet, Montana. They continued up the west side of Rock Creek for one mile to where the trail crossed back to the east side.

43. After crossing Rock Creek they went up the east side five miles, crossed back to the west side just above the mouth of Red Lodge Creek, and went up Red Lodge Creek to their evening camp.

stream [Red Lodge Creek] that we encamped on for two miles, then the road took the hills. then we came the ballance of the road up hills and down into valleys which were very fertile and cherrys were in abundance. Arived on a fine stream of pure water [Rosebud Creek]. Plenty of wood and grass. The Indians are burning the grass on the oposite side of the river with the intention of starving our cattle. I prospected this river and found gold. Travelled this day 13 miles.

August 19. We started at 7 a.m. and crossed the river [Rosebud Creek] where we had encamped on last night, then travelled over a hilly country for 10 miles and then came on another stream [Stillwater River],[44] quite a large stream near the foot of the snow caped mountains. We lay here that night. Grass, wood and water plenty. Distance travelled 10 miles.

Aug. 20. We started at five this morning and came about five miles and crossed a small creek of good water. No more water for nearly 15 miles untill we struck the Yellow Stone. We travelled this day 21 miles. We are now encamped on the [Yellowstone] river.[45] We here found a small train of 10 waggons. From this to the place where we first struck the Yellow Stone 91 miles.

Aug. 21. We lay in camp this day.

Aug. 22. This morning we moved out at 7 a.m. Travelled through a fine fertile country on the Yellow Stone River.[46] Crossed two dry river beds. Arrived on a fine stream [Boulder River]. A fork of the Yellow Stone. Met several other waggons on this stream. The people are talking of wintering here.[47] Distance from the first place we struck the Yellow Stone 104 [miles].

Aug. 23. We started up the [Yellowstone] river this day, a fine road and a beautiful valley. Crossed the Yellowstone after travelling 18 miles. Distance travelled on the [Yellowstone] river 117 miles. Crossed in the evening and came on 4 miles farther. Struck a hot stream

44. After crossing Rosebud Creek they went northwest over the hills to the Stillwater River.

45. They camped on the bank of the Yellowstone River just west of Bridger Creek.

46. They traveled all day up the south bank of the Yellowstone River.

47. It is not known who these people were, but they moved on. No emigrants actually stayed this far down the Yellowstone during the following winter. The closest mining camps were in Emigrant Gulch, several miles above present Livingston, Montana.

of water [Hunters Creek]. Encamped on this river or creek for the night. During the evening I started up towards the source of it and found it [Hunters Hot Springs]. The prairie surrounding it is generally level. It springs up in 8 or 10 places, boiling so that I could not hold my finger in it a second. It is strongly impregnated with sulphur, which smells strongly on my approach to it. Also we saw this day a [Mackinaw] boat containing nine men, going down the [Yellowstone] river for the States, having left Virginia City about one week previously. Distance to the Yellowstone 4 miles.

August 24. This morning we struck out about one mile to a cold spring, where we breakfasted. Our cattle would not drink it from the hot stream. We then came on a good road for 9 miles, where we struck the Yellowstone again. Here a large party of Crow Indians came to us. They seemed very friendly and are good looking Indians. We dined here then we started out again and ascended a very high hill [Sheep Mountain], one mile long, very rugged. Then came over the bluffs to a stream [Shields River] which flows into the Yellow Stone. I found some gold in this stream. Distance travelled this day 16 miles; [from] where we struck the Yellowstone 137 [miles].

Aug. 25. We left camp all well and travelled a hilly country untill we came to a very steep descent. Very rugged. Then we came on the Yellow Stone again and came along its banks to the entrance of the large kanyon [First Canyon of the Yellowstone], ascending the snow clad mountains. Here we found men who belong to a party of miners who are at work 28 miles from here [at Emigrant Gulch].[48] We imediately sent a party of men up there to see whether it will be advisable for us to move up there or go on to Virginia City. Distance travelled this day 12 miles. Where we first struck the Yellow Stone 149 miles.

48. Gold was discovered in paying quantity in a long, narrow, rocky gulch twenty-five miles south of present Livingston, Montana, on August 30, 1864, by Bozeman Trail emigrant David B. Weaver and two others in the Townsend train. Because most of the miners who rushed to the gulch were Bozeman and Bridger trails emigrants, it became known as Emigrant Gulch. In fall 1864 the population of the Emigrant Gulch area was reportedly three hundred people. Mining claims and cabins extended for several miles up the gulch, and a settlement developed on Emigrant Creek a mile below the mouth of the gulch named Yellowstone City.

Mining in Emigrant Gulch boomed in 1865, but at the end of the season miners began leaving for gold strikes in other areas. In spring 1866 increased danger from Indian raids caused the remaining miners to leave. At the end of summer David Weaver reported that the entire Emigrant Gulch area was totally deserted.

Aug. 26 We lay in camp this day awaiting the return of our men. Here we parted with Shorthill and the other boys. Divided everything. Now George [Travis] and I are with a party of Germans. Have two good oxen and 1 good cow. Trout are very plenty in the [Yellowstone] river. One man can catch a hundred pounds per day if he chooses, easy. Sold at Virginia City 75 cents per pound.

Aug. 27. Lay here all day.

Aug. 29. Lay in camp all day.

Aug. 30. Our men came in tonight and advise going to Virginia [City].

Aug. 31. We broke camp today and proceeded on the way for Virginia City. Travelled up a small stream [Billman Creek] for 8 miles and encamped for the night. This is a very fertile country and well watered, but hilly. It rained nearly all day.

September 1. This morning we moved out at 8 and came through a very lovely country [Bozeman Pass]; at noon we halted on a small branch of the Gallatin River [East Gallatin River] at the edge of the valley. Grass knee deep. We then moved forward and arrived at Bozeman, a city consisting of one log house, three others in course of construction. this is a lovely valley and very fertile. Many people are now beginning to settle here. Gold in most of the streams. Two white men has killed two of the Indians and the whites are afraid of retaliation. Distance to the Yellowstone about 21 miles.

Sept. 2. We lay here all day.

Sept. 3. We moved out this morning. Crossed over a fine valley. At 7 miles came on a small stream of water. Here our company divided again. Three waggons went ahead. We came on about 4 miles and crossed the Gallatin River, quite a large river. Encamped on this side of the river for the night. Killed a fine antelope. Enjoyed it finely. I cannot find any gold on this river, although there may be plenty. Distance travelled 11 miles.

Sept. 4. We broke camp at 8 a.m. and travelled over a very good road. A fertile country. Arrived on the Maddison River. Distance from the Gallatin to the Maddison about 17 miles. This is a large stream about one hundred yards wide. No fish in this river, nor any of the small tributarys. Distance travelled 17 miles.

Sept. 5. At 8 a.m. we crossed the Maddison River and travelled over a mountainous country, but fine valleys between the mountains. Most of the valleys are ocupied by white settlers, mules and oxen. Looks well. We camped on a small stream [Hot Springs Creek] for the night. Distance travelled this day about 12 miles.

Sept. 6. This morning we started early and came on through a hilly country for about 17 miles and encamped on a small stream of water [Meadow Creek] by a ranch. On the right of the road are the Norwegian miners They do not pay well, the miners leave daily. Grass very scarce. Distance travelled 17 miles.

Sept. 7. We moved up a very steep hill and halted there. No grass. We are now within 5 miles of Virginia City. Distance travelled 3 miles.

Sept. 8. We went into the city this morning and we heard on the way that Shorthill has made a discovery up the Yellow Stone [at Emigrant Gulch] and they are hunting up the men of our train to go back. We walked about the town and mines, this day. Lay in an unfinished house that night.

Sept. 9. We start off early this morning. Back for the Yellow Stone, travelled about 20 miles and encamped for the night.

Theodore A. Bailey

DIARY, 1866

THEODORE BAILEY traveled in one of the earliest trains that took the Bozeman Trail in 1866, passing over the trail weeks before the Eighteenth Infantry appeared on the scene. Leaving his home in Michigan, Bailey traveled by train and stage to Council Bluffs, where he engaged his passage to Virginia City, Montana, for twenty-five dollars with an Iowa man named J. S. Bicking. From Omaha, Bailey's train took the north-side Platte road. It is evident from his entries that he had a copy of John L. Campbell's guidebook, which he consulted often until the guide was no longer accurate.

On first examination, Bailey's diary has all the appearances of a trip journal, with daily entries written in the present tense. However, it is actually a rewritten version, copied sometime in the following spring of 1867 from the original journal kept on the trip. Bailey does not say this, but the title includes the phrase "Consisting of Extracts from the Private Journal of . . . Theo. A. Bailey." Furthermore, Bailey's handwriting does not vary from entry to entry, as one would expect it to in a journal written under the conditions of overland travel. Finally, an entry containing retrospective information provides conclusive evidence that Bailey wrote this text after completing his journey. His entry for Friday, June 22, concerns the Fetterman Fight that did not occur until December 1866. Bailey could not have written this entry any earlier than spring 1867, when news of the disaster first reached the settlements in Montana. Bailey probably rewrote his diary in late March since, in the supplementary section of comments, the last temperature he recorded is for March 15, 1867.

Bailey left no personal information about himself, but some important facts can be deduced from his journal and verified. He apparently

SOURCE DOCUMENT: Theodore A. Bailey, Diary, 1866, original, Small Collection 1438, Theodore A. Bailey Diary, 1866–1867, MHSA.

Main Street, Helena, Montana Territory, ca. 1866.
MONTANA HISTORICAL SOCIETY PHOTOGRAPH ARCHIVES, HELENA

began his trip at Monroe, Michigan. He never specified which state the Monroe he left from was in, and he twice mentioned meeting people from Monroe, Wisconsin. But later in his diary, he compared several rivers he crossed to the Raisin River at Monroe, which is the river that passes through Monroe, Michigan. Also, he traveled from La Salle to Monroe to begin his trip, and there is a La Salle near Monroe, Michigan.

The 1860 federal census for Monroe County, Michigan, lists the Louis E. Bailey family as living in Monroe.[1] Louis, sixty-one, was a baker, born in New York. His wife Eliza Ann was forty-five, and she was born in Michigan. A daughter, also named Eliza Ann, was fifteen. A son, Theodore, was twenty-two years old in spring 1860, making

---

1. 1860 Michigan census, Monroe County, City of Monroe, First Ward, p. 12.

him twenty-eight or twenty-nine in summer 1866. His occupation was listed as "RR Baggage Man," and he had a personal estate valued at two hundred dollars.

That Bailey was a fairly young man on his Bozeman Trail trip can be surmised from his diary. He appears to have been a single, unencumbered young man, saying goodbye to his girl and setting off for the goldfields. From his diary it would seem that the other members of his party were all men, traveling fast. He makes no mention of women until the end of the trip when, upon arriving in the Gallatin Valley, he makes the surprising revelation that three women had traveled in the train.

Another indication of Bailey's youth is that, during the trip, he was particularly energetic and agile, frequently jumping into raging rivers to rescue struggling men and animals. He appears to have had few possessions, as shown by his concern over losing his blankets. Worse, he kept his most valuable papers in the pocket of his coat, which he lost early in the trip. Among the most revealing features of his diary were his frequent references to the dollar value of his and others' losses and his cynical comments about the high cost of goods along the way.

Bailey had some degree of education, as he was literate. Although not excellent, his spelling is passable, and some of his variations were commonly used at the time. He was a Mason, which we know from his mentions of visiting a Masonic Lodge in Omaha as well as losing his Masonic diploma later. He was always alert to the possibilities for the future of the West, and although he was impressed with the potential for mining and agriculture in the areas he traveled through, he was overly optimistic about the future of the Bozeman Trail. His concluding remarks show that he had a harsh, ethnocentric attitude towards Indians, typical at the time. He elaborated on the popular view that the Indians would have to make way for advancing civilization, but added that those who tried to exterminate them would "find a big job on their hands."

Bailey's writing reveals many of his personality traits. He obviously disapproved of drunkenness, as when his companions got drunk one evening. On the other hand, he was fairly tolerant of most other forms of behavior and did not continually list all his fellow travelers' faults, as some diarists tended to do. But he also seems to have been a bit self-righteous. When so many of the men abandoned the train in their haste to get ahead, he readily concurred with the few remaining who made a pact not to let any of the deserters back in the group and not to help them if they got into trouble. In addition, he was independent and at times appears to have been aloof. He rarely refers to his traveling companions by name, although he willingly joined working and hunting parties. In all, Bailey was probably a welcome traveling companion. He was hardworking, enthusiastic, and sociable.

Theodore Bailey's diary had never before been transcribed. Very fragile, it was handwritten in ink in a 4 by 6 1/4 inch, paperbound notebook. Bailey's spelling variations and idiosyncratic punctuation are preserved, with the exception that I have substituted a comma for his mark, which looks more like a period, for clarity, since this mark usually indicated a comma. He mostly used two periods to indicate the end of a sentence, although he sometimes used only one period or an elongated mark indicating the end of a sentence or phrase. Following another common nineteenth-century custom, Bailey split a word at the end of a line, wherever it occurred in the word—sometimes leaving only one letter to carry over—and not at a syllable break as is done today.

Bailey's diary offers an observant, articulate, and humorous view of the Bozeman Trail experience. Unfortunately, the diary stands alone as the only written record Bailey left. His diary was passed down in the family to Wesley Bailey Van Cott, perhaps through Bailey's sister Eliza Ann, to whom he dedicated it. In 1967 Wesley Van Cott's widow donated the diary to Reed A. Stout, San Marino, California, who sent it to the Utah Historical Society. Realizing its significance to Montana's gold-rush history, the Utah Historical Society sent the diary to the Montana Historical Society.

No biographical information about Bailey is in the Montana Historical Society file containing his diary, and I only uncovered one further reference to him. He was enumerated in the 1870 Montana territorial census.[2] The census listed him as T. A. Bailey, thirty-two, a miner living at the Cedar Creek mines.[3] Sadly, after ten years working in the mines, he still declared a personal estate of only two hundred dollars.

---

2. 1870 Montana Territory census, Missoula County, Cedar Creek mines, p. 31.

3. The Cedar Creek mines were on Cedar Creek, fifty miles northwest of present Missoula, Montana. Gold was discovered there in October 1869, resulting in a rush of three thousand people into the little gulch in spring 1870. By 1873 placer mining had exhausted the gold vein and only a few miners remained. Merrill G. Burlingame, *The Montana Frontier* (1942; repr., Bozeman: Big Sky Books, Montana State University, 1980), 92–93.

THEODORE A. BAILEY DIARY

PERSONAL NARRATIVE: OR BOULDERS BY THE WAYSIDE, CONSISTING OF
EXTRACTS FROM THE PRIVATE JOURNAL OF A TENDER FOOT.

BY A PILGRIM TO HELENA[4]
THEO. A. BAILEY

Owing to a misfortune I met with on the 14th day of May, by which I lost my coat at Shoemakers point on the Platte River,[5] I have to trust my memory for that portion of the trip as far as Fort Reno, on the Powder River.. that being the first opportunity I had of obtaining another book..

Monday April 23rd 1866. Left Lasalle this AM for Monroe,[6] & remained in town during the day & night, Saying my good byes to friends.. went to see my girl in the evening

[Bailey traveled by railroad and stage to Council Bluffs, Iowa. There he paid J. S. Bicking of Mitchelville, Iowa, twenty-five dollars for his passage to Virginia City. Paying a fixed sum for board and assisting with the work was a typical way single men obtained overland-trails passage.]

Tuesday May 8th 1866. Left the Military Bridge [in Omaha][7] at 7 am & camped at [Peter] Reeds Ranche dis[tance] 16 miles..[8] roads very muddy & hilly

Wednesday May 9th 1866. Started at 8 A.M.. passing through Elkhorn city & Bridgeport both small frontier towns.. camped at Fremont[9]

Thursday May 10th 1866. We entered the valley of the Platte today, which is to be our guide for a long distance westward.. the valley is as level and smooth as a floor for nearly all the distance to Laramie.. on Monday May 14th we had a specimen of the winds of the plains.. which cost me the loss of my best coat, which was lieing

4. "Pilgrim" was a common contemporary term for an emigrant or traveler.

5. Shoemaker's Point was a popular road ranch and campground on the north-side Platte road, 143 miles from Omaha.

6. Monroe is in the southeastern corner of Michigan, twenty miles south of Detroit. It is on the Raisin River, near Lake Erie. La Salle is five miles south of Monroe.

7. The Military Bridge was one of several bridges constructed in 1857 on the Omaha to Fort Kearny Military Road. The bridge Bailey refers to was a mile and a half west of Omaha, possibly at Black Mud Creek. It was located at the present intersection of 24th and Cuming Streets.

8. Peter Reed came from Pennsylvania and established his ranch sixteen miles from Omaha in 1857. Reed commanded Company A of the Second Nebraska volunteers during the Civil War. After the war he worked for the Union Pacific Railroad and managed the section seven miles east of Columbus, Nebraska. David Anderson, "The Early Settlements of the Platte Valley," *Collections of the Nebraska State Historical Society*, 16 (1911), 203.

9. Richard Owens passed through Fremont May 23, 1864.

10. Losing his Masonic papers was significant as these papers offered a certified introduction into a new community.

11. The 1866 treaty council at Fort Laramie on June 5 and 6 was intended to obtain permission to use the Bozeman Trail and protect the emigrants from Indian attacks. Bailey shared a commonly held view that the treaties, rather than curtailing Indian warfare, encouraged it.

12. An American war hero, General Winfield Scott died May 29, 1866. A leader in every major war, beginning with the War of 1812, he ended his military career as the first commander in chief of the Union Army in the Civil War.

13. It is more likely the emigrants died from disease than that Indians killed them.

14. They camped on the bank of the North Platte opposite the site of Fort Fetterman, near where the Bozeman Trail turned north off the emigrant road. Many 1866 travelers referred to it as Bridger's trail after Jim Bridger, who had guided Connor from this new turnoff the year before. Most travelers did not know that this was a new route and not the one Bozeman and the other emigrant trains had traversed in 1863 and 1864.

15. These were the Winnebago soldiers of Company A, Omaha Scouts, who had been

loose under the wagon sheet & blew off.. in the pockets were my Journal letters Masonic Diploma[10] etc. went back on a mule about 10 miles, but could not find it.. we arrived at Fort Kearney on Wednesday May 16th and laid over for 2 days [waiting] for a larger train.. left Kearney Friday May 18th   wrote home today from two miles west of Kearney & sent letter to the Fort by a teamster.. from Kearney to Fort Laramie we had good bad & indifferent roads, some of the way very sandy hills.. had to double our teams   we are travelling on the north side of the north Platte, passing Chimney Rock & Scotts Bluffs & arriving at Fort Laramie, Dacota Territory on Saturday June 2nd.. we found the country in the vicinity of the fort swarming with Indians belonging to the Sioux & Shianee [Cheyenne] tribes they are here for the purpose of making another treaty with Uncle Sam so they can go on the war path again.. (how are you indian treaties)[11]   heard of the death of Gen Scotte [General Winfield Scott][12] today & wrote home..

Sunday June 3rd 1866. We broke camp today & went about 8 miles west of the fort for feed for our stock as the Indian ponies have ate all up in the vicinity.. camped in a beautiful nook on the banks of the Platte, at the lower end of which we found several graves of Emigrants killed by Indians several years since..[13] From Laramie we continued up the Platte for about 80 miles over roughf rockey hills & camped for the last time on the banks of the Platte at the forks of the Bridger cutoff on Monday June 11th..[14] a company of Cavalry [the Omaha Scouts] passed us today on their way east from Fort Reno. the privates were Winebago Indians.[15] here we leave the old California & Oregon road & take the new Bozeman route to Montana. the road was laid out in 64 but not travelled last year on account of the hostility of Indians.[16] but as one train has passed on ahed of us this year we are bound to try it..[17] The country between the Platte & Ft Reno is beautifuly undulating & grass good but water very scarce.. Arrived at Fort Reno on the banks of Powder River on Saturday June 16th 1866.. got a book here in which I shall keep the balance of my journal.. bought a 1/2 lb of tobacco <u>stems</u> at the modest price of $2.00 per pound.[18] left Reno at 10 A.M. camped about 14 miles west of the fort for the night.. we have been in sight of the Big Horn Mts for three days. their tops are covered with snow..

Sunday June 17th 1866.[19] Broke camp at 7 A.M. & travelled 11 miles to Crazy Womans fork of the Powder River.. the ford was very muddy & banks steep, had to hitch ropes to the wagon tongues & help the teams out by manpower. camped here for the night. we do not intend traveling on Sunday but the feed was so poor at the fort we had to today.. Spent the afternoon in washing & mending..

Monday June 18th 1866. Left Crazy Womans Fork at 7 AM camped at noon at a sink hole where we found a little water Camped for [the] night on the banks of Clear Creek, a beautiful mountain stream, water cold as ice & gravel bottom. our road to-day was first rate & country lovely

Tuesday June 19th 1866. We missed it in not fording the creek last evening as on getting up this A.M. we find the creek much higher than yesterday owing to the melting of the snow in the Mts yesterday & a warm rain in the night. we did not try to ford at the crossing but found a much better place about a mile below & started at noon for it. it prooved very good & by 2 P.M. all the teams were across when we went into camp as the next water is said to be 20 miles dis[tan]t.. Killed a large Spotted Rattle Snake today & found a vein of coal in a bluff, about a mile from camp cropping out about 12 ft wide Saw some beautiful Specimens of Ising-glass

stationed at Fort Reno all winter. They left the fort on June 6 and were on their way to Fort Laramie when they passed Bailey. Margaret Carrington recorded in her diary that the Eighteenth Infantry command she was with passed them on June 17 just west of Fort Laramie. Margaret I. Carrington, *Absaraka: Home of the Crows* (1868; repr., Lincoln: University of Nebraska Press, 1983), 94.

16. The Bozeman Trail was closed to emigrant traffic in 1865, and General Connor's Powder River Indian Expedition campaigned in the region.

17. At least four trains were ahead of them on the Bozeman Trail.

18. The sutler store at Fort Reno was operated by A. C. Leighton and John W. Smith, business partners in emigrant and sutler sales at Kearney City, immediately west of Fort Kearny. Leighton was the junior partner in the Smith and Leighton firm. In August and September 1865 Al Leighton accompanied Connor's Indian campaign in the Powder River Basin as field sutler.

At the end of the campaign Leighton was appointed sutler at Fort Reno, the post Connor had established on the Powder River, but Smith went to Fort Reno instead of Leighton that winter. Al and Jim Leighton returned to Fort Reno on June 21, 1866, bringing supplies to replenish the stock at the Fort Reno sutler store and for sutler stores they planned to open at the other proposed Bozeman Trail posts.

19. Colonel Henry B. Carrington's Eighteenth Infantry command left Fort Laramie on this day, June 17, to establish two additional Bozeman Trail forts.

20. Mica, popularly known as isinglass, was often noted by nineteenth-century diarists. Mica is a group of chemically and physically related mineral silicates that characteristically split into flexible sheets. Thin sheets of mica were sometimes used as a substitute for glass in western frontier windows.

21. Fort Phil Kearny was established here less than a month later.

[mica] in a bank by the roadside..[20] four Antelope were killed by our party today.. weather very warm during the day nights cool & pleasant..

Wednesday June 20th 66. This has been a day of events to our train.. Directly after getting over a range of hills we entered a beautiful little valley through which meandred a creek with a very rapid currant which we forded three times & then came to a larger one at the farther extremity [Piney Creek].[21] we camped for noon at the third ford, & after dinner eight Arrapahoe Indians came into camp & by signs gave us to understand they had a lodge about 4 miles ahead, & that they had come to collect tribute of us (begging) which we paid in Tobaco, Coffee Sugar etc.. about 2 P.M. we resumed our march & in about an hour came to the ford of Piney River which we found very high & dangerous. a train ahed of us commenced crossing first & by Six they were all safely over.. after crossing one or two of our heavy wagons some smarty proposed lashing two light wagons together but no sooner than they had reached the swiftest & deepest part than the front one broke in the reach & the wheels parted company. the front ones were pulled ashore by the men on the opposite bank the front end of the wagon swung down stream the upper hind wheel revolved in the current & in a moment more the wagon careened over & deposited its contents in the boiling stream.. on this wagon which belonged to F. Van Wagenen of Monroe Wis. were two men one E'd Van Wagenen & Fred Loutze before the wagon turned E'd was taken off by a man on horse-back, as he could not swim & by his excessive fright gave signs of jumping overboard. Fred was taken off by a rope passed to him from shore.. I had placed my blankets on this wagon for safety as our wagon was very heavy & as I had the cool satisfaction of seeing them going down stream at a 240 rate, I considered myself out & insured [uninsured] to the extent & value thereof.. but as the river was very crooked I thought to make an effort to save them & other property if possible so started down accompanied by about 20 naked Arrapahoes, who plunged in the current at the bends of the stream & saved nearly all of the floating property, including my blankets.. the other wagons crossed safely, only wetting some of their loads a little.. We accomplished the fording by taking a rope across & men enough to pull a wagon over. the stock had to be driven over loose.. as the Indians had been so honest & efficient we gave them several presents, I very reluctantly parting with my pocket knife.. it was 9 P.M. when we formed camp on a beautiful bench on the <u>other side</u> [of] <u>Jordan</u>.. as we were all more or less tired & wet, some of the boys got a gallon of whisky of [from] a freighter at the small price of fifteen dollars per gal.. <u>when they began to make the welkin ring</u>.. & they succeeded admirably   Several were very <u>much how came you so</u>..[22]

Thursday June 21st 1866. Left camp (<u>Bacchus</u>) at 8 A.M. & camped at noon on a beautiful creek [Prairie Dog], dis[tance] about 10 M.. Left at 2 & traveld about 15 M.. our road to-day was good but very hilly..[23] we are having good feed & water, the grass is knee high.[24] an antelope was killed today. just after camping we had a thunder storm

Friday June 22nd 1866. On arising this A.M. we saw the Mountains above us covered with Snow that had fallen during the night   Left camp at 7 & made about 8 miles to Piney Creek [Goose Creek], which we find very high. had to block up the wagon beds & ride the stock over.. one small wagon upset & broke a wheel got all across at noon, occupying three hours on the ford.. camped for the night on the bank for repairs. rained at 5 P.M. P.S. Fort Phil Kearney has since been built in this neighborhood[25] & last Dec. 98 Soldiers & three officers

22. Bailey is using euphemisms to refer to his companions being drunk. The phrase to *make the welkin ring* was apparently commonly used at the time, but it is not clear whether Bailey is using it in a new sense. Incidentally, fifteen dollars for the whisky was a very high price. In comparison, at that time an army private's salary was about fourteen dollars per month.

23. They traveled over Lodge Trail and Fetterman ridges.

24. A year later haying parties from Fort Phil Kearny came to this area.

25. Fort Phil Kearny was built between Little Piney and Piney creeks, where Bailey camped two days earlier.

were surprised & massacred by the Sioux & Shianees.. Lieut. Grummond formerly of Detroit was one of the killed[26]

Saturday June 23rd 1866. O[n] awaking this AM my ears were greeted by the sound of rain prattling on the tent. it rained untill about 9.. during the storm we were above some of the clouds & heard the thunder below us.. our road today has been over some of the highest hills & nearer the main chain of Mts than before.. at noon we came to a creek [Wolf Creek] about 2 rods wide & 3 ft deep which we had no trouble in fording. camped here for [noon] dinner.. resumed our march at 2 & one hours drive brought us to Tounge [Tongue] River..[27] found a small train here that seceded from us yesterday the river being so high they did not attempt to cross, untill we came up. then they took a wagon apart, & making a boat of the bed sent two men over in it. three men having previously crossed on horseback, one of whom was washed off but swam ashore.. on sending the bed back it swamped & the fording was abandoned for the day.. We saw two Buffalo across the river today, being the first we have seen, altho signs have been plenty.. the seceding party saw a bear last evening.. more antelope were killed.. we are in a lovely little valley tonight, surrounded by timber.. & grass good, the creek banks lined with wild roses.. & bounded on all sides by the everlasting hills & mountains covered with a white mantle of snow. the weather has been very cold today & overcoats were fashionable

Sunday June 24th. After breakfast a fiew men went up & down the creek to find a better ford. the upper party returned at 10 A.M. & reported a passable ford 3 miles above.[28] broke camp at 12 & arrived at 1 [P.M.] & immediately commenced fording.. all safely over at 4 P.M.. 4 ft water & very rapid stream about 2 miles from creek saw a herd of Buffalo & some Elk. Snatching our rifles about 10 of us went after them, had a long chase.. after crossing the first range of hills found a little valley

26. Lieutenant George Washington Grummond was one of the three officers killed in the Fetterman Fight on December 21, 1866, near Fort Phil Kearny. His widow Frances Courtney Grummond later married Colonel Henry Carrington, after his first wife Margaret died. Frances C. Carrington, *My Army Life and the Fort Phil Kearny Massacre* (1910; repr., Boulder, Colo.: Pruett Publishing Co., 1990).

27. They camped on the Tongue River, halfway between present Ranchester and Dayton, Wyoming. Campbell's guidebook noted that the Tongue River was thirty-five miles beyond Powder River, but it is actually about one hundred miles.

28. This ford was at present Dayton, Wyoming. The later military cutoff between Fort Phil Kearny and Fort C. F. Smith crossed the Tongue River there. Jim Bridger opened the military cutoff in spring 1867.

alive with Buffalo.[29] I think one thousand a low estimate of the number. we chased them about 3 miles & killed three bulls. they were larger than any oxen I ever saw.. during the chase I became detached from the rest of the party in chasing a bull & got so far away from the road that I did not find it again untill near sundown & so far west of camp that I had to walk untill 9 o'clock before getting in..[30] during my walk I saw about fifty Antelopes & heard the wolves howling in all directions.. this is perhaps the best hunting ground in america   weather warm & roads good

Monday June 25th 1866. Got an early start & about 9 AM forded a small creek [Crazy Creek]. at 12 M [noon] arrived at the South Fork of Little Horn [Lodge Grass Creek], where we had recourse to our ropes again to make the ford.[31] river narrow & about four feet of water. got all across by 2 P.M. & camped for noon. Started at 3, & an hours drive brought us to a small creek [Willow Creek] which we forded without any trouble.. camped at 6,30 PM on Trout creek [Rotten Grass Creek].. Saw more Buffalo today. weather very cold in the A.M. but pleasant this evening.. Buffalo steaks for Supper..

Tuesday June 26th 1866. I am on guard tonight, for the last time I think.. had a good road this forenoon. camped at noon on the banks of a small creek [Soap Creek] water cold as ice & clear as crystal.. Saw four Cinnamon Bears, one of them was Killed & the others got away.. about an hour after, saw a band of Elk. there was twelve large ones & three calves. a long grey wolf was killed.. roads very hilly this afternoon. at one place had to lower our wagons by hitching a rope to the hind axle & the men easing them down.. camped at 6 PM at a Spring.. Saw a fiew Buffalo & passed four prararie dog towns.. Bear meat for Supper..

Wednesday June 27th 1866. Left camp early & one hour bro't us to Big Horn River.. found Cap't Siglers

29. Going north from the Tongue River, the trail ascended a high plateau and then dropped down to a valley, about five miles south of the Wyoming-Montana state line.

30. Bailey walked many miles through the hills and valleys west of the road. In the evening he found the train camped on the Little Bighorn River, twenty miles north of the Tongue River.

31. The party used the same method they had at Piney Creek on June 20. Ropes were taken across the stream and wrapped around a tree, and then the wagons were attached and pulled across.

32. This was John A. Zeigler's train of forty-five wagons. Zeigler had lived in Montana for three years. In the spring he had returned east and was now bringing his family over the Bozeman Trail to live permanently in Montana. *Virginia City Montana Post*, July 21, 1866.

33. The drowned men were identified as a man named Whiston and Dr. Storer from Illinois. Ibid.

[Zeigler's] train here.[32] the river is so high they cannot cross. day before yesterday he lost a man out of his train.. he was riding in the river hunting for a crossing. on coming to deep water he washed off the mule & sank to rise no more. he was from Pennsylvania. I could not learn his name.. yesterday they lost another by the upsetting of a raft they were using, made of two dugouts lashed together & wide enough to hold a wagon bed.. neither of the bodies could be recovered..[33] our train will join Siglers [Zeigler's] & commence crossing in the AM.. The river is falling a little tonight   it is as large as the Raisin at Monroe [Michigan] & four times as rapid.. Two small parties that left us at the last ford came up this afternoon. they commenced making a large canoe & are crossing their loads in it.. the river is so bad that stock cannot be driven in so they take them over by leading them by the haltar from the canoe. in attempting to take two mules & a horse at one time they had to let go of them & one mule was drowned the others came back to this shore again.. after which they took one at a time with success.

Thursday June 28th 1866. I commenced working at the ferry today, rowing on one of the rafts   everything works well today & we have got another raft running.. got all the goods & wagons over by 2 PM. commenced on the stock.. got all over by sundown.. the single canoe has been running all day with stock.. & owing to starting to[o] low down stream they got in some very bad rapids & drowned two very valuable mules.. the other trains have not crossed yet & are to have our rafts in the A.M. about 300 Arrapahoe Indians are camped near here & came to our camp tonight loaded with furs & robes   & some of the boys struck up a lively <u>trading post</u>   the handsomest robes I ever saw were bought for a pair of common soldier blankets. a cup of flour bought a pair of beaded mocasins.. & one man bought a grey wolf robe for twelve matches..[34] Some of our party prospected on

34. This was a typical accommodating encounter. Significantly, matches, used to make percussion caps for their guns, were a valued trade item.

the dry bank of the river & found gold in nearly every pan, but <u>Montana on the brain</u> prevents us stopping..[35] I have no doubt this is a good mining country..

Friday June 29th 1866. Started at 8 1/2 A.M. & struck for the road as our ferry was about 3 miles above the crossing.[36] after getting over the bluffs we came into a very roughf & barren country, abounding in Sage Brush, Chaparell & prickley Pears.. & [water] very strongly impregnated with alkali.. one pool of which was as thick as cream [bentonite].. met a party of men bound for the Big Horn to establish a ferry & prospect for gold..[37] made a dry camp to-night on an alkali flat   grass very slim.. very warm day

Saturday June 30th 1866. Cool & pleasant this A.M.. our road has been very roughf & through an alkali country, with deep gullies every mile or so.. camped at noon at a spring of good cold water which is very acceptable. grass good & some wood.. road very roughf this afternoon, country barren   camped on Nez Perses fork [Pryor Creek] tonight.. caught a Silver cat fish weighing 3 1/2 lbs   musquitoes are plenty.. rain to-night

Sunday July 1st 1866. Owing to loosing so much time at the streams we are to travel on Sundays.. So we start this AM & travel over some of the roughfest hills I ever saw.. often we are on a narrow ridge just wide enough for a wagon   & again pulling up a steep acclivity by means of ropes & letting down again by the same means. at 12 M [noon] we got our first view of the Yellow Stone River, as we were on the top of a very high hill..[38] the view was magnificent.. embracing the river & valley for several miles.. & at 2 P.M. we descended to it [Yellowstone River] down a sidling hill on a grade of about 45 degrees or less.. we had to lower the wagons by ropes.. camped on the banks in a beautiful grove of Cottonwoods..[39] just above us an arm of the river jutting up to the bluffs forbade our passage up the valley so we

35. *Montana on the brain* and *Bannack on the brain*, expressing an overwhelming eagerness to get to the goldfields, were popular expressions during the Montana gold rush. A similar widely used expression was *gold fever*.

36. Their ferry was at an alternate crossing, three miles above the usual ford at Spotted Rabbit Crossing. The ferry that operated later in the season when Fort C. F. Smith was established was three miles above this one, or six miles above the usual emigrant ford. After crossing, Bailey's party went back downstream and intersected the road at the former ford.

37. The men were Mitch Boyer, Louis and John Richard, Big Bat Pourier, and Juan Jesus Luis, who were coming from Bozeman to run a ferry on the Bighorn River.

38. They were on the bluffs lining the south side of the Yellowstone River opposite present Billings, Montana.

39. Bailey's train seems to have taken a different route than the preceding trains. His description suggests they descended from the bluffs farther downstream, probably at the mouth of Bitter Creek. The bluffs lining the south bank of the Yellowstone west of there blocked their passage upstream, and they were forced to go back up the bluffs and continue northwest to another descent to the river.

go back to the mountains again, passing over the brows of hills.. often in imminent peril of upsetting. lowered into a ravine by ropes & out again by the same means   it was a very fatuiging way of spending the Sabbath.. camped at 7 P.M. on the banks of the Yellow Stone in a forest of Cottonwoods⁴⁰   grass good..

Monday July 2nd 1866. Our road this A.M. led us up the [Yellowstone] valley for a short distance & then we had to climb the hills again but found them less abrupt than those of yesterday. had a very good road today & desended to the [Yellowstone] valley by an easy grade at noon & camped on the banks of Clarks fork of the Yellowstone.⁴¹ after dinner we left the valley & passed over the hills on a very good road & at 3 P.M. commenced to desend again, when we found we had come to the ford of Clarks fork⁴² & it [was] very high & as large as the raisin at Monroe [Raisin River at Monroe, Michigan,] or larger & [had] a very swift but smooth currant.. I performed the very foolish freak of swimming across & found it all I wanted to do to get back. I was nearly benumbed.. we divided our train into parties of 8 wagons each to make a raft & get across the best they could.. we have been in sight of a very high chain of Mts [Pryor Mountains] all day, clad with snow as far as the eye can reach   I presume they are the main chain of Rocky Mts.. weather very warm.. no rafts are finished tonight

Tuesday July 3rd 1866. Arose early & went to work on our raft & by 8 had it in the water.. it is built of six logs 14 ft long & 1 ft thick lashed together.. with this unwieldy craft we have eight wagons & their loads & passengers to take across.. we had no bad luck & at dark had all our party over except the stock. there was eight rafts built by the train.. two of which were wrecked & landed on an island below. their loads were saved. one party made a canoe & it done first rate untill it colided with a raft, which upset it & lost the wheels of one

40. They camped on the south bank of the Yellowstone River two miles below the mouth of Blue Creek.

41. During the morning they went two miles up the Yellowstone bottom, turned south and went eight miles over the hills and back to the Yellowstone River at the mouth of Duck Creek, and then went five miles up the bottom to Clarks Fork.

42. After their noon stop they turned south again, went three miles over the hills, and came back to the Clarks Fork ford three miles above its mouth.

wagon & the axle of another.. both the property of one
man. about four some commmenced to swim their stock
over by riding one & forsing others to follow. one man
in attempting to cross was unhorsed & the horse turning
back for shore. in his endeavors to controll him he
became exhausted & was drowned before he could get to
shore[43] his body has not been recovered. it was said he
had a $1000 in his pocket.. 14 wagons belonging to a
train that we left at the Big Horn came up to-day..
weather very hot..

43. The drowning death
of Jerome Shimel, a
member of Orville
Royce's train, was
reported in the *Virginia
City Montana Post* on
July 21, 1866.

    Wednesday July 4th 1866. Independance day.. we
began ferrying early in the A.M. & worked all day. all the
goods & stock of our train was safely across by 5 P.M.
Murrays train came up to-night & one wagon belonging
to it hired one of our rafts & overloading it, it went
down with about $3000 of goods   nothing but a small
satchel of clothing was saved.. our train is becoming
demoralized   Several teams that crossed first are leaving
us & going ahead on their own hook.. 7 mules got on an
island & I with three others had to swim over & drive
them off. we were the only four in the train that would
own they could swim—weather very warm.. we fired a
National Salute with guns & pistols this evening & had
very good music from a band of 2 violins, bass viol &
brass horn.. the river has been rising all day..

    Thursday July 5th 1866. We left Clarks Fork of the
Yellow-Stone at 6,30 A.M., without any desire of forming
any further acquaintance.. but found that our road led us
[south] across the bluffs and to the river [Rock Creek]
again..[44] where we camp for dinner   about four miles
back we came into the greatest clouds of grasshoppers I
ever saw. they obscured the light of the sun & had eaten
up every blade of grass & leaf & were so thick on the
ground as to scare the horses & mules.. we kept along the
[Rock Creek] bottoms for two hours, when we came to
another branch [Red Lodge Creek] to avoid fording we

44. After crossing the
Clarks Fork, the trail
turned to the south and
went up the west side of
the Clarks Fork to Rock
Creek, coming to its bank
a few miles above its
junction with the Clarks
Fork.

go on the bluffs & pass around it as it is an arm of the
main stream.. did not get back to the road today
camped on an island.. the stream we are on prooved to be
a fork of Clarks fork [Red Lodge Creek] & not the main
stream. a buffalo was killed today & we have fresh steak
for supper   the day has been very warm but in the
evening became cloudy & finaly rained

Friday July 6th 1866. We got an early start & drove
up the Island about 3 miles & came to the ford, where we
crossed without any difficulty.. good road to-day
camped at noon, at a brook [Beaver Creek] fed by
springs.. water clear & good.. we have made the fastest
time this A.M. of any on the trip.. left at 2 & one hours
drive bro't us to the ford of Little Boulder [East
Rosebud Creek].. found a party here that left us
yesterday.. they have been ferrying all day & have six
wagons over, when we arrive.. they got all over safe & we
commence   the river is rising very fast, & is the swiftest
we have met yet & about five feet deep. some of our
party cross to-night & some back out, thinking the river
will be lower in the morning.. five crossed all right when
a small wagon was let in & nearly across, when one
wheel broke, & in less time than I can write it was torn
to pieces & carried down. nothing but the gearing &
mules were saved.. after this catastrophe, the vote was
unanimous for crossing in the A.M. grasshoppers have
filled the air & covered the ground all day

Saturday July 7th 1866. Commenced to ford at 7 AM
& at 9 all across, but one small wagon, which setting
to[o] deep in the water was upset & all the contents
deposited in the stream. a considerable [amount] of the
load was caught below. left Little Boulder at 9,30 A.M. &
one hour came to the Nes Perses fork of Big Boulder
[West Rosebud Creek]. this we forded without any
difficulty & camped for noon on the west bank. broke
camp at 1,30 P.M. & at 3 came to the Big Boulder River

[Stillwater River] a very large & swift stream. here we find all the teams that have left us. they are building rafts & canoes. one raft was launched & sent across with 3 men. after landing on the opposite side it got away & went downstream this stream is not very wide but deep & swift & will be very difficult fording. I caught some very beautiful Speckled Trout here.

Sunday July 8th 1866. The fording of Big Boulder [Stillwater River] was commenced at 9 AM by some of the teams in advance of us & by noon they had all of their party over.. two other parties were fording at the same time. about 2 we got one of the rafts & commenced to cross & were safely over by five.. very warm day..

Monday July 9th 1866. Left Big Boulder [Stillwater River] at 5,30 A.M. & made very fast driving, as our stock is all fat & in good plight & the men are getting very anxious to get to our journeys end.. every one on his own hook is the order of the day.. roads very good, only a fiew steep hills.[45] camped at noon on a small creek [Bridger Creek] water clear & good.. directly after dinner we came into the valley of the Yellowstone & had a very beautiful road.. made a very long drive today & camped on the bank of a large stream [Boulder River] of which we have no account in our guide book [Campbell's guidebook]..[46] here we found a train that left Leavenworth on the 4th of March last & have been here since the fourth of July.. they have lost one man & six mules in attempting to ford & have abandoned the attempt intending to wate untill the river falls they have offered $500 to be put safely over, & no takers.. they are very heavily loaded freighters.. we are finding so many streams not on our guide or maps, that I am at a loss to find the right name & many of them are not named at all..[47] to-night I hear we have not come to the Boulders yet, but I think it a mistake.. Grasshoppers very thick & fast destroying the grass.. weather very hot..

45. During this day they crossed the high plateau—now known as Stockade Hill—on the south side of the Yellowstone River west of present Columbus, Montana. The Bozeman Trail crossed Stockade Hill and descended to the Yellowstone River just above the mouth of Bridger Creek, crossed Bridger Creek, and continued north a short distance to the Yellowstone River.

46. This was a long drive indeed, at least thirty-five miles.

47. They were at the Boulder River, near present Big Timber, Montana. None of the rivers they crossed since Clarks Fork were listed in Campbell's guidebook.

Tuesday July 10th 1866. Our train is divided into two squads & gone to work on rafts. the river is about a foot higher to-day than last night, which makes it utterly impossible for us to ford.. on taking a walk up & down the river to-day I find seven camps on the banks quite enough to make a good sized town.. our rafts will not be done to-day.. our stock are on good grass & getting fat.. the weather has been insufferably hot..

Wednesday July 11th 1866. The day opened cool & cloudy & finaly culminated in a shower. the river [Boulder River] is about as high as yesterday.. a party headed by Roice [Orville Royce] went up the river about four miles & at noon we heard they had not been able to get a cable across the river.. we got a large lot of rope of [from] the freight train & made a cable & got it across today & got our raft launched, but owing to the rapidity of the current only small loads can be crossed.. commenced at 2 P.M. & at 8 P.M., had 7 wagons & loads over   Cool & pleasant evening..

Thursday July 12th 1866. Commenced rafting early & at noon had all our wagons over & every alternate load for the freight train.. at 2 P.M., as another train were ferrying the connecting rope between the cable & raft broke & downstream went the raft & its load & three men   but they stuck to it & got ashore about one mile below.. our train has dwindled down from sixty five to fourteen wagons, as every ferry has made a good opportunity for men to show their dispositions. some of them as soon as they got over would leave the train. we passed a resolution not to let them back or help them in the least.. left at 4,30 PM & unexpectedly arrived at the ferry of the Yellowstone at 8,30 PM   all of our party came up by 11 PM   by them we learned of an accident at the Big Boulder after we left by which two wagons & four horses & the loads were lost..

Friday July 13th 1866. Breakfasted early & by 6 A.M. our wagons were all over the Yellowstone & joined by those that forded the Big Boulder above us. left the ferry at 7 A.M. the ferry is owned by Bozeman the man that laid out this route[48] & from him I learn that the last stream we crossed was the Big Boulder. the price of ferrying was $10.00 in greenbacks for each wagon & 50^c for each horse.. here we see the first white settlement since leaving the Platte & that only one log house occupied by the ferry men camped at noon on the banks of the Yellowstone & had splendid sport catching Trouts. the river was alive with them. I caught about 25 with my spoonhook while the train was at dinner.. left at 2 PM & forded 25 rod creek [Shields River] on a good ford water only about a foot deep & gravel bottom camped at night on a small brook. rained in the morning & twice in the afternoon. roads good except a fiew high hills..

48. John Bozeman operated a ferry near the ford for a few months in 1866.

Saturday July 14th 1866. Started early & camped at noon on a little brook [Billman Creek]. good feed & water. Scenery magnificent.. left camp at 2 PM & crossed the divide between the Yellowstone & Missouri [Bozeman Pass].. desended to the valley of the Gallatin River down the sides of a ravine [Kelly Canyon], & crossed a creek [Kelly Creek] several times.. very muddy at the crossings.. entered Gallatin valley about 5 P.M. & saw the first fence & farm since leaving Fort Kearney.. arrived at Bozeman <u>city</u> at 7 P.M. this <u>city</u> contains a grist mill, saw mill, whisky shop, & two log houses grasshoppers have been in clouds along the road all day.. rained in the evening..

Sunday July 15th 1866. The morning opened clear & beautiful we are to lie over today, but most of the party go on to Virginia City they left us at 7 A.M. dist.[ance] to Virginia City 75 miles, to Helena 90 miles.. there are some splendid crops of wheat & potatoes about here but the grasshoppers are destroying them very fast..

Monday July 16th 1866. Very cool last night.. rained this morning & cold & cloudy.. left Bozeman at 7 A.M.,

arrived at the ferry of the east Gallatin at 9 A.M. & find so
many teams ahead of us & the ferry so slow that we will
no[t] be able to cross untill near night. went up the river
about a mile to a ranch & saw the first <u>woman (except
three in our train)</u> since leaving the lower Platte.. Crossed
at 6 P.M.. & camped on the west side.. price of ferriage $6
per team.. this evening I visited a Mr. Matchell   he lives all
alone & has been here 25 years, trapping & hunting..

Tuesday July 17th 1866. Our course to-day has been
down the Gallatin Valley, passing a ranche every fiew miles.
this valley is a splendid grazing country   the cattle are very
fat.. the crops of wheat potatoes etc. look very fine   at
6 P.M. arrived at the ferry of the Missouri at Gallatin <u>city</u>
which contains one house, population two men that run the
ferry. it was laid out to be the head of navigation of the
Missouri, but as no boats ever succeeded in <u>climbing</u> the
great falls of the Missouri the town <u>broke</u>..[49] this is the
junction of the three forks of the Missouri.. Gallatin,
Madison, & Jefferson [Rivers], which uniting form that
river [a blank space] miles from its entrance with the
Mississippi.. the Missouri here is about half the size of the
Raisin at Monroe, with smooth currant.. very warm day..
if Mosquitoes counted as the population Gallatin City
would outnumber London or Paris..

Wednesday July 18th 1866. Left Gallatin at 7 A.M. &
camped at noon on a small creek, left at 4 P.M. & camped
at a ranch for the night, where we got the first water
from a well since leaving Ft Kearney. Saw a lot of sluice
boxes by the roadside which indicates we are
approaching the Gold regions.. prospectors are at work
in the M'ts above us. rained this evening

Thursday July 19th 1866. Left at 7 & camped at
noon on the banks of the Missouri at the Confedrate
Gulch ferry.[50] left at 2 P.M. & camped at night on Beaver
Creek at Major Campbells ranche..[51] roads good,
weather very warm..

49. Gallatin City was
located at the headwaters
of the Missouri River, at
the confluence of the
Gallatin, Madison, and
Jefferson rivers, near
present Three Forks,
Montana. The first
community sprang up in
late 1862 as a prospective
real estate development
just above the mouth of
the Gallatin River, on the
west bank of the
combined Madison and
Jefferson rivers. The
location proved
unsatisfactory, and a new
town grew up on the east
side of the river.
Beginning in 1863 ferries
were operated on the
rivers in the area. Gallatin
City declined rapidly in
the 1880s after the
Northern Pacific Railroad
bypassed it, and the town
no longer exists.

50. The Confederate
Gulch ferry across the
Missouri River was
twenty-five miles
southeast of Helena. The
site is now submerged in
Canyon Ferry Lake.

51. Campbell's Ranch
was on Beaver Creek, six
miles from the Confeder-
ate Gulch ferry on the
road to Helena.

Friday July 20th 1866. Left Campbells ranch at 7 & made one drive to Helena arriving at 3 P.M. & camped on Academy hill..[52] Helena far exceeds my expectations, being a very large & <u>fast</u> mining camp situated principaly in 'last chance' gulch—there are three business St[reet]s lined with the usual variety of Stores, Banks, Saloons, gambling houses, assay offices, Restaurants etc to be found in all new mining towns.. the times are dull at present especialy for <u>Tender Feet</u> & the streets jam full of idle men..

Saturday July 21st 1866. Passed the day in looking about town, & see evidences that this is (or <u>had</u>) been a rich mining camp, but, the drawback now is a scarcity of water (I <u>wish they had a little of that we had to encounter on the road, we could have spared some just as well as not</u>)

Sunday July 22nd 1866. Sunday in the mines.. those who have never been in a mining country would not believe their senses if suddenly placed in a thriving camp on a pleasant Sabbath morning.. it is the day for everyone to visit <u>town</u>, & transact the business of the week   miners & ranch-men come to purchase their week's <u>grub</u>.. does Jack who is mining in Confederate [Gulch] wish to see his friend Bill from Nelson [Gulch] he goes to town on Sunday & ~~hardly~~ rarely fails of meeting him.. as a natural consequence every merchant, Saloon, Gambling den, Hurdy house [hurdy-gurdy][53] & all the allurements to part fools & their [gold] <u>dust</u>, do more business than any other day of the week. music greets the ear from the open doors of gamblers hells, auctioneers crying their wares from every "<u>cheap Ings, Sheap Clodings</u> house" & he who squeezes his way through the lenght [length] of Main St on Sunday should have his elbows iron plated..

Monday July 23rd 1866. Left Helena to-day at 2 PM for St Louis Gulch..[54] arrived at 6 PM   our driver got drunk & lost the road.. dis[tance] twelve miles..

52. Academy Hill, located between present Broadway and State (formerly Bridge) Streets, is now known as Catholic Hill. The earlier name of Academy Hill referred to the Helena Academy, one of four schools in Helena at that time. The academy was located on Rodney Street on the eastern side of the hill. The principal of the Helena Academy was E. Webster Stone. In 1867 the school reportedly had seventy pupils who were charged $1.50 each per week. Burlingame, *The Montana Frontier*, 314. The frame Academy building was torn down in 1868, and subsequently the hill became known as Catholic Hill after the Catholic church and Catholic hospital located on its crest.

53. The hurdy-gurdy, or dance hall, was a popular type of saloon in western mining camps. Andrew J. Fiske arrived at Helena later in the 1866 travel season than Bailey. He noted in his diary on October 7, "In the evening I went around to the several 'hurdy gurdys' or 'dance houses' where for the sum of $1.00 in funds you could have the pleasure of dancing with a girl and the whiskey thrown in." Montana Historical Society, *Not in Precious Metals Alone: A Manuscript History of Montana* (Helena: Montana Historical Society Press, 1976), 151.

54. St. Louis Gulch was one of the mining gulches near Helena.

Tuesday July 24th 1866. Today I have done the first placer mining in my life, ground Sluicing in St Louis gulch..

Friday August 10th 1866. Commenced working for the ten mile mill & lumber Co today & worked untill Nov 17th when we froze up..

FINIS.

Supplimentory..

The distance from Omaha city to Helena Montana, by the route we travelled is called eleven hundred and fifty miles.. Six hundred miles of which is on the old Platte route & five hundred & fifty on the new Bozeman & Bridger routes.. If it were not for the numberless Streams flowing from the chain of Mountains that bound the route on the west.. this would be by far the best route, as feed for Stock is found in abundance, with the exception of two or three days travel in the bad lands. all the large streams on this route will ultimately be provided with ferries.. last season there was but one.. at the Yellowstone..

On arriving at Bozeman city, the first settlement in Montana, we first heard of the Indian massacres of emigrants in our rear. I can only account for our not being attacked by the fact of nearly all the Chiefs & Warriors of the Sioux, SChianee [Cheyenne], Arrapahoe, & Blackfeet were at or on their way to Laramie to make a treaty with the Government   & on their terms not being complied with they took the war path & massacred a great many emigrants on this road that were out late..

Roumors have been afloat in this country, to the effect that there is to be a general Indian war this summer [1867].. well let it come. the Indians have got to clear out & it might as well be done first as last. but where are they to go as this is their last northern strong hold.. exterminate them say some but they will find a big job on their hands.. they are more numerous than many suppose..

My impressions of Montana as a mining country improve every day of my residence here. several new gulches were found late last fall and nearly all reported to be rich.. the only draw-back is the long winters, which puts a blockade on gulch mining   but as the mines become developed to a greater debth, they can be drifted in the winter, preparitory to washing the dirt in the Summer

As an agricultural country Montana will in a fiew years be self-sustaining. the country is spotted with valleys all of them containing the best of land. in the Gallitin over one hundred thousand bushels of wheat was ra[i]sed last season, some land producing as high as seventy five bushels per acre.. Potatoes & all the garden vegetables grow well

As a Quartz mining country she is yet in her infancy, only a fiew mines being sufficiently developed to take out pay rock but if one hundredth part of the quartz claims allready located & claimed prove good she will be the richest mineral Territory in the Union..[55]

In regard to healthfulness she is like all of the mountain states & territories—very fiew if any diseases are known to any extent   the mountain fever attacks <u>Tender feet</u> if they are exposed much on first arriving to the cold nights & hot days of Summer..[56] Ague is entirely unknown & colds a very rare thing.[57] one half the exposure that some undergo here would if in the States give them a cold for a lifetime..

Weather Record 1866 X 7

Dec 25th Christmas 1866. The first snow fell to-day & continued all day. —not very cold..

Jan 1st 1867 New Years. Thermometer 20 deg[rees] below zero

Jan 2nd	18 "	"	"
" 5 "	10 "	"	"

55. Bailey is describing the mining of gold from gold-bearing quartz lodes as opposed to placer mining of gold deposits along a stream or old streambed. Quartz mining refers to mining a body of ore, or the quartz lode containing gold. The ore was crushed in a mill (most quartz mills were stamp mills) and then washed to recover the gold.

56. Mountain fever was originally a general term applied to a variety of febrile diseases occurring in the Rocky Mountain area, but eventually a common pattern of symptoms differentiated it as a specific disease. Mountain fever occurs primarily in the spring and early summer. It is characterized by one to three episodes of fever lasting about forty-eight hours, separated by two to eight days of seeming good health. Other symptoms include chills, severe muscle and chest pains, joint pain, and headache. In 1906 it was demonstrated that this febrile disease is transmitted by the bites of wood ticks. It has been known as Colorado tick fever since 1926 and has recently been found to be an arbovirus infection.

57. Ague is a nonspecific term referring to fever and chills. In the nineteenth century, ague came to be synonymous with malaria, a prevalent disease that manifested these symptoms, but it was also applied to any condition for which the symptoms were primarily fever and chills.

Feb 18th   22 "   "   "
 " 20th   10 "   above   "
March 1st to 13th the longest cold snap of the winter,
from 10 to 25 deg below zero
March 14th thawing to-day
 "   15th Snowing to-day
good Sleighing since Dec 25..

DEDICATORY

To my Sister E.[liza] A.[nn] Bailey Devaney, this
[diary is] the child born of idle moments by the wayside
& in the miners cabin, is affectionately dedicated by her
roving brother.

Theo A Bailey

P.S. Strictly private & in no case to be shown outside of
the family.. & preserved, as the original will be destroyed

Ellen Gordon Fletcher

DIARY AND LETTERS, 1866

ELLEN LOUISE GORDON FLETCHER, known throughout her life as Nellie, traveled with her family in one of the last trains in 1866 before the July Indian raids changed the nature of travel on the trail. She was born at her father's farm near Rushford, Allegany County, New York, on September 1, 1841. She was the oldest of ten children born to Fordyce Foster and Sarah Ann Smith Gordon: Ellen Louise, "Nellie," born 1841; William Reiley, "Will," born 1843; Blanche Eugenia, born 1845; Mary Emily, born 1847; Catherine Virginia, "Genie," born 1849; Emma Smith, born 1852; Charles Bower, born 1854; Leon Luther, born 1856; George Smith, born 1858; and Rollin James, "Rollo," born 1861.[1]

Nellie Gordon was educated at Rushford Academy, a public school in Rushford. Rushford Academy was established in 1851 to provide a broader education than the public elementary schools (then known as common schools) and secondary schools afforded at the time. Nellie Gordon's grandfather and several uncles were on the academy's board of trustees and were instrumental in the founding of the school. Rushford Academy was one of the first academies of its type in western New York, drawing students from a wide area. More than three hundred students were enrolled in the academy at the time Nellie attended. In 1853 the family moved about fifteen miles south to Cuba,

---

SOURCE DOCUMENTS: Ellen Louisa [Louise] Gordon Fletcher, Letters, 1866, typed transcripts, Small Collection 78, Ellen "Nellie" Fletcher Papers, 1866–1870, MHSA; Ellen Louisa [Louise] Gordon Fletcher, Diary, 1866, Small Collection 1977, Francis D. Haines Papers, 1966–1971, MHSA (hereafter SC 1977). Published in *A Bride on the Bozeman Trail: The Letters and Diary of Ellen Gordon Fletcher 1866*, ed. Francis D. Haines (Medford, Oreg.: Gandee Printing Center, 1970).

1. Information on the Gordon family is from SC 1977; an obituary for Fordyce Foster Gordon in *Cuba (N.Y.) Free Press*, February 20, 1908; the 1860 New York census, Allegheny County, Cuba (listing for Fordice F. Gordon and family); and Billy and Nellie Fletcher's great-granddaughter Carol Jo Thompson, Bozeman, Montana.

Ellen "Nellie" Gordon Fletcher, just before she left for Montana Territory.
PHOTOGRAPHED BY W. F. PAGE, CUBA, NEW YORK. COURTESY OF CAROL JO THOMPSON

also in Allegany County, which was close enough to Rushford for her to continue attending the academy.

After graduating from Rushford Academy in 1863, Nellie Gordon passed an examination and earned a certificate allowing her to teach in a common school. The common schools in and around Cuba and

Rushford were generally held for brief periods, depending on the weather and available money. While teaching in a common school, both male and female teachers received room and board in the homes of students or trustees. Male teachers were paid twelve to eighteen dollars per month, while females received one to three dollars per month. Gordon taught first in Madison County, New York, near her mother's relatives, for a few months. She then taught near the village of Allegany, southwest of Cuba, from January through March 1864, again in December, and for a period in spring 1865. When she was not teaching, she lived at home with her family in Cuba.[2]

In late fall 1865, Nellie Gordon met a neighbor who had just returned from Virginia City, Montana. His name was William Asbury Fletcher, but he was usually called "Billy." He was born in Wilna, Jefferson County, New York on March 24, 1829, the son of Samuel and Hannah Emily Johnston Fletcher. The Fletcher's eight children were Millicent Teressa, born 1827; William Asbury, "Billy," born 1829; Dorreska A., "Deckie," born 1831; John Townsend Peter or Penoir, "J. T. P." or "Towny," born 1833; Rachel Emma, "Chell," born 1843; Henrietta Mary, "Retta," born 1846; Josaphine, born 1850; and Ambrose, born 1854 (Josaphine and Ambrose did not survive to adulthood).[3]

Billy Fletcher had married Zilpha Wakefield on April 17, 1854, in Portville, Cattaraugus County, New York. They moved to Nebraska in 1856 and settled at Bellevue, where he farmed and worked as a butcher. Their daughter Ellen, known as Ella, was born in 1857. By early 1860 his wife and a newborn infant had died, and his sister Dorreska was living with him, presumably to care for Ella.[4] In 1863 he and his younger brother Towny Fletcher went to Bannack, Montana. After a year there, they went to Alder Gulch, and Billy opened a butcher shop in Highland, halfway between Virginia City and Summit. The brothers returned to their parents' home in Cuba, New York, in summer

---

2. A copy of the teacher's certificate issued by the State of New York to Miss Ellen Gordon, dated April 15, 1863, is in SC 1977, MHSA.

3. Sources for the Samuel Fletcher family include the SC 1977, MHSA; the 1850 New York census, Cattaraugus County, Hinsdale, p. 138 (listing for Samuel Fletcher and family); and Carol Jo Thompson, Bozeman, Montana.

4. The 1860 Nebraska Territory census, Sarpy County, Bellevue, p. 7, lists William A. Fletcher, 31, farmer; Ella, 3; and Dorreska A. Fletcher, 29. Dorreska was his younger sister. In his statement to a Hubert H. Bancroft employee who was collecting material for Bancroft's historical works, Fletcher said that he married Zilpha Wakefield in 1866. He was probably referring to his first wife Zilpha but made a mistake in the year he married her, since he married Nellie in 1866. Hubert Howe Bancroft, "Montana Dictations, Madison County, 1884–1885," Bancroft Library, University of California, Berkeley.

1865, accompanied by their cousins Dell Allen and John Lefever, who had been in Montana with them.

Nellie Gordon, a neighbor of the Fletchers, became acquainted with Billy Fletcher, and their friendship soon grew into love. In January and February 1866, Billy was seriously ill with typhoid fever for four weeks. During these weeks while Nellie nursed him, he proposed. Nellie had misgivings at first and wrote in her diary on January 22: "He asked me how long it would take me to get ready to go back to the mountains with him. I could not help a sort of shrinking when I thought of going but I love him dearly & know that he loves me too." She wavered while he was desperately ill, but two weeks later, when his recovery was assured, she talked with her mother about going to Montana. "She cried some while I was talking with her & said that she would prefer to have me settle near home, but if I liked Wm. better than anyone else to marry him."

Billy and Nellie were married in late March, and soon afterward they left New York for Montana. Billy was thirty-seven and Nellie was twenty-four. Their traveling party included Billy's nine-year-old daughter, Ella Fletcher; Billy's sister Rachel "Chell" Fletcher, twenty-three; Billy's younger brother J. T. P. "Towny" Fletcher, thirty-three; Nellie's younger brother William "Will" Gordon, twenty-three; and Billy's cousins Dell Allen and John Lefever. They traveled by railroad and steamboat to Bellevue, Nebraska, Billy Fletcher's home before he had gone to Montana in 1863. They arrived at Bellevue on April 18 and moved into an old house, with few furnishings, until they left for Montana.

On May 14, the Fletcher party left Bellevue and traveled seven miles north to Omaha, where they camped and the men bought the remaining supplies for their trip. The next day they left Omaha, and like most of the 1866 travelers, they took the north-side Platte road. They were usually only four or five days behind Theodore Bailey (whose diary immediately precedes Fletcher's in this collection) the entire trip to Montana. At Fort Laramie, they formed a larger train to pass the tightening military inspection and elected J. C. Caldwell captain. In spite of the warnings and precautions, they encountered no Indian problems, but Fletcher's was the last of the diarists' trains to pass through the Powder River Country before Red Cloud's War began.

Fletcher's diary and letters are the only known detailed accounts written by a woman while she traveled the Bozeman Trail. In contrast, Margaret Tomlinson's 1864 diary is much briefer, and the 1864 reminiscences of Adelia French and Mary Kelley were written many years after the journey. Her writings offer a great deal of social history as well as give an extraordinary glimpse into the female experience on the trail. She wrote about social occasions and visits with other women in the trains. She described the emigrants' food, clothing, and camp life. She carefully noted what time every one else in her party got up in the morning and who cooked the breakfast, as she usually slept late. In all, her writing reveals a young woman who led a pampered and sheltered life, in keeping with the ideology of domesticity that defined the contemporary feminine ideal of the middle and upper classes. Also in line with nineteenth-century etiquette, she never mentions the fact that she was pregnant the last six weeks of the journey. Her daughter Blanche, named after her sister, was born March 5, 1867.

Extremely sociable and interested in her fellow travelers, Fletcher wrote detailed descriptions of domestic activities and social interactions. She did not record the numbers of miles traveled or the water and feed available for the animals like most men, but rather wrote about what interested her, such as gathering and pressing flowers, what clothes both men and women wore, and the preparation and serving of meals. She graphically expanded upon the "woman in green" who was going to Oregon, a tuberculin young man and the companion he hired to take him to Montana, and the reaction of the other members in the train to Mr. Smith, the wife-abuser.

Fletcher was also sensitive to the Indians' situation. On June 16, while she was at Fort Laramie, she wrote an insightful analysis of the treaty negotiations going on there at the time, indicating that she was well informed and understood the conflict between the Indians' demands and the government's intentions concerning the new road to Montana. After she crossed the Bighorn River on July 1 and was surrounded by a crowd of Arapahos, she wrote an ingenuous yet astute comment that conveys the nature of the Indians' and emigrants' perspectives of each other, revealing that in one respect they apparently viewed each other exactly the same way. She wrote that the Indians were "gazing at us as though we were a curiosity," while at the same time she described them as fantastic and exotic.

The Fletcher party arrived at Virginia City on July 27. Billy and Nellie Fletcher settled in Highland, in Alder Gulch, three miles south of Virginia City, and Billy built a house for them there, into which they had moved by the end of September. He opened a butcher shop in Summit, three miles farther up Alder Gulch. On December 31, 1866, his sister Chell married Israel M. Wolf, and the Wolfs subsequently moved to Crete, Nebraska, where they lived for the rest of their lives. In 1868 Billy and Nellie, together with his brother Towny, moved to the Madison Valley and homesteaded south of McAllister, on a creek now known as Fletcher Creek.[5]

In the early 1870s they moved to a ranch on the river bottoms of Meadow Creek, south of the mining districts of Red Bluff and Sterling. Billy engaged in farming and running a butchering business, and Towny continued mining and eventually went into ranching. Billy and Nellie Fletcher had nine children: Blanche, Samuel, Mary, Winifred, Ruth, William A. Jr., Carl, Margaret, and Florence. Towny married Nellie's aunt Julia E. Gordon, a younger sister of her father, in 1875. He lived on a ranch on Norwegian Creek for the rest of his life.[6] Billy died in May 1905, and Nellie died in November 1919.[7]

Throughout the trip, Nellie Fletcher wrote letters to her family at home as well as keeping her diary. She wrote her letters in diary form, and in many cases the letters continue where the diary stops. The transcriptions of the diary and letters made by Francis D. Haines, Fletcher's great-grandson, are presented here. Haines transcribed from the original diary, but he had to rely on family transcriptions of the letters because the originals no longer exist. He preserved Fletcher's spelling and only made changes to the letters where they disagreed with the diary. Fletcher was a devout Methodist and began each diary entry with verses of Scripture, which Haines omitted. The diary is the primary document presented in this collection. It is supplemented with passages from the letters, which are inserted into the diary text in italics.

---

5. The 1870 Montana Territory census, Madison County, Virginia City post office, p. 241, lists William Fletcher, 41, butcher; Ellen, 28; Ella, 14; Blanch[e], 3; and Samuel, 2. In the next dwelling were John [J. T. P.] Fletcher, 37, miner, and three other men.

6. A biography of J. T. P. Fletcher is in *Progressive Men of the State of Montana* (Chicago: A. W. Bowen and Co., 1901), 816–17.

7. A brief biography of the William A. Fletcher family, written by their grandson Donald Evans Fletcher, is in Madison County Historical Association, comp., *Pioneer Trails and Trials, Madison County 1863–1920* (Great Falls, Mont.: Blue Print and Letter Co., 1976), 56.

ELLEN GORDON FLETCHER DIARY AND LETTERS

May 14, Monday. William [Billy] was up this morning as soon as day break. Had an early breakfast. It was'nt five o'clock when Will got up & breakfast was nearly ready. I helped Billy pack some of the bedding & dishes. Got everything packed & the horses ready before noon. They all had to work hard & especially Billy. Will went with me over to Mr. Thayers & I got me a new calico dress at 25 cts. pr. yd. & a dollar's worth of Coats' thread.[8] Mrs. Clark called to bid us good bye & Mrs. Wilcox. Mrs. Oliver very kindly offered to get dinner for us. We all took dinner there. Chell's trunk was put on the outside & she was mad & cross because her trunk was'nt in our wagon. We started at 20 min. past twelve, reached Omaha about 4 o'clock. Had quite a pleasant ride. Finished my letter to Blanche on the way.[9] Will went into a store with me & got a pair of buckskin gloves. Two dollars & a quarter. We have camped for the first time just a little way out of Omaha. There are a good many other wagons camped all around us. Billy got sausage for supper & we warmed up some potatoes.

Bellevue, Half past nine in the morning

Good morning, girls [sisters].
Here I am sitting on a roll of rubber blankets, surrounded by my household goods. Everything is torn up and packed, only waiting to have things put aboard the wagons. We have got a trunk of bread and soft ginger cake, etc. packed, or rather a small quantity of the said article in the trunk.
Half past twelve in the wagon, bound for Montana.

8. Calico is a plain-weave cotton print fabric with small designs, used for aprons, dresses, curtains, and quilts. Coats thread was a brand of sewing thread and is still a major brand today.

9. She wrote to her younger sister Blanche, who was twenty years old.

10. The "Debarge dress" was probably made of barege, a sheer fabric woven of silk or cotton and wool. Barege was originally made at Barèges, a town in southern France. A sacque was an unfitted or semi-fitted bodice, jacket, or robe.

11. Delaine is a light dress fabric made of wool or cotton and wool. It can be either printed or plain.

12. Gingham is a plain-weave cotton fabric of light or medium weight that is woven in stripes, checks, and plaids.

13. A "wrapper" was a loose full-length work dress, developed as an alternative to more fashionable attire for housework. It was a one-piece garment with an under-bodice for bust support. Its front hook-and-eye closing for the under-bodice and a top button closing made it ideal for pregnancy and nursing.

14. Nothing is known about this ranch, which was probably located at present Cole Creek, a branch of the Little Papillion Creek. The road crossed Cole Creek at the southern edge of present Benson Park in today's northwest Omaha. Richard Owens camped at Cole Creek two years earlier. Owens diary, May 21, 1864.

15. The ranch at Papillion Creek was thirteen miles from Omaha.

Will and Chell are sitting on the seat in front, while I am back inside of the wagon almost shut out, or rather in, from the outside world. Billy is walking, driving our cow, to get her accustomed to following the train. Ella sits on the bottom of the wagon peeking out between Chell and Will. Chell has got on her Debarge dress, tucked up short, a large calico apron, and her buff [color] sunbonnet and water-proof sacque.[10] She looks like a little girl. I have on my black and white delaine [dress],[11] a new green gingham apron, my turban and water proof.[12] Will has on his old short coat and Scotch plaid pants and vest and broad-brimmed hat. Ella has on her calico dress and sunbonnet. I have my calico wrapper in the wagon, a large bib apron made of that blue calico, and a new green gingham sunbonnet, so you can see I am armed and equipped.[13]

May 15, Tuesday. Had breakfast at about seven o'clock. Billy was up before 5 o'clock. It seems rather odd to be cooking out of doors. There are plenty of neighbors. Will & Dell went down to the city after breakfast. Will bought three very pretty camp chairs, one arm chair at ten shillings, the other two at $3.00. Billy got Chell some gloves like mine last night & a tin churn. They milked into the churn & put it right into the wagon. Some little specks of butter gathered on the top. We started at half-past eight. The first ranch we came to was Mud Creek Ranch, sometimes called Robbers Roost.[14] Next came to the little Papio [Little Papillion Creek], which was a small stream emptying into the Papillion Creek or river. Then came to the ranch of the large Papio [Big Papillion Creek],[15] & Reeds Ranch.[16] The country we passed through was very pleasant, the grass is greener than any I have seen. Saw some very pretty cottages back in [the] groves near Elkhorn City. I should'nt call it much of a city. The location is beautiful on high ground, but only a few houses.[17] We camped down across Elkhorn river in among the trees. A camp of about 30 Indians are not far away. Mr. Hazen, an acquaintance of Wm.'s called on us at night. They opened a bol. [bottle] of blackberry wine which Mr. Clark presented.

    May 16, Wednesday. Billy got up about four o'clock, made biscuit for breakfast. Town cooked the snipe, which he killed yesterday for Chell & I.[18] It was very nice. Mr. Hazen called while we were eating breakfast. He invited us to call on his wife. He was on his way to Omaha. It is a beautiful day, quite cool, but comfortable. About two or three miles from the Elkhorn river we came to a small stream called Rawhide. It received its name from a circumstance which happened a number of years ago, [during] the Cal. emmigration [California gold rush]. A man from Ill. I think made a threat that he would kill the first Indian which he came across. Accordingly to fulfill his promise he shot a squaw. The Indians wanted revenge & followed the train with which he was connected. They demanded the man. He was given up & skinned alive before their eyes.[19] This stream empties into the Elkhorn & the E.[lkhorn] into the Platte at Elkhorn City. We had a fine view of Platte river in the distance. At noon we camped out on the prairie two miles from Fremont city on the right was the boundless prairies, in front of us to the west & south was the Platte river. Only a mile south of us. The feed was better than any we have seen. The grass was from 6 to 12 & 18 in. high. Camped near Mr. Hazens at a little past four. It is a beautiful place smooth, level prairie as far as the eye can see. The R.[ail] R.[oad] is [in] sight & to the south is Platte river & the rough ragged bluffs beyond & only a little way from us. Mrs. H.[azen] invited us in to tea. We had cups ready but Billy, Towney,

16. Peter Reed's ranch was sixteen miles from Omaha. Theodore Bailey also mentioned Reed's ranch. Bailey diary, May 8, 1866.

17. Elkhorn City was twenty-two miles west of Omaha. Today the town is named Elkhorn and has a population of approximately 1,400.

18. A snipe is any of several kinds of game birds living mostly in marshy areas.

19. Rawhide Creek is said to be named for the skinning alive of a white man after he shot a female Indian, a popular and widely reported trails legend. All of the emigrant accounts describing the incident share the same basic elements as the story of Dave Bailey, which was published as an authentic account in the *Stanton (Nebr.) Picket*, January 20, 1905. Bailey was twenty-two in 1849 when he joined an ox train of men from Iowa to go to the California gold rush. At the start of the trip he declared he would kill the first Indian he saw. When his wagon was about to cross a creek in Nebraska, he saw an Indian woman and girl sitting on a log. He shot the woman just as his wagon reached the water. That night the wagons were surrounded by Pawnees who wanted revenge for the killing, threatening to kill the emigrants if they did not turn the killer over to them. Fearing the

consequences of not complying, the men allowed the girl and a few Indians to come into the camp and find the shooter. The girl identified Bailey, and the Indians dragged him from the camp, stripped him, and tied him to a tree by the river. Then they stripped the skin from his body with sharp knives, and he died in the process.

20. Fletcher's maiden name was Gordon.

21. Contemporary guidebooks noted that the road from Omaha came to the Platte River at North Bend. Today the small town of North Bend, Nebraska—established in 1856—is located here.

22. A smudge is a smoky fire. The smoke from a smudge does not frighten mosquitoes, but it is an effective repellent.

Ella, Chell & I went in, found her very kind & pleasant. Her mother was a Gordon.[20]

May 17, Thursday. Started out about seven o'clock. Mrs. Hazen was over to see us before starting. Traveled along the Platte valley in sight of the river & the bluffs & also the R. R. [railroad] Passed some beautiful groves. In the afternoon a Pawnee Indian came up with us at Great Bend. No town only a name for the bend in the river.[21] The Indian had a sort of Tomahawk with a pipe in the end. The handle was the stem. He lingered near the camp. Said that it had been two sleeps since he had eaten anything & he was heap sick. We gave him some biscuit & tea & he said that he felt heap better. It has been very warm. Built a smudge to frighten away the musquitoes.[22]

[As they continued traveling up the north side of the Platte, Fletcher described their sleeping arrangements in a letter on May 18:]

I sleep as sweetly as at home. Our beds are very comfortable. I have a straw bed and feather bed and pillows, one sheet and two blankets. Chell has the same, only no feather bed. Their beds, Chell's and Ella's, are in one part of the wagon, and Billy's and mine in the other. He puts boards across to fill out where the trunks do'nt come, and the beds are very comfortable.

Noon Camp near Fort Kearney,
May 23rd, 1866

May 21st. Well, as I said before, the clouds were very dark and threatening. I had been watching the lightning playing over the clouds for some time. It was a grand and beautiful sight. Pretty soon the blacksmith who lived close by came over and said that if we would bring over a little bedding to cover us with, the ladies were welcome to a bed of husks, and he thought it might rain *hard, but Billy had put everything under shelter and got our beds all nicely made, so that he thought we would be well protected, and we thought we would stay at home. He had'nt more than got home when it commenced sprinkling. We immediately fixed for bed.*

Soon the storm was upon us in all its fury. "The wind blew, and thunders roared, and the lightning flashed." The mules and horses were tied out near the wagons, and the thunder was so heavy, the storm, lightning and all raised a regular panic among them. The mules snorted and screamed and the men had to run out to fasten them more securely. They were just going to bed when the tent blew down. Will had got undressed and the wind and storm beat in upon him furiously. He started when he could get out, and went over to the blacksmith's, where they gave him a dry shirt, and he stayed there all night. They fixed up the tent and slept comfortably the remainder of the night. Their bedding did'nt get wet.

In the wagon we were not particularly inconvenienced, only by the rocking of the wagon. The rain turned to hail and blew and beat against the wagon sheet, but we did'nt get wet. The flashes of lightning made it seem like a blaze of light in our tent, or rather wagon, which shook and rocked like a cradle.

We have plenty of everything good in our large wagon. We have dried apples, peaches, prunes, and currants, canned peaches, two cases of them, each case containing two dozen cans, canned green corn, oysters (steamed I believe), a case of blackberry wine, and I do'nt know what all. Oh, besides, we have sixteen quarts of tomato catsup. William got it of a Mrs. Oliver, who lived next neighbor to us in

Bellevue. We have five hundred-pound sacks of flour, bacon, ham, and codfish, potatoes and butter, plenty of tea, coffee, <u>sugar</u> and <u>molasses</u>, vinegar not left out. We have a little keg of Golden Syrup, which is very nice. We have'nt opened any of our canned fruit yet, and used only dried apples a few times.

Perhaps you would like to know what we have at our meals. Well, at night we usually camp at four or five o'clock. Four is the usual hour. Our little cook stove is unloaded from a rack made for it at the back part of the wagon. The fire is built and tent up in quick time. We sometimes boil potatoes, but usually warm up some which are left in the morning. We then pick up some codfish and cook it with milk. Billy usually washes the potatoes and gets them cooking, and I make a large batch of biscuit. I mix them in a pan and make them with my hands as we do bread biscuit (we use cream [of] tartar and soda).

We have tea for supper—take the end board of our large wagon which is quite a large board, put it across two provision boxes, put around our tin plates, cups and knives and forks, set our spider of fish on the table, and the kettle of potatoes either on it or by the side of it, set on our dripper of biscuit, butter, etc. Our tea is then ready without any further preliminaries, and we proceed to seat ourselves wherever we like to eat. We have three chairs and several small boxes, used to feed the horses in, so we make out very well for seats.

For breakfast we have coffee and warm some of the biscuit baked the night before. At noon we usually camp at eleven o'clock, and stop an hour and a half or two hours. We do'nt cook dinner. They only take off our trunk which [we] carry provisions in, and they eat biscuit or bread and milk.

*Wednesday, [May] 23rd. Started early on our
journey. Camped at noon nearly opposite Fort
Kearney. Townie was going to cross over the river
then to see if there was any letters for us, but he
got a little into the river and found it so deep that
it was almost impossible to cross. Then, several
different channels to the river were there, and it is
quite a difficult crossing, so I wrote a letter to the
postmaster, directing him to forward any letters
which might be there for us, and a man there
kindly offered to take our letters and send them by
the stage.*

May 27, Sunday. I fell asleep this morning after Billy
& Chell got up & did'nt wake until breakfast was nearly
ready. The sun was shining beautifully. It was clear & the
air so still. It seemed so hushed & holy as if nature too
was observing the Sabbath, but lo' the change. The wind
blows, the sky is completely cast over with clouds. A
lady, the one in green, is washing today. The Oregon
wagons have gone on to the river. A new wagon came in
this afternoon & has stopped here. There are six wagons
of us all. The day has been very long & I fear that I have
not spent it as I should. Have read some in Townie's
Testament. Ella & I went on the bluffs. They are mostly
sand. We gathered some beautiful flowers. *I have pressed
some of them and will send them home.* Had oysters for
supper & Billy made some biscuit with yeast powders.
They were very good. It is very cold, the coldest day
since we left home, I should think. Our first Sabbath
camping. A strange Sabbath. How well I should like to
have spent the Sabbath in Cuba at my own sweet home.
May 29, Tuesday. Started at 23 min. past five. Road
rather sandy. We had'nt gone far before we had sand in
abundance. We had to go over some sandy bluffs which
were very steep & hard pulling for the horses. Chell, Ella

& I walked several miles through the sand. Will was riding the pony & driving the cow & he helped me on the pony to ride over some of the sand hills. The woman in green walked & led their racer. I had a nice ride on the old gray, my first horse-back ride since I left home. Will found a deer horn, a nice smooth one, & a gutta percha pipe.[23] Billy showed me some soap-grass [yucca] & I gathered some. *It looks like a large hill of broad grass, with a sort of white edge. The point is sharp as a needle and quite thick. It is sometimes used to make soap of.*

23. Gutta-percha is a plastic substance from the latex of several Malaysian trees of the sapodilla family. It resembles rubber but contains more resin.

May 30, Wednesday. Started out at half past five o'clock. I did'nt get up until breakfast was nearly ready. It was just sunrise & the sun shining upon the bluffs made them beautiful, part in shadow & part in sunshine, which made them look all mottled with brown & gold. The morning came off pleasant with some floating clouds. We saw some white clouds over the bluff which some of them thought was Pikes Peak. They did look like mountains in the blue distance but they soon lost their form. Had good roads part of the forenoon. Traveled about 15 miles. Camped for noon near the river. Saw a prairie wolf. More sand in the afternoon & again in the afternoon it began to blow & rain. Had some thunder & lightning. The storm increased instead of abating & we had to go quite a ways in the storm. The road was very sandy for a short distance. Camped in the rain on the bank of a pretty, clear winding stream. It was a narrow stream & our wagon stood on the very edge of the bank. The boys set the stove in the tent. Billy made the biscuit & Townie got the potatoes & meat, *bacon*, over it. Did'nt rain long. Townie & John watched the stock. We are very comfortable. The boys got wet.

June 2, Saturday. Started out in good season. Very cool in the morning. Not quite as many mosquitoes & gnats as last night. I waked in the night, from the smarting & itching of their bites on my face. It has been a beautiful day. Billy gathered some flowers for me that I had not seen before. I have enjoyed the ride so much today. It was so sunny & we saw so many beautiful flowers & beautiful scenery. In the afternoon we had some sharp lightning & the clouds grew thick & black. The wind blew & we had every prospect of a severe storm.

We saw a camp of [Sioux] Indians down near the [North Platte] river. They had 7 wigwams or lodges & over 30 horses. As we came along opposite their camp they came running up to the road to see us. One very large Indian savage looking & painted red came around in the middle of the road with a sabre & revolvers & waved his hand for us to stop. [He] *wore two large heavy brass rings in each ear, nearly or quite as large around as my wrist. One was in the lower part of his ear, and one a little above.* The rest of the men were armed— or some of them. It looked like hostility at first, but they only wanted to talk with us. We had a little storm.

We had'nt more than got camped when the Indians came rushing along, squaws, papooses & all. *They were friendly Indians and brought written papers from Fort Laramie to that effect, recommending them to the protection of loyal men. They wanted to trade with us,* "swap," *they called it.* One of them had [a] little antilope which he wanted to trade for something. One begged for some whisky of Billy. Said he would give two ponys.

The squaws came along too with their children and papooses on their backs. Some of the little boys were quite pretty and had their bows and arrows. The arrows had steel points. Some of the little boys were entirely naked, except a small piece of buckskin or something around their body. Some of the little children had necklaces of beads and shells and long strings of beads and other ornaments with a shell at the bottom, in their ears. They would come clear down on their shoulders, and would be enough to break through any white persons ears, I should think. The

*squaws, some of them, had on a sort of skirt of buckskin
with blankets around them, and trimmed up with every
imaginable ornament. All of them wore something in their
ears and around their necks. I could hardly tell a squaw
from an Indian. They all wore blankets.*

June 8, Friday. The wind was blowing very hard
when I waked this morning. It continued to blow until
we started. Has been quite windy all day. We have had
the wagon sheet up tight in front nearly all day. Townie
had to go off three or four miles after Sutlee pony. The
beans which Billy put over last night, he left a good fire
under them & they were done when breakfast was ready.
We camped at noon *near* [Fort] *Laramie* near an Indian
camp & the Indians flocked around as soon as we
camped. We have traveled today in sight of some
mountains. Laramie Peak is the one we see, I suppose.
This afternoon we could see the snow on the top.[24]

*We shall reach Fort Laramie sometime this afternoon.
There are large numbers of Indians there now, as they
are about to make a treaty.[25] I suppose this may be the
last letter I can send you before I reach Virginia City.
Will was going to write today, but after seeing the
Indians, he has lain down on the bed beside me and is
taking a nap. His apetite is excellent and health good. We
are none of us lacking for apetite. We ate dinner of cold
beans, tomato catsup, cold biscuits and butter, and golden
syrup. We have plenty of milk which the boys generally
eat at noon. We carry it in a little tin churn.*

June 9, Saturday. Waited a while this morning after
we were ready for the men to find some stray stock. I
wrote a few lines home to complete my letter. We sent
six to the office by Town who went over after the mail.
Started at 7 o'clock. Had a fine view of [Fort] Laramie. It
looked like quite a village.

*As we neared the place, a soldier came out to meet us
and inquired for the captain of the train. On being told*

24. Laramie Peak, the
highest peak in the
Laramie Mountains
at 10,274 feet, is fifty
miles west of Fort
Laramie. It was visible to
emigrants up to one
hundred miles away.

25. The treaty council
with Oglala and Brulé
leaders was held on June
5 and 6. On June 8, the
day Fletcher was camped
nearby, prominent Oglala
leaders Red Cloud, Red
Leaf, and Man Afraid Of
His Horses left the fort
and returned to their
camps. Their departure
marked the beginning of
Red Cloud's War against
the Bozeman Trail.

that there was none, he informed us that we would be
obliged to organize before proceeding further, as they
were not allowed to pass with less than thirty men.[26]

There are a great many Indian lodges, or tepees as
they call them, all around near Laramie. We saw a good
many Indians, some of them herding their stock and some
around their lodges. They have a great many ponies. We
saw some of the squaws riding horseback, sitting on the
horse man fashion [astride the horse], with their blankets
around them.

You ought to see their ornaments. Some wore large
bracelets of brass, and some had beads of tin around their
arms. They were dressed in style, I tell you. As for "rats"
[hair ornaments], you would see the fashion carried out to
an extremity. I saw both Indians and squaws with them
on, one young Indian with his face all painted up and
ornaments around his neck and ears. He had on rats.
They were made of strips of flannel wound up into a roll
and fastened into his hair, one red and the other blue.
They were nearly a foot in length.

One thing attracted my attention more than
anything else, and that was to see the squaws build their
tepees. They had long poles, three of which were
fastened together at the top and then set up. They then
set the rest of the poles around them, same as they set up
top poles. They then take the tent material which is
stretched up on the poles, the wind helping them some.
It is soon spread all around the poles. They fasten it
down, drawing it tight, and their house is complete.
They were made of elk skins nicely pieced together, and
looked very novel and pretty to me, with the poles
sticking out of the top.

Government is about making a treaty with the
Indians which was the reason of there being so many
about the post. The treaty is to come off this month.[27]
They have chiefs of nearly all of the tribes at the fort

26. The soldier was
enforcing General Pope's
General Order No. 27,
which required a train to
have at least twenty
wagons and thirty armed
men before it was given
permission to proceed.
U.S. Senate, General
Order No. 27, in
"Protection to Trains on
the Overland Route," 40th
Cong., 1st sess., 1867, Ex.
Doc. 2, Serial 1308.

27. The Fort Laramie
Treaty of 1866 was
concluded when a few of
the Oglala and Brulé
leaders known to be
peaceful and dependent
upon the traders signed it
on June 27, and even
fewer Cheyennes signed
it on June 28. The treaty
was not ratified by
Congress and therefore
was never officially
recognized.

now, and it is costing the government considerable to feed them as they furnish oxen for their meat.

We camped a short distance out from Laramie to organize. A Mr. [J. C.] Caldwell was elected captain of the train, and a paper was drawn stating that he had been chosen by the train, and signed by all the men. Mr. C.[aldwell] took this and went back to the fort to report to the provost marshall. Townie came before noon with our letters which were very welcome, I assure you. Chell had two from Retta and one from cousin Julia Carver. I had the two from home. Will had one from Bro. Page, and Billy one from Dr. Allen, and Dell one from his father which completed the list.

June 10, Sunday. It rained considerable in the night. Was cloudy when I got up which was not until breakfast was ready. They got the teams all ready to start & it looked so much like rain that Mr. Colwell [Caldwell] did'nt want to start. We went on five miles to the Oregon camp.

Camped between five wagons bound for Oregon and a wagon and cart bound for Montana. It was raining when we reached the Oregon camp, and we stopped awhile.[28] *It was about eight o'clock in the morning, and in one of the tents they were having morning prayers. It was a sound which I had not heard before on the plains and brought many hallowed memories. There is a large family of them [the Eakins], the father and mother and seven [nine] children, a cousin, and the grandfather and grandmother, who are nearly eighty years old. It was a pleasant sight to see them there and hear them sing the old familiar hymns.*

They had been obliged to lie by on account of an accident which happened to a little child four years old. He fell out of the wagon and the wheels ran over his head and thigh. His head was badly cut and his thigh broken. They had been there several days and the little boy was getting better. He is a sweet little fellow, and

28. The "Oregon camp" was the party of Stewart B. Eakin, traveling from the town of Bloom, Cook County, Illinois, to Oregon in five mule-drawn wagons. There were sixteen members in the party: Stewart B. Eakin Sr., his wife Catherine, and nine of their ten children; Stewart's parents, John and Betty Eakin; and three young men employed as drivers. Three diaries were kept by members of the party: Stewart B. Eakin Sr, age fifty; his daughter Jane "Jennie" Eakin, sixteen; and Stewart B. Eakin Jr., nineteen. All three diaries are in Shirley Ewart, Jane Anderson, and John Anderson, eds., *A Long and Wearisome Journey: The Eakin Family Diaries* (Bend, Oreg.: Maverick Publications, 1991).

reminded me of Rollo.[29] *His eyes were just as black. Poor little fellow, he had to lie in the bottom of the wagon (which was a sort of carriage and quite comfortable). He had a box made for his leg, and it had to lie there.*[30]

June 11, Monday. It was a most glorious morning, *such days as only come "after the storm."* Such a morning as gives one strength & vigor. I rode Billy horse & drove the cow 3 or 4 miles. Had a nice ride. Had to go over high steep hills [Emigrant Hill]. We were walled in by hills [in Rocky Pass].

Camped down by the [North Platte] *river. There is an old deserted blacksmith shop here. It is a low sandy place a few large cottonwoods and a plenty of rose bushes and fragrant currant.*

June 12, Tuesday. Was up early this morning as usual but *one of the wagons broke down yesterday, and they had to go back to the fort to get it repaired,* [and they] did'nt get in until 7 & they had to rest. Towney & John staid over across the bluff with the stock & did'nt get in until after breakfast. Ella went off & gathered some beautiful flowers. I mended Billie's pants for him, put patches of antilope skin on the knees, *just such kind of patches as father would like. He looks nice with his white patches.*

We started out before the rest. Had some hills but the road was very smooth & nice most of the way. Saw some beautiful large pieces of agate, *too large to pick up and carry so far when we are "mountain bound."* Camped where it was said to be only 9 miles. Wm. thinks it is 15. It was 22 min. past 3 when we stopped. There are some trees of box elder & a splendid spring of clear water [Boxelder Springs]. Still it is a rather dismal looking place walled in on either side by steep banks which look as though they might have been built for fortifications. Opposite us on the top of the bank are four graves.[31] Chell & I went over to see the little Oregon boy who was hurt. He appears to be getting along finely. He is a

29. Rollo was Fletcher's brother Rollin James Gordon, age five.

30. The injured child was four-year-old Walter Eakin. He fell out of the wagon he was riding in soon after starting out in the morning on June 5. The wheels of the wagon rolled over him, and his left thigh was broken and his head was badly cut. They put a splint on his left leg and sewed up his cut, and then his mother and father took him ahead of the others to Fort Laramie, forty miles away. He was kept in the post hospital for a few days, where "the Surgeons dressed the leg & head under chloroform," and a stretcher was made for him. On June 9 he returned with his parents to the rest of the party, who were waiting about eight miles west of Fort Laramie. Ewart et al., *Long and Wearisome Journey,* 91–96.

31. Boxelder Springs were about twenty-seven miles west of Fort Laramie, on a stretch of trail that went away from the North Platte River to avoid an impassable canyon upstream. Several graves were at the springs, which prompted one diarist to comment that it was the most dangerous place on the route. However, Indians killed few if any of the deceased, and most of them were victims of accident or disease.

sweet patient-looking fellow of four years. I did washing for Will, Billy & myself.

June 13, Wednesday. Had breakfast before 5 o'clock. Started at half-past five. My clothes were nearly dry this morning. It has been pleasant but cold, with quite a strong wind. We were a little behind when we started but soon caught up & went past the rest of the train. There are now 35 wagons *in the train.*

We reached the camping place earlier than the ox trains, and camped outside of the correll, near the [North Platte] *river, in such a pretty, cozy place. The grass is green and nice where our tent stands. We have trees to shade us and plenty of shrubbery in the shape of rose bushes, etc. about a mile back from the camp are high, scraggy piles of rock rising up 200 feet. Chell and I went out there after supper and climbed part way up one of them, where we carved our names, "Nell and Chell." Chell left the "h" out of her name and scratched it out again, declaring that she was'nt there. It is a sand colored rock* [sandstone], *and we could easily mark our names.*

[June 16, Saturday] *We camped down on the bank of the river for noon. It looked very pleasant as we came down off the rough mountains, to see the green valley below with its winding river and green trees. We came to a new road called "Bozeman's Cut Off" this afternoon. It is a much shorter distance by that road than by the other called "Lander's Cut Off."*[32] *The Indians do'nt like to have us travel this road as it is called their best hunting ground. The only thing which they do'nt seem to settle* [at the treaty council] *is about this road. They* [the Indians] *want to have this road thrown up and not allow any travel there. They say that they will give up anything else, but this they will not. They* [the Indian commissioners] *intend to hold the chiefs at Fort Laramie until they yield to the proposals made by the Government. If they do'nt they will detain them until most of the emigration is over.*[33]

32. They were at the mouth of Sage Creek, opposite and two miles west of the site of Fort Fetterman, where the Bozeman Trail turned off from the main Platte road. The Lander Road was a cutoff west of South Pass to Fort Hall and was the conventional overland route to Montana in the 1860s.

33. Fletcher's comments reveal that most emigrants were well-informed not only about the Indians' attitudes toward the Fort Laramie treaty negotiations but also about the Indian commissioners' intentions to impose federal policy on them whether they agreed to it or not.

June 17, Sunday. We started this morn at half-past six.
Billy put the gray pony in with one of the mules & put
one of the hackers in with Sutlee. They worked very
well. We drove until about eleven o'clock when we
camped near a spring of water. I was glad to have even a
part of the Sabbath to rest from our ordinary labors. It
has been a beautiful day, but quite warm. It is cool &
pleasant now & some of the boys in the train have got
Townie with them playing ball.

June 18, Monday. Started at half-past five o'clock.
Pleasant but very warm. The road has been a little rough
part of the way & part of the way the traveling was good.
Hav'nt seen any trees since we started until tonight.
Good feed all of the way, the land is a little rolling with
occasionally quite a hill to go over. At noon wrote some.
Mrs. Light came over. Had a pleasant chat with her. We
have corrolled for the night not far from a small stream
of water. It is pleasant down there under the trees which
we scarcely see now, only as we sometimes find them by
the water. Kate Caldwell brought us over a plate of
antilope meat. We shall have it for breakfast.

*Mr. [J. C.] Caldwell is captain of our train, and a very
pleasant man, formerly from Penn. He has been in
Montana for a few years past, farming. Last fall he went
back after his two daughters [Kate and Narcissa], both
young ladies. His wife is dead, and the girls are going to
keep house for their father.*[34]

June 19, Tuesday. Started this morning at half-past
five. Road a little rough. Traveled 18 miles in the
forenoon & 8 or 10 in the afternoon. In the forenoon
some man from another train overtook us. The train
camped for noon only a little way from us. We have
concluded to join them, *the ox train* [Caldwell's] *travels
so slow.*[35] Kate Caldwell was over to see us at noon. I was
writing home. Chell & I went home with her & they
showed us their Photograph Albums. Kitty, Little Kitt as

34. The 1870 Montana
Territory census, Missoula
County, lists J. C. Caldwell,
farmer, and Narcissa,
twenty-four, keeping
house. Both were born in
Pennsylvania. By this time
Kate was no longer living
with them and was
probably married.

35. They joined a freight
train with ox teams
belonging to the firm of
A. C. Leighton and John
W. Smith, which was
taking supplies to Fort
Reno. Leighton was
traveling with the train.

36. There were four women in the Caldwell train: Mrs. Light, Kate and Narcissa Caldwell, and Kitt.

they call her, gave me a beautiful bouquet of flowers. *She is with a brother, and is a shy little thing.*[36] Will Turner says he wonders if he can't tie up Billy [horse] to the wagon in order to keep him. We saw quite a number of antilope in the forenoon. Townie, Dell, Will & some others went out after them but did'nt get them. Camped about 5 o'clock with the new train. They formed a circular correll & placed the tents inside. It is quite pleasant on an elevation of ground, a few trees in sight near the small stream where we get water.

June 20, Wednesday. Pleasant today, made only one drive. Camped at 2 o'clock with the new train. *Rode in view of four buttes as they call them. This is a name which they give to small mountains standing out alone from other mountains. They sloped evenly each way up to the top where it was perfectly level for quite a distance. They were called Pumpkin Buttes.*[37]

37. The Pumpkin Buttes, noted landmarks for travelers on the 1865–66 route of the Bozeman Trail, are three orange-colored, flat-topped buttes that can be seen for miles in the Powder River Basin. The buttes are erosional sandstone remnants of the Oligocene White River formation that once covered the area.

There are 25 wagons in the [new] *train now, and over sixty men. They are very pleasant people, most of them. A good many families in the train. Mr. Cooper, the captain of the train, has family along, a wife and two children. They appear to be very fine people. Mr. Caldwell's train camped just below us tonight. They sent us up a meal of antilope meat. Camped at about two o'clock. The snow-capped mountain range is in full view. It is a grand sight, the lofty mountains covered with snow. We frequently see it snowing on the mountains.*

June 21, Thursday. Started at quarter past six this morning. Pleasant but warm, & now in the middle of the day it is very warm, uncomfortably so. Mr. Colwell's [Caldwell's] train started at a little past four. Had rather rough roads today, made only the one drive of 17 miles to reach the Fort [Reno]. Only stopping to water the stock as we came to water. Reached our camping place a little after noon. It is in a grove of rather rough looking trees. It is shady but sandy & not very pleasant. Became a little acquainted with Mrs. Capt. Todd *of the train*, her husband was a captain in the army. She is a young bride married a month later than I was. She seems to be a very quiet & pleasant woman. *They were from Springfield, Ill. I found out that she was a bride. She was married in April, starting her journey the next day after they were married.* Several soldiers were down *from the fort* to our camp. *There are only 80 men there. Two gay young lieutenants are all the officers in command at the fort.*[38] Also Mr. Layton [A. C. Leighton] the Sutler he [Leighton] went on to the fort last night on horseback. Chell went over to Capt. Coopers this eve with Mr. & Mrs. Todd.[39]

June 22, Friday. We were waked in the night by the sound of men around & found that the soldiers had been around the camp, *instead of Indians*. Townie, Dell, Johnie & nearly all the men were up. They said that they arrested one man. We crossed the river & passed the fort at a little distance, a short time after starting. Fort Reno is located on the Powder river, a dark muddy stream. It consists of several low log buildings & looked very little as I should imagine that a fort would look. Chell rode with Mr. Todd around to the fort. Several of the teams went around them, overtook us at noon camp. Drove until dark tonight. For water had to go down a bad steep place just before camping.

Camped at "Crazy Woman's Fork," a small stream or river. It was a beautiful spot near the stream in a grove of large trees. The men had blazing fires soon, & it was a pretty sight the white topped wagons & tents & the blazing fires shining through the trees, and the moon looking down quietly upon it all. Over our wagon is a large tree bent over like an arch.

June 23, Sunday [Saturday]. Billy was up as usual lately, as soon as light. Breakfast was all ready by the time I was dressed. And before me spanning the

38. Captain Edwin R. Nash and the Omaha Scouts left Fort Reno on June 6, so that when Fletcher arrived at the end of June, the fort was depleted to a garrison of 104 men of Companies C and D, Fifth U.S. Volunteer Infantry. The commanding officer was Lieutenant Daniel W. Dana, Company D. The only other officer present was Lieutenant Thomas G. Stull, Company C. After Colonel Henry B. Carrington and the Eighteenth Infantry arrived at the fort on June 28, the Fifth Volunteers left on July 6 for Fort Laramie to be mustered out of service.

39. Fort Reno sutler, John W. Smith, wrote about Fletcher's train in a letter that was published in the *Denver Daily Rocky Mountain News*, July 19, 1866. He reported that the train had more than one hundred wagons and nearly two hundred men, and he continued: "Among the emigrants were several western officers who more or less distinguished themselves during the late war [the Civil War]. . . . several young ladies also accompanied the expedition. Success to the 'crinoline.'"

heavens was a most beautiful rainbow. It soon commenced raining, rained quite hard for a few minutes, had several little showers. Was ditained from starting on account of the rain. Townie went down & caught 8 fish, *enough for our supper.* He dressed them when he came up. We had to cross the river soon after leaving camp. It was bad crossing too, *it was marshy and bad coming up from crossing the river,* 2 wagons got stuck on the bank & another just after getting across. We crossed without difficulty. It has rained some this forenoon the country after leaving the river has been fine. Billy says it is splendid farming land. It stretches out into broad waving fields of green. Some hills but not high. *Camped by the side of a cool mountain stream called Clear Creek.*

June 24, Sunday. Had breakfast at seven o'clock, considerable later than the usual hour. *Last night the captain took a vote among the men to decide whether we should start today or not. The majority were in favor of resting. Accordingly we have the day to ourselves.* It was a beautiful morning & has been pleasant all day. Very warm. Nearly every woman in camp except ourselves have been washing today. Quite a number of the men among them Townie, went out prospecting for gold. It has been pretty quiet from most of the men who were about camp. That is I heard no loud swearing. A man in camp has been shoeing horses & mules nearly all day.

In the tent next to us is an invalid man. He is an unmarried man of about 26 years of age, and has the consumption [tuberculosis]. *He is a young lawyer from near Chicago, very quiet and gentlemanly. He has been in our tent quite a while today. He has no friends along, only a young man, an acquaintance, whom he takes through, bearing his expenses there and back, for taking care of him, cooking, etc. The young man is very kind, but the sick man looks now as though he was almost past*

*help, though it seems as if this mountain air would make
him feel strong and well if anything would.*[40]

June 25, Monday. Was waked in the night by Billy
getting into bed. He was on guard. I did'nt know it last
night. There was quite an excitement in the train this
forenoon. Suddenly the cry came, "A woman is killed."
Mr. Smith has killed his wife

The train was immediately stopped and the men
rushed back to see if it was true. "Hang him, stretch him
up to the first tree," were some of the cries which greeted
our ears. They found that the woman was not dead, only
stunned. Her brutal husband had struck her with the
butt of his whip. Those who were acquainted [with him]
said that he had been in the habit of whipping and
abusing her. He was compelled to travel in the middle of
the train. The captain informed him of the feelings of the
train, and gave him to understand that if he did the like
again, he would be treated accordingly.

*Had to cross another stream called "Big Pine Number 2"
[Piney Creek]*[41] *just before camping, which was full of
large stones. Camped on a hill on the opposite shore.*[42] *Billy
got a couple of camp kettles for me and took them down
close by the water to do some washing   It was cool and
pleasant there. It was nearly dark when we went back to
camp. I almost wanted to stay there all night. Our blazing
camp fire made it so pleasant among the trees. Some of the
men saw five bears a little distance on the hills. They all
fired away but did'nt kill either of them.*

June 26, Tuesday. Did'nt get started until nearly seven
o'clock. It was a beautiful morning & my clothes were
quite dry. In the morning the road wound around
through the mountains [Lodge Trail Ridge and
Fetterman Ridge]. Once we went over one side of a
mountain. The roads were quite steep. Saw a good deal
of burnt rock [scoria]. Up on the mountains one of them
looked as if it had burst open by some volcanic eruption.

40. It was the common
belief in the nineteenth
century and through the
1930s that the dry
climate in the mountain
West would cure
tuberculosis, leading to a
thriving health industry
that lasted until medical
cures were found.

41, Prior to the
establishment of Fort
Phil Kearny, the trail
went through a gap
farther west, crossed the
Little Piney, passed north
of the site of the fort, and
then crossed Piney
Creek.

Fort Phil Kearny was
established on a high
piece of land between the
forks of Piney Creek
about three weeks later.

42. They camped at the
base of the slope leading
up to Lodge Trail Ridge.

Passed through some beautiful green valleys, by the side of cool mountain streams. Camped just across quite a good sized stream of water [Prairie Dog Creek].[43]

June 27, Wednesday. Was up early this morning, had breakfast & started at a quarter of six. Early for this train. They wished to get ahead of the ox train which has kept up with us for several days. We had to retrace our steps for a few miles as we went three miles below where we should have crossed the river.[44] We had to cross Tongue river [Goose Creek] in the morning. It was quite deep & they raised some of the wagon boxes to keep out of the water. Crossed without difficulty but it delayed us about an hour. Soon after that Capt. Cooper saw a bear in the brush near the creek & over 30 men rushed out with their guns. Billy was among the number. This delayed us another hour & the men came back without their bear. Camped for noon near Eve creek [Soldier Creek]. The country passed thro' was beautiful, especially near Tongue river [Goose Creek].[45] There was trees all along & green waving hills & the white capped mountains beyond.

In the middle of the afternoon the lead team belonging to the two Mr. Smiths came rushing back with the alarm of Indians. We correlled immediately, & the Indians [Arapahos] soon came to camp, refusing to take anything unless we went down the hill. *This looked somewhat like hostility, as it was a bad hill to go down, and a narrow pass at the foot of the hill.*[46] *However as we could get rid of them in no other way, they started on down the hill. The ox train came up in the meanwhile and went on with us. The Indians stood in line down at the foot of the hill. Instead of 200, there were about 90 in number. They were armed with bows and arrows and a few of them had guns, and some of them had long spears. They did not offer any molestation, and we drove on a little ways and camped in a beautiful little valley. A small stream [Wolf Creek], thickly shaded was close by.*

43. They crossed Prairie Dog Creek ten miles from the Piney Creek crossing and camped on the east side.

44. Ten miles from camp they came to the fork in the road where the Bozeman Trail turned west and went across the divide to Goose Creek. They continued straight ahead, on Connor's 1865 trail, and had to turn around and come back to the fork. Another train made the same mistake two weeks earlier and probably left a visible trail that confused them.

45. The Goose Creek crossing was just northwest of present downtown Sheridan, Wyoming. Ten years later General George Crook established his headquarters camp nearby, between the forks of Big and Little Goose creeks, during his summer campaign.

46. They were on present Keystone Road west of Sheridan, a few miles southeast of the Tongue River crossing where Arapahos attacked the Sawyers train the preceding year. Her description of a "bad hill" and "narrow pass" at the base suggests they were approaching the North Dry Creek ravine.

The ox train corrrelled with us, forming a long circle.
Quite a [large] space was enclosed. The Indians followed
us on their ponies all the way, and on either side of the
wagons were men [in the train] who walked carrying
guns on their shoulders. Townie came in [from hunting]
safely, but did'nt see the Indians until he had reached the
creek at the foot of the hill. He concealed himself in the
bushes and the Indians rode past him close by his head.
We were afraid something had happened to him when he
was gone so long. They gave the Indians some bacon,
sugar, flour, etc., tied the horses and mules inside of the
correll, appointed a double guard and retired for the
night. These Indians were Rappahoes [Arapahos]. The
ones we saw last night were Cheyennes.

Thurs. [June] 28th. The Indians did'nt disturb us any
through the night. I slept soundly and found everything
safe in the morning. The Indians led the way around for
us to cross another bad stream [Tongue River], and rode
along with us nearly all of the forenoon trying to swap.
More came up from near the river, and one old chief
made the captain of the train a present of a nice buffalo
robe. We got rid of the Indians when we came to the next
stream [Twin Creek]. Pleasant roads part of the day
when we had to go over the bluffs again.

June 29, Friday. Started at six o'clock, found rough
roads most of the way.[47] *One of our wagons broke an*
axle tree just after noon. Fortunately, it happened to be
near some good timber. Two of the men went right to
work at it, and had it fixed ready for starting the next
morning. We washed and baked bread.

Saturday, June 30th. Pleasant today, but warm. Passed
through some very pleasant country, and toward night
we came in sight of the Big Horn River. There is a large,
beautiful valley before we reach the river. Just as we came
into the valley we crossed a small stream of water, about
a mile or so before the river. There are trees along the

47. On this day they went
through hilly country and
crossed Little Bighorn
River and Lodge Grass
Creek and camped on
Rotten Grass Creek.

river, and the valley stretches out broad and very level, hundreds of acres of which is covered with wild oats. They look almost like the oats which we cultivate. We have seen some wild wheat. I should think it would be fine feed for stock.

As we neared the river we found that there were already trains there ahead of us. We drove down and camped in a grove of large, scraggly trees. It was very pleasant but sandy. We found that we should be obliged to lie over there for a chance to cross the river. One large train had been there two weeks and another train had been there four days and had got about half of the train across. Still another, an ox train, had just come up. There we were, four trains of us, and a part of another across, and the rest on this side of the river.[48] *There are Indians [Arapahos] on the other side of the river. The mountains are in sight. Behind us the broad, green valley, and in front the river.*

July 1st, Sabbath. William and Townie found some old mountain friends[49] *of theirs last night who were just crossing the river. They were very much pleased to find them. They had been anxious to go in company with them when we started, but they could'nt wait, and started fifteen days first.*[50] *It proved, however, they gained nothing by it, as there was a good deal of rainy weather, and the streams were all of them very high. They had to raise their wagon boxes and had bad times in crossing several streams which we crossed without any difficulty.*[51]

Mr. [John] Reed, captain of the train, owned one of the boats, and as he was a particular friend of the boys, he said that they should go over with his train. We were glad to accept of his kind offer, as we learned from the men that two men had been drowned in crossing the stream, from the train ahead, and that they lost mules and wagons.[52] *All were impatient to cross, and as Mr. Reed crossed the remainder of his train this morning, we were taken across*

48. They were at the Bighorn River middle crossing, about three miles above the emigrant ford at Spotted Rabbit Crossing. Theodore Bailey crossed here on a ferryboat two days earlier. Bailey diary, June 28, 1866.

49. The "mountain friends" were men the Fletcher brothers knew in Montana.

50. The captain of the waiting train was John Reed. A member of the train, Richard W. "Dick" Clarke, wrote a reminiscence that was published in the *Billings (Mont.) Gazette*, June 25, 1933. Clarke related that crossing the Big Horn River was the most difficult part of the trip. Reed's train was there about ten days, most of which were spent building rafts out of cottonwood logs.

51. The earlier trains experienced high runoff in the mountain-fed streams, whereas the water levels had subsided by the time Fletcher's train crossed them.

52. Storer and Whiston, two men in John Zeigler's train, drowned while attempting to cross the Bighorn on June 25 and 26. Theodore Bailey also recorded the accidents. Bailey diary, June 27, 1866.

*by them. It was a busy day for the Sabbath and ill
accorded with my feelings, but there seemed no
alternative. The men worked busily and faithfully the
whole day in getting the remainder of their train and our
wagons across. Four of the men were at our tent to dinner.*

They had three boats which consisted each of two
long, large logs hewn out, and lashed together. This made
one boat. The wagons had to be unloaded and the things
carried across in the boats. Only a few things were left in
our large wagon. The wheels were taken off and the box
set right across the boat. Chell and Ella rode across in the
large wagon, and I stayed until the last load which was
the wagon in which we ride. The beds were left in the
wagon   when the boat came near the shore, men hauled
it up to the landing with ropes   and on the other side a
span of mules were sent in the water to draw the boat
ashore. The stream was quite broad, but the voyage
across was very short.

*We found plenty of [Arapaho] Indians over on the
other side who thronged around, gazing at us as though
we were a curiosity.*[53] *They were dressed in every
fantastic style imaginable. Most of the Indians wore
buffalo robes around them. Some of them wore blankets.
I found Ella surrounded by about a dozen children who
were trimmed off with beads and the teeth of animals.
They all want to swap. One little girl handed Ella a pair
of moccasins, and said "meat" meaning she wanted
something to eat for them. Ella got her a piece of bread
and kept the moccasins. One old squaw brought me a
pair and wanted a cup of sugar. I took them of her. Dell
got a pair of plain ones for Chell. Mine only have a few
pink, blue and white beads. They did'nt bring any very
pretty ones. Some of them are made of antilope, some of
buck and buffalo skin.*[54]

*July 2nd. It is very warm and the Indians as thick as
ever. It is impossible to keep them away. Billy bought*

53. This was the large
band of Northern
Arapahos who traded
with emigrant trains
between the Tongue and
Bighorn rivers.

54. Fletcher was the last
diarist in 1866 to interact
with the Arapahos prior
to the military occupation
of the trail. Like the
experience of the earlier
travelers, hers was a
trading and exchange
encounter that typified
the accommodating
relations between the
emigrants and Arapahos
in that period. Although
she does not mention
trading the highly sought-
after matches, the Indians
also valued the American-
made food items traded.

some moccasins for himself and three buffalo robes. Chell washed and I baked a large batch of bread. The men have been at work all day getting the trains across. Capt. Cooper's family are now across. Their tent is near ours. They are very pleasant neighbors. It is a great task to get the mules across. They take two or three at a time and tie them to the boat and row across. It is quite difficult to get some of them in[to the water] at all, especially the mules who are headstrong creatures at any time. We are all safely across. It is quite a relief to think of it, as there has been two men and five mules drowned in the train ahead [Zeigler's train]. Tomorrow we expect to start with these mountain boys. Mr. C.[aldwell]'s train is not yet across.

July 3, Tuesday. I was surprised this morning when I waked to find that I had the bed all to myself. I had'nt waked since I went to sleep last night. It was a very warm night, uncomfortably so   when I went to bed & for some time we could hear the Indians screaming & making considerable noise. I found that they had been to breakfast when I got up & a large group of [Arapaho] Indians were just going away. Billy had got a nice Buffalo robe of them. Another very warm day. Went in to see Mr. Cooper a little before we started. Was sorry to go off & leave them. If Mr. Mandeville gets over today they want to start on to overtake us. Started at seven o'clock & drove until quite late. The roads were very bad in the afternoon. So many deep places to cross. Found the molasses bottle broken & the catsup spilled over the box. We drove quite a distance to find good water but finally camped in a dreary place where there was but very little water & that not fit to drink hardly.[55]

July 4, Wednesday. The musketoes were very thick last night & troublesome. Waked very early. Started at half-past five, glad to leave that place of sage brush & alkali water. One of the wagons broke an axle but it was soon fixed. Had a good many bad pieces to go over.

55. They were probably at Little Muddy Creek, about eighteen miles from the Bighorn River. Fletcher was one of the last emigrants to take this route. All subsequent Bozeman Trail travelers took James Sawyers's new cutoff west from the Bighorn River to the Clarks Fork, bypassing Bozeman's circuitous route by way of the Yellowstone River.

Steep hills, traveled until about twelve & camped for noon just across a dry creek. There are a few trees & an Eagles nest in the top of a large one. Mr. Reed sent over a nice box of lemonade or rather sugar of lemons prepared for lemonade. Townie brought it to me with Mr. Reed's compliments. Mr. Mills a man who is with Mr. Reed brought us a large piece of cheese & another a nice piece of antilope. The men are all very kind & generous. This is the 4th of July! how little to remind one of this great national anniversary. Passed a long range of rocks which looked like walls which had been built. They extended from 5 to 10 miles.[56] There was a regular gateway & one could easily fancy that some olden city might appear beyond were we to enter the gateway. Camped in a cozy place near a cool spring of water which was very refreshing to us all. I could hardly drink enough.[57]

July 5, Thursday. Started at half-past five. Had bad roads most of the way, though a little way we had nice green grass. Crossed a clear stream of water [Pryor Creek] when some of the men took their gold pans & washed to see what they could find. About two miles beyond this an axle to one of the wagons broke & we had to stay there the remainder of the day. It is a dull dreary looking place, nothing to be seen but bleak looking hills covered with sage brush. The water is very poor, & we all feel tired being warm & some musketoes. Had a shower just at night. Chell found enough gooseberries for tea.

July 6, Friday. Had to wait a while in the morning for the men to finish fixing the wagon, which made it late starting. We came to a very steep place about noon. The road had been over hills but we then came to some of the roughest wildest looking hills we have had to pass over.[58] I had been sleeping & Billy waked me to get out & walk. Will & I started out & went over a long ridge of sandy looking rough.

56. Rock outcrops resembling walls stretch five miles along the east side of East Fork Pryor Creek.

57. The spring, now known as Wagon Box Springs, is on East Fork Pryor Creek, seven miles southeast of the Pryor Creek crossing. The spring is near the sandstone rock-wall formation stretching along the east side of East Fork Pryor Creek in this area. The spring and rocks are in the Crow Indian reservation.

58. They were in the rugged hills on the south side of the Yellowstone, opposite present Billings, Montana.

59. There is no entry for
July 7 in either the diary
or letters. On this day
they came to the
Yellowstone River
downstream from the
mouth of Blue Creek,
went two miles up the
bottom, turned south and
went ten miles over the
bluffs, and came back to
the Yellowstone at the
mouth of Duck Creek.

60. They went five miles
up the Yellowstone
bottom to near the mouth
of the Clarks Fork, turned
south and went over the
highlands, and returned to
the Clarks Fork three
miles upstream from its
mouth.

61. They were at the
Clarks Fork upper
crossing, three miles
above its mouth.

62. Theodore Bailey's
train constructed
ferryboats here on
July 3 and 4.

July 8, Sunday.[59] It was a lovely morning. Started at
half-past six after traveling a couple of miles the road
again went up over the bluffs.[60] Found it quite level and
pleasant. On the right was a steep bank which
overlooked Clark's Fork & Yellowstone rivers. C's Fork
[Clarks Fork] empties into the Yellowstone near here.
Had a fine view of the snow capped mountains this
morning. We could see them for a long distance. Traveled
8 or ten miles & found upon reaching the river [Clarks
Fork] that we should be obliged to cross by boats as at
the Big Horn.[61] Some one from the train ahead of us
have built some boats & stopped to ferry trains across.[62]
We laid over after reaching the river [Clarks Fork]. It is
very warm & the musketoes are plenty. Billy has built a
smudge all around the tent & the wagons. I tried to find
a cool place in the shade but the musketoes drove me
away. Mr. Welch went hunting. Killed two antelopes.
Townie has been playing cards & everybody seems to
have forgotten that it was Gods holy day.

July 9, Monday. Very warm. The men have been at
work down at the river [Clarks Fork] all day. I have done
quite a large washing & Chell made a large batch of
bread. Billy told us that we must be through all by noon
in order to cross but we did'nt have to go. Billy made
some dumplings for breakfast. They were nice & light. I
washed Ella's & my dress & they were dry in a few
moments. In the afternoon we had a nice quiet time to
sew. I had plenty of mending for Ella & myself & the
day passed swiftly away. Several of the wagons have
crossed, but we are yet on the wrong side of the river.

July 10, Tuesday. Billy was sick with a terrible
toothache, nearly all night. The night was warm & today
the heat is oppressive. Our wagons were the first to
cross. The boats are not as large nor as good as those at
the Big Horn. We could'nt ride across in the wagon box
but sat on some boxes in the boats. Had no difficulty in

crossing before we crossed the Cooper train came up.
The most of them came down to see us. Mrs. C.[ooper],
Mrs. Mandeville & [Mrs.] Todd. They seemed very much
pleased to see us & had a sad story to tell. Mr.
M.[andeville] lost part of his wagon, all of his fruit, tea,
coffee, all of his provisions except the flour & bacon.
Mrs. M.[andeville] said that two or three hundred
D[olla]rs [were lost].

July 12, Thursday.[63] Had a little shower in the night.
Warm when I waked in the morning, & plenty of
musketoes. Just as we were all hitched up ready to start
we had a little rain again. Ella begged of me to go up on
the top of the hill with her to see the rocks & river. Said
that she would pick off all of the burrs & sticktights if I
would go & after combing my hair we went up there. I
felt well paid for the trouble of climbing the hill & the
annoyance of those prickly grasses. There was large flat
rocks piled & tumbled around in profusion, one higher
& larger than the rest. We climbed upon [it] & had a nice
view of the river far below. I could hardly see how they
got down to the river after water. It was rocky. Had
some bad places to go through. Had to cross a river [Red
Lodge Creek] which they supposed to be the Rosebud
twice. Chell rode Mr. W[elch]'s pony a while in the
afternoon. Towards night the road left the river [Red
Lodge Creek] & we drove for several miles over high
green hills or bluffs. Did'nt find water until late. Mr.
Coopers train was just behind us all the afternoon,
camped beyond us.

July 13, Friday. Billy was on guard last night until
midnight. The morning was quite cool & pleasant. Mr.
Cooper started out some time before us. We only drove
four or five miles when one of the wheels to Mr. Reeds
wagon burst, & we have correlled to fix it. It is quite
early not more than nine o'clock. Stopped two or three
hours. Joe Smith came over after some sugar & Billy got

63. The entry for July 11 is
missing. On that day they
went south up the Clarks
Fork to Rock Creek and
then up Rock Creek to
Red Lodge Creek.

him to shoe one of the mules. Had several bad places to go over this afternoon. At about 3 o'clock we camped beside a swift stream of water [Rosebud Creek]. They hesitated about crossing but it is pleasanter on this side, & they will be obliged to block up the wagons [to cross]. It is very pleasant here beside the musical river. I have been washing. Before I got my clothes

July 16, Monday.[64] We were up early & the men were soon crossing the river. We crossed the first of any.

July 17, Tuesday. Started at about six o'clock. A clear cool morning. Chell rode Mr. Welch's pony. Did'nt camp for noon until after two o'clock. Had a long tiresome ride, passed over some very high hills, had some bad steep stony places to go down.[65] Crossed one clear cool stream of water [Stillwater River]. Saw some Elk up on the hill at the left of the road. Mr. Mills wounded one & we could plainly see him limping off down the hill. Two wagons stopped to get the elk & did'nt get in until nearly time for starting again. It is rather pleasant here in this grove, but the trees are large & scraggly & the ground is rough. Mr. Welch took dinner with us. It was nearly four when we started for afternoon. Chell lost her thimble, it dropped out of the wagon & they looked in vain but could'nt find it. She felt very badly as it was a present from her mother. Camped near the Yellowstone. Very warm & musketoes.

July 18, Wednesday. Started in good season. Cool & pleasant, we now have the cool fresh breeze from the mountains, which seem to be only a little distance. We see the snow peaks before us, & to the left. Reached quite a large rapid stream [Boulder River] at about eleven o'clock. Mr. C[aldwell]'s train was crossing, had some of the wagon boxes raised. Mr. Reed brought his watch & pocket book for me to take care of. It was quite pleasant at the crossing. A large grove of trees on one of which was a piece of bark nailed up informing us that the water

64. There are no entries for July 14 and 15, when they camped on a branch of Rosebud Creek.

65. This was the steep descent at Sandborn Hill where the trail descended to the Stillwater River.

was full of rocks so we had'nt better raise the wagon boxes too high. Mr. R.[eed] had us women get into one of the large wagons to cross. We crossed without difficulty & so did Townie   but Billy started with only the team which he drives & just as he was nearly across the mule began to act bad & finally threw himself. Billy jumped in & for a few moments we expected the mule would drown. Billy too came very near going, but ropes were thrown him & he got out safely. The men helped all they could. Townie had to wade in & at last they succeeded in getting the wagon safely out, [and] except the loss of a neck yoke & some trim about the harness, nothing was hurt, not even wet enough to do any harm.

July 19, Thursday. Morning cool & pleasant. We reached the [Yellowstone] river [ferry] at about 8 o'clock. Mr. Cooper's train had just got across. A large rope is strung across the river & the boat is swung across by means of ropes & pulleys. Two wagons crossed when we did, so were only a few minutes crossing. The price for ferrying across is $10 per wagon & fifty cts. for each mule or horse. A small cabin on this side of the river, occupied by the ferryman [John Bozeman]. A few large trees, under one of which I am sitting to write. The bark is cut off a good many of the trees & names written with pencil.[66] Chell went fishing with Mr. W.[elch]   She had 3 trout & Mr. W. gave us all he had caught. We only went on a few miles. The roads very good. Camped early.

July 20, Friday. Was up & started in good season. Found very rough roads most of the way. Had to go up over some very high steep hills, to the left of us was a deep rocky gulch. If one of our wagons had gone off there it would have been gone. The sun shone very hot, & at noon camped in the midst of the prickly grass. In the afternoon had quite a large stream of water to cross, which our men called 25 yd. creek [Shields River]. There was quite a pleasant valley & just across the stream was

66. See Davis Willson's diary entry for August 28, in which he noted some of the names and messages.

67. This was probably a Blackfoot or Nez Perce lodge.

an Indian lodge.[67] The boys found some of their mountain friends there prospecting. Two of them came down to our camp & Billy has left the gray pony in their charge. Just before camping we came to the most sideling place we have seen yet. The men had to put ropes on the wagons to keep them from tipping over.

July 21, Saturday. It was after sunrise when we got up this morning. One of the wagons had an axle burst yesterday & the men had to unload & distribute the freight around among the other wagons. This delayed us for some time. The morning was cool but soon grew very warm & the musketoes swarmed around in abundance. Did'nt travel far today. Came up just to the divide in the mountains [Bozeman Pass] & camped. It is a wild rough looking place, mountains on every side of us. A little to the left & back of us are some rocky, snowy peaks, & all around on every side mountains some of them covered with a low growth of evergreen trees & some of them green & grassy. Billy is on guard tonight. It is a lovely evening, clear & cool, & bright moonlight.

July 22, Sunday. Was up in pretty good season this morning, but did'nt get started until seven o'clock. I walked over the divide. It was quite steep but not at all as I had imagined it to be. I supposed that it would have been much rougher & higher. Chell rode Mr. Reeds pony & after a little ways I rode our Sutlee pony. He is a very good riding horse, not quite as easy as the gray but I had a nice ride. I enjoyed it so much going down the narrow mountain roads through the trees & across bad places. I overtook Mr. R.[eed] & Chell, had a very pleasant chat with him. We passed some beautiful mountain springs & streams of water clear as crystal & cool.

July 24, Tuesday. I was waked this morning by having Mr. Reed around to each wagon, saying "grub fires." Went down or rather up the [Gallatin] river a mile or so to find a crossing. We had several channels to cross. It was right in the woods & the road was some of the time very rough through among the large streams. It was quite a distance before we came out onto the road as this was a new crossing. As we came out a small cabin appeared to view, completely shaded by trees and surrounded by out buildings. A winding path led down to an outside cellar which was built in a bank. Mr. Gay [John C. Guy] occupied this ranch.[68] We stopped & Townie introduced us. Mrs. G.[uy] invited us in & we stopped half an hour. It looked quite neat & tidy there. A homemade bedstead, large cupboard & table were in the room. There were several children. The youngest came in & I asked his name & what was my astonishment to hear him reply Jeff. Davis. His mother told him not to be ashamed of his name so I could see what their sentiments were. We camped about a mile from there for noon, it was opposite a large field of wheat. We also saw green peas & cabbage & potatoes growing. Camped for night about three miles from Madison river.

68. John C. Guy came from a Colorado mining camp and settled near Bozeman in the fall of 1864. He was elected sheriff of Gallatin County in 1866 and served in the position for six of the next eight years. In 1868 he built a two-story hotel in Bozeman, the Guy House, and operated it until 1877, when he moved with his family to the Yellowstone Valley. Rosa Beall, "Montana's Early History," *Contributions to the Historical Society of Montana*, 8 (1917), 302.

Noon camp, July 26, 1866

My dear friends at home:

We are now within eighteen miles of Virginia City, and have camped for noon in the valley of the Madison. It is very pleasant here. The snow-capped mountains are in front and on every side of us. We crossed the Madison yesterday morning. Now where we are, there is a sound as of the rushing of wind through the forest. I looked out of the wagon and the air was literally filled with grasshoppers, as far as you could see. Their silvery wings fluttering in the sunshine give them the appearance of snow flakes. . . . Fortunately for us they did'nt all come down to the ground, but passed over in an hour.

While I am writing this, sitting in the front of
the wagon, in comes Billy and throws himself upon
the bed beside me, pinching me and tormenting me
generally. There he has taken the pen out of my
hand, and taking a small iron ring he placed it on
my paper and marked around it. I wish some of you
girls would pull his ears for him. So much for my
letter today. He says to tell that is his love. "Round
is the ring that has no end. So is my love."[69]

69. These words were
from a popular song of
the time.

July 27th, Friday eve. Again I seat myself to finish
this letter. It is just sunset now. We have been to tea,
and Chell and I have seated ourselves outside of the
tent to finish our letters home. We have camped in a
wild, picturesque little spot not much larger than our
correl. Around us on every side are high undulating
hills, smooth and green, and some of them covered
with low evergreens. Beyond and towering up above
these, old Summit Mountain rises up rough and
rocky with spots of snow.

Two or three of the men have been writing
home, but have laid it aside. Some of them are
getting their supper, some in little groups sitting
and lying around on the grass chatting away as if
they already had nothing else to do. Just opposite
me a man has his sleeves rolled up and is mixing
biscuit with all his might. Will has been lying
under the wagon reading your letters and his
papers, but now he has taken towels and soap and
gone down to a little stream close by to wash. Dell
is somewhere around camp, and Billy and Townie
have both gone down to their shop at Highland,
which is only three quarters of a mile distant. . . .[70]

70. This was the butcher
shop that Billy and
Towny Fletcher had
established in 1864 in
Highland, a mining camp
three miles south of
Virginia City in Alder
Gulch. They were
camped in Alder Gulch,
less than a mile north
of Highland.

We reached Virginia City at about noon
[today]. I can hardly tell you what my feelings
were, or what my impression of the place, as I
reached at last that long talked-of, long looked-for

place. It certainly did'nt surprise me with its broad streets and splendid edifices. It looked strange and new to me, and different from anything which I had ever before seen. It is quite a large place, though it does'nt show off prepossessingly at first sight. The city is situated in a hollow or basin like, entirely surrounded by mountains, not green and fresh looking, but brown and bare, the numbers of stock in and around the city having eaten off all of the grass. There is'nt a tree in sight. All have been cut down for wood, and all about the city, the ground is cut and dug up by the mining which is constantly going on. All this gives the city at first sight, a rough, bare look.

As you enter the city and pass through the business streets, it shows to much better advantage. There are some very fine stone buildings, quite stylish and city-like, but mostly small. The streets are narrow and the dwelling houses small, the greater portion being built of logs. The outside streets consist entirely of log cabins, some of them the littlest bits of houses that I ever saw, and built right on the mountain side. It reminded me more of a row of hen coops than anything else to see the little low cabins stuck down on the hill side. The place seemed very lively, though they say there is not near as much business carried on there at present as there has been. Billy stopped in the city only a few moments to buy a few tin pans and some flour and butter. Small pans were only $1.50 apiece, flour $14.00 per sack of 100 lbs., and butter $1.25 a lb. We reached our camping place without any accident, glad enough to find a quiet place to rest the remainder of the day.

Davis Willson

DIARY, 1866

DAVIS WILLSON traveled over the Bozeman Trail with eight friends and relatives from his hometown in New York. His train was in the middle of the many trains scattered from the North Platte River to Fort Reno during the week in July when Indian raids occurred all along that part of the trail. His train was raided three times, and although the raids did not result in any major loss or casualties, his diary is an important source of information concerning this significant period.

Davis Willson was born July 17, 1841, in Canton, St. Lawrence County, New York. He was the second of seven children of Ambrose and Julia Hill Willson.[1] Until he was sixteen, he attended a public school in Canton. After working in a printing office, he was a member of a brass band for about a year, until he became ill and had to leave his job. He returned home to recuperate, and during the next several months, he worked in the post office at Canton. But because he was still ill, he went to California in 1859 to recover his health. He stayed in California for eighteen months, part of the time with an uncle, returning home in 1861.

Beginning in 1861 Willson attended St. Lawrence University in his hometown Canton, New York, for three years and Oberlin College, Oberlin, Ohio, for one year. He also worked for two newspapers while attending college. In 1864 his brother Lester, who was two years older, found him a position in the Union Army's commissary department in Washington. He worked there until the end of the year, and then he joined the Union Army, serving until May 1865. After the war he

SOURCE DOCUMENT: Davis Willson, Diary, 1866, original and typed transcript, MS Collection 1076, Davis Willson Papers, 1861–1915, Merrill G. Burlingame Special Collections, Renne Library, Montana State University, Bozeman (hereafter MS 1076, MSU).

1. The Ambrose Wil[l]son family is listed in the 1860 New York census, St. Lawrence County, Canton Village, p. 90.

Davis Willson, 1872.
MERRILL G. BURLINGAME SPECIAL COLLECTIONS, MONTANA STATE UNIVERSITY, BOZEMAN

returned home to Canton and was employed as a clerk in a dry goods store for seven months.[2]

In spring 1866 a group of men organized in Canton to go to the Montana goldfields. The principal organizer was Charles V. Rich, Davis

2. Kim Allen Scott, "The Willson Brothers Come to Montana," *Montana The Magazine of Western History*, 49 (Spring 1999), 58–70. A biography published when he was forty-four years old, is in Michael A. Leeson, ed., *History of Montana, 1739–1885* (Chicago: Warner, Beers & Co., 1885), 1172–73. Manuscript biographical material on Davis Willson is included with the diary in MS 1076, MSU.

Willson's cousin.[3] Born in Morley, New York, in 1832, Charlie Rich went to Illinois in 1850, worked there two years cutting timber, and in 1852 went overland to California, returning to New York in 1855. The next year he married Melinda M. Taylor. In 1861 they moved to Illinois, where he farmed until he enlisted in the Union Army in 1864, serving for nearly two years in the quartermaster department.[4] One of the first men Charlie Rich enlisted in his Montana venture was Loren W. Tuller, who had served with him in the army. Tuller became Rich's business partner in buying a stock of goods to open a store in Montana.

In preparation for the trip, Charlie Rich and L. W. Tuller recruited the rest of the party to help transport the goods. In addition to Davis Willson, the other young men who made up the traveling company were Charlie's nephew Franklin W. Rich, eighteen; Frank Harper; Charles C. Caldwell, twenty-two; Perry Earl; J. Hopkins Taylor; and John Hershaw.[5] The business ledger of the Tuller and Rich Company reveals that each of the young men paid $150 for passage to Montana. Some of them paid for their passage in installments during the trip. The ledger also indicates that Tuller and Rich paid some of the men for work they did en route to Montana.[6]

Charlie Rich was the captain of the company of nine men that set out from Omaha on May 31 on the north-side Platte road. They traveled in at least two mule-drawn wagons, joining with others to form larger trains when necessary. They turned onto the Bozeman Trail on July 20. On July 22, while Davis Willson's party was nooning at Sand Creek, Indians tried to stampede their stock, but the men successfully repulsed them. That evening they camped at Antelope Creek. The next morning they surprised another attempted ambush of their stock, driving the Indians away with only a few shots. They laid over to rest the animals, and again the next morning they discovered and thwarted an

---

3. This relationship of cousin is assumed from the fact that Charles Rich's mother was Sallie Willson Rich. *Progressive Men of the State of Montana* (Chicago: A. W. Bowen & Co., 1901), 815.

4. Leeson, *History of Montana*, 1154, 1157; *Progressive Men . . . of Montana*, 815–16.

5. Of these six young men, only Frank Rich is known to have written an account of the journey. The *Billings (Mont.) Gazette* published an article by Rich containing excerpts from what is identified as a diary but appears to be a reminiscence. Rich's account contains some accurate descriptions of the journey, but for the most part, it dramatizes and exaggerates events, especially encounters with Indians. Frank Rich, "Diary of Franklin W. Rich," *Billings (Mont.) Gazette*, September 7, 1941, September 14, 1941.

6. Loren W. Tuller and Charles V. Rich, Ledger, 1866–1867, MS Collection 632, Willson and Rich Records, 1866–1871, MSU.

ambush attempt. They moved on to Fort Reno, fortunately without encountering any more Indians, and arrived there two days later. On the way, they passed where an emigrant had recently been killed and went by his grave about ten miles farther on.

At Fort Reno Willson heard "awful stories about Indians murdering and plundering trains in good earnest." Although his train was a typical Indian target, it had come through relatively unscathed. He noted in his diary that they had been fortunate in fending off the Indians' intentions because they had been extremely cautious and watchful. This was a successful strategy because the warriors were intent primarily on capturing unguarded stock and attacking small parties or individuals separated from the trains. Willson's party had posted ample guards, and their caution enabled them to surprise the Indians lying in wait for them when they herded their stock in the mornings. Above all, they had been lucky, as in the case when the men who had gone hunting during the noon stop returned just as the Indians attempted to drive off the herd, and consequently the combined force of emigrants staved off the raid.

Willson was among the large group of emigrants and freighters who gathered at Fort Reno to proceed ahead together. His party was in the large combined train that followed the one Perry Burgess had been in, a result of the military attempt to impose some degree of control over the flood of trains passing between the forts. Charlie Rich was elected captain of the combined train, which was made up of six trains of more than two hundred wagons and three hundred men. One can only imagine how difficult it was to lead such a train, and by the time they reached Fort Phil Kearny, Rich had decided that he did not want to be overall captain any longer. E. R. Horner was elected to replace him as captain to lead the train to the Bighorn crossing.

For the rest of the trip to the Gallatin Valley, Willson's train experienced no more problems with Indians. To their dismay, however, interpersonal problems among the Bozeman Trail travelers escalated. Congestion along the Bozeman Trail was at its height, and the trains began competing with each other for the best place in the long lines of wagons and particularly at river crossings, where they faced huge, tension-filled bottlenecks. Willson's train often traveled with the Phillips and Freeland freight train, which soon deservedly gained a reputation for unruly and aggressive behavior. Willson's diary reveals his total disdain for the captain, William Phillips, and at the same time he describes the efforts by everyone in his own group to distance themselves from Phillips at every opportunity.

Upon his arrival in the Gallatin Valley, Willson recorded his poignant feelings as the group of nine "good jolly boys" broke up and scattered. He was particularly sad that his boyhood friend Charlie Caldwell had gone to find work in Helena, and he knew he would probably never see him again. He wrote, "We have been boys together, and mingled our boyish dreams. All this is done away now and we stand against the stiff realities of manhood, naked and alone." He ended with a long nostalgic reverie about his home, family, and friends, as if to brace himself for the start of a new life.

Once he arrived in the Gallatin Valley, Willson did not travel any farther. He settled in Bozeman, where he lived for the remainder of his life. Charlie Rich and Hopkins "J. H." Taylor also settled in Bozeman and became prominent figures in the community. Frank Rich later settled elsewhere in Montana. The rest eventually returned to the East.[7] At first, however, Rich and Tuller set up their store in a tent in Bozeman, and the rest of the men tried to find work.[8]

In the fall Willson became the first public school teacher in Gallatin County. He taught in the home of Joe Miravalle, John Richard Jr.'s father-in-law, during the winter of 1866–67.[9] In 1867 Davis's brother Lester came to Bozeman and began a prosperous career as a retail merchant. Lester Willson was known in Bozeman as General Willson because of the brevet rank he attained in the Civil War. Davis worked as a clerk at the Rich and Willson general store and continued teaching school during the winters until 1869. He then worked at various bookkeeping and clerical jobs, including an appointment as deputy collector of internal revenue in 1870–71. In 1876 he was appointed registrar in the General Land Office, a position he held for ten years. From the beginning of his residence in Bozeman, Davis Willson contributed numerous articles to Montana newspapers, most of which he signed simply "D. W."

Willson returned to Canton following his father's death in the early 1870s, and while he was there, he met Martha Van Allen. Martha subsequently traveled to Montana by railroad and stagecoach, and she and

---

7. Frank Rich eventually settled in Dean, Montana. L. W. Tuller sold his interest in the Rich and Tuller business to Davis's brother Lester Willson in 1867 and returned to the East. The remaining members of the traveling group presumably also left Montana within a relatively brief time.

8. Five of the original group were still living in Bozeman in 1870. Davis Willson, Charles and Frank Rich, Hopkins Taylor, and Frank Harper are listed in the 1870 Montana Territory census, Gallatin County, Bozeman.

9. Rosa Beall, "Bozeman's First Schools," *Contributions to the Historical Society of Montana*, 7 (1910), 307.

Davis were married on May 18, 1874, in Virginia City.[10] Davis and Martha were the parents of one son, Frank G., who became a civil engineer. Sometime in the 1870s Lester and Davis's youngest brother, George, also moved to Bozeman, making three Willson brothers who made their homes in Bozeman and were integral to the community's development.

Willson's life took its final form in Bozeman, particularly as the result of becoming actively involved with the Presbyterian church. He was one of the founding members of the First Presbyterian Church of Bozeman in 1872, and he was subsequently involved in every aspect of the church's development. In 1889 he was ordained as a minister, serving for twenty-three years as the pastor of two Presbyterian churches, at Hamilton and Springhill, and he was known as pope of the Gallatin Valley.[11] His wife Martha died in Bozeman in 1906. Willson died in Newtonville, Massachusetts, in April 1915 at the home of his son Frank. He was buried in the Willson family plot in Bozeman.

Willson wrote legibly in his small, leather-covered diary. I have made very few changes in his entries. I did reform the longest entries into paragraphs and I substituted lower case where he irregularly capitalized letters at the beginning of words, in both cases for readability. As evidenced by his diary, Willson was extremely personable, observant, and articulate. And perhaps explaining why his diary is such an enjoyable document to read, Willson was described as a "gentle, white-haired, lovable man" in his later years.[12] His delightful personality is evident throughout, and his diary offers one of the most light-hearted, humorous, and yet discerning views of emigrant group dynamics. It is a memorable account of friendships, of sharing good times and bad, of facing life-threatening danger, and, above all, of growing into manhood through a challenging experience.

---

10. George Edwards, "Presbyterian Church History," *Contributions to the Historical Society of Montana*, 6 (1906), 327.

11. Davis Willson's prominent roll in the Presbyterian Church in the Gallatin Valley is described in ibid., 290–329.

12. Quoted in an unidentified obituary for Davis Willson in MS 1076, MSU.

DAVIS WILLSON DIARY

Monday, May 7 1866 =

The morning found me up at an early hour, the household all astir with preparations for my leaving home. I was to start for the new territory of Montana. A company had been formed and we were to leave our little village of Canton on the 4 oclock, afternoon train.

My dear sisters & younger brother were flying from room to room performing little acts of kindness which were to be the last tender services for years—we knew not how many. But as quite everything had been done for me that could be—a little dark haired sister (begging with her large blue eyes that all the rest had done something for me but she) having finished the sewing of a button on my shirt—this busy searching about for more to do, & wandering from room to room, was more for the purpose of keeping back the tears & making my departure as cheerful as they might. At last the carriage drove up, which my father was to drive himself and my mother, to detain the parting as long as she could, was to go with us to the village. Then came goodbye to sisters— the last kiss & kindly spoken word,—but the tears would come! And as we drove rapidly away the choking in my throat was all that I could bear.

[Willson and the others in Charlie Rich's party left Canton, New York, on May 8 and traveled by railroad to Chicago, where they spent a day sightseeing. They continued on to St. Joe, Missouri, by railroad, arriving on May 12. They immediately boarded the steamboat Denver *for Omaha. On the boat Willson became acquainted with Oscar E. Penwell, a resident of Bozeman, Montana, who had traveled east on a visit.]*

13. The Herndon House hotel register for 1866 is in the collection of the Douglas County Historical Society in Omaha, Nebraska. A photocopy of the register for May 14 lists L. W. Tuller, Charles Caldwell, F. Harper, J. Hershaw, F. Rich, and D. Willson in room four. Oscar E. Penwell, a Montana resident whom Willson met on the steamboat, was registered in room thirteen; and General William Tecumseh Sherman was in room forty-one. Although Davis describes it as "a miserable place," the Herdon House was considered by some to be the best hotel in the region, and it was the largest. It was a four-story brick building that occupied a city block. There was no running water, and only a few rooms had stoves, for which there was an extra charge.

Monday, May 14.

Reached Omaha City about 5 o'clock. Staid at "Herndon House" a miserable place.[13] I & Charlie went to find Ed Collins. Found him at the office of the Pacific R. R. [Railroad] Gen[eral] Sherman & staff were at the hotel. Tuller knew him. He introduced our whole party to him. Had a long talk with him in regard to the Montana country and our enterprise out there. He had been out on an inspection tour. Gave us some good information. He had a reception in the evening & was serenaded. Hotel was jammed full. Some speeches made

Thursday, May 31.

A bright fine morning. Making preparations to start across the plains. Went to town—wrote a few letters, and at noon came back to camp. The boys had got the tents down and everything packed—eat lunch, and Charlie Rich left us to go on as soon as we could while he went off to buy a Saddle Mule. We got everything ready and left camp about three oclock. We were now fairly on the way for Montana.

The country so far was all a rolling prairie. About three miles out came to a more level country. I never before appreciated a prairie. A beautiful rolling meadow reaching off to the South West as far as the eye could trace until it gradually receded into the blue distance and touched the sky. The prairie being rolling we soon lost sight of this view, and saw nothing but hills around us. Did not go far however—about five miles—when we encamped. Pole Creek [Cole Creek] was the name of the little stream I believe. About dusk Charlie Rich came up with his new Saddle Mule.

[At Rawhide Creek, Willson wrote: "Several years ago, a party coming through here, one of them from Pierpont N Y said he would shoot the first Indian he saw. Arriving at this place, he saw a Squaw fishing in the creek near by and fired killing her instantly   The party were followed by the

Indians, over taken about three miles, and they caught the man and skinned him alive."]

Sunday, June 3.

. . . [We] are encamped about a mile and a half from Fremont, a little town of about 200 inhabitants. The country is perfectly level here, only walled in upon the sides by high bluffs that can but just be seen in the distance. We are between the Platte River and the Elkhorn and close by the Pacific R. R. Wrote a letter home this evening. The mosquitoes were <u>painfully numerous</u> ~~that night~~ could scarcely sleep. But I have got the start of the boys in having a <u>mosquito net</u> with me, which before starting the boys laughed at me for. Now I am offered $3.00 for it but I hate mosquitoes to[o] bad to accept of it.

Monday, June 4.

The sun was shining brightly & we were all up at an early hour and off. Charlie C.[aldwell] made a great deal of fuss about the mosquitoes last night—swore some, but was careful to say nothing but "<u>damn</u>". Stopped in town—(Fremont)—to get wagon tongue mended which was broke the morning before, by one of the mules falling down upon it. Did not get under way till noon.

In the meantime Charlie C.[aldwell] [Hopkins] Taylor Frank Rich and myself went to the Post Office— a private dwelling—to mail some letters. Post master was a fine specimen of the New England emigrant. We sat down, read his papers and had a long talk with him. He was a man of quite superior intelligence—possessing the true New England characteristics by being some what <u>opinionated</u> and abundantly supplied <u>with "ideas"</u>. A black, slouched hat covered a high, venerable forehead very broad at the organs of Ideality and Mirthfulness, & full & round at Causality & Comparison. Underneath the Reflectives, largely developed, projected the line of Preceptives, betokening a pretty sound knowledge of

14. Willson's appraisal of the man's character is based on phrenology, a popular nineteenth-century system of analyzing a person's characteristics from the configuration of his or her skull.

everything that came under his observation.[14] A pair of large spectacles rested astride a nose of monstrous size, and from out a homely countenance reflected a pair of mild bright eyes, that, while conversing, were lighted with a beam which if it did not make it handsome gave to it something of deep interest. A few thin gray hairs mixed with dark, hung from under his hat and he sat with coat off, leaning against the wall. From the religious papers lying round and the manner and tone of conversation as he proceeded I judged he was not only the worthy Post master of the town, but he was the leading Deacon. Charlies quick perception discovered something of the ministerial about him & as Charlie always wants to know everything, he commenced laying plans to find out his man. It was rather amusing to see the process.

Taking a piece of paper from his pocket & drawing a pencil very deliberately & wisely therefrom [Charlie C.] began inquiring the principle features of the town & writing down each answer. First how many stores, Hotels, blacksmith shops, and then the Churches. How many & what denomination and lastly who supplied the pulpits. By this little piece of strategy his curiosity was gratified by the discovery that this remarkable individual was not only the worthy Post Master of Fremont, but was pastor of the Congregational Church. He was formerly from Massachusetts but emigrated to one of the far Western states over 20 years ago.[15]

15. Reverend Isaac E. Heaton was the pastor of the Congregational Church in Fremont, Nebraska, from 1857 to 1869. Reverend Heaton and his family were among the first settlers in Fremont in 1856. L. J. Abbott, "History of Dodge County," *Transactions and Reports of the Nebraska State Historical Society*, 2 (1887), 269–70.

I talked with him about Henry Ward Beecher. He then started off with a long account of him & his family. Of some of his works [and] also of Miss Stow[e]'s [Harriet Beecher Stowe], and quoted long passages from each, showing that the acuteness of his memory was wonderful. He thinks there is not a man living who utters more truth than Beecher but thinks he is not a man of sound judgment.

We got under way about noon. Came about three
miles, when it commenced to rain and went into camp. It
broke up about six and I got out my violin. Played
awhile, when an old man came along on horseback. He
was dried up wrinkled and barefoot. Short, white beard
grew on his chin & upper lip resembling bristles. He
drove up, looked for a moment, winked, snifted up his
nose, and said, "Mighty putty teaune". Hesitating a
moment, then winking & snifting again said "Whear ye
from". "New York" we answered Then with another
wink & sniff, said "Will ye please play a mighty putty
teaun now?" Rather pleased at finding such an
appreciative listener, I struck up one of my favorites,
thinking that with all his uncouthness he is a dear lover
of music and may have a refined soul within him in spite
of the rusty covering. This thought was some what
shattered however on looking up to find him very
keenly eyeing our mules & then quietly riding off in the
middle of the strain.

The rain and the cool air had completely demolished
the mosquitoes and it bid fair for us to have a good
nights sleep. Charlie C[aldwell]—says "boys they were
a little thick for comfort last night," which, at the
memory of whose antics ~~the previous night~~ brought
forth a hearty laugh.

Tuesday, June 5.

Slept rather late—rained all night. Charlie C[aldwell]
& Perry [Earl] on guard Some jocularity. Rained nearly
all day. Roads bad & could not move. We lay in the tent
~~nearly~~ all day. In the forenoon, sang nearly all the time
from Hopkins Singing book About noon [Loren] Tuller
and I went up to the _hotel_ (a little nasty log house) and
wrote. Had but two meals. Diner at half past 4. Rather
cool but clearing off in the West. Got out violin Charlie
[Caldwell] promised to grease my boots if I would play.

Soon Charlie Rich and "Blow-hard" came. Charlie R.

and [Hopkins] Taylor sang and I played accompaniment "Blowhard" thought it was "perfectly charming!" "Beautiful" &c &c. "Blowhard" is a great big, fat, greasy man whom we run on to the other day and is going to Montana with a load of alcohol. He rides a horse and "<u>his man</u>" as he calls him (another fat greasy fellow) drives his ox team. He makes himself rather familiar, is a regular ignoramous but thinks he is a man of more than ordinary capacity and has a <u>fine appreciation</u> of the "fine arts" & the "beautiful"!! He "counts" a great deal on being worth some money. Will have a great claim when he gets to Montana unless he "should lose it" for there is some dispute about it in regard to some points of law but [he] aint much afraid but he'll come out ahead (of course) All he had got to do is to go there settle down and <u>make friends</u>, which he has a peculiar faculty to accomplish. He is quite a lady's man too. He left a great many feeling bad where he come from. Had a hard time getting away from them. <u>Charlie Rich</u> tells him it's the <u>very idea he first formed of him</u>(!) He is about 45, his fat face a little one sided, teeth black and not many of them & a little irregular but he has a full black eye one turned down a little, which is probably that remarkable feature about him that is <u>so attractive to the ladies</u>.

Wednesday, June 6.

Was on guard last night. Dark and cold. It came nigh about the longest night that ever darkened the country. But morning always comes. The sun was out and shining brightly. Waited awhile that the roads might dry and pulled out about eleven o'clock. "Blowhard" said he wa'nt going till two in the afternoon, so we bid him an <u>affectionate</u> goodbye, hoping to meet him again when we arrived in Montana. Traveled pretty fast. Overtook train of oxen & passed them at a little frame Hotel where they stopped to feed. We waited there till our wagons came up. I sat leaned against the house and slept. Rode the mule, nearly fell asleep while riding. Came into camp about 4, close to the Platte, made my feet sore walking. Was never so tired in my life. Went to bed early. Slept well.

Thursday, June 7.

Broke camp early. Cool & cloudy. Good day to travel. Roads were rather heavy. Stopped where there were three good looking ladies & got water. I & [Frank] Harper rode ahead and halted to feed until the rest came up. Passed train bound for Kearney at a house eating diner. Drove to the banks of the Platte & stopped for lunch, noon. Put the saddle mule into the harness and took one out to ride that had never been saddled. Had lots of fun. Charlie Rich tried to ride him but [it] would stand still & kick up. [Loren] Tuller broke him so that in the middle of the afternoon he went first rate. I then got out & rode him the rest of the way. Saw some houses made of <u>Sods</u>. Also a Sod fence.

Going through a bad place the wild leaders broke their bars and run away. I was on ahead & would have got run over if they had not hallooed to me. Caught them, rig[g]ed up and came on. Looked like rain and went into camp. Wind blew horridly. Sun went down and the shower went round us. I was grinding coffee and the boys most of them were lying down [Hopkins] Taylor and [Loren] Tuller getting supper when who should ride up but the inevitable "Blowhard" with his team & "his man" behind him. "Glad to see you" "How do you do?" "Thought you was dead" &c &c He went on and selected his camp.

After supper, Charlie Rich thought he would go out and make a visit. Asked him where he was going. Said he was going over to tell lies with Blowhard. At dusk another wind & another shower. I never saw it lighten so in my life. It would remain as light as day for almost a minute. Frank Rich was on guard. Oh, gracious how the rain poured, & the wind almost took our tent off. We were a little frightened, but [it] soon passed over.

Friday, June 8.

The mosquitoes drove us out of bed this morning at three o'clock. The air was literally thick with them. Charlie C.[aldwell] [Loren] Tuller & [Hopkins] Taylor "hung to" until sunrise by keeping the blankets over their heads. I got my mosquito net on and went to work getting breakfast. Sun up and the wind rising blew them away. Saw two Indians pass. One on horseback. They are the first we have seen since starting.

"Blowhard" pulled out about half=past eight. He has got ahead of us, and we shall no doubt have the pleasure of his company for some ways yet. We had some sport trying to milk a cow. The owner of Miss Bossy came along and put a stop to our depredations. Charlie C.[aldwell] says, "Why, that cow belongs to the hearders back here." "She does hay?" says Mr Owner "Perhaps I dont know who she belongs to" which created quite a laugh and bids fair to become a "by word" with us by the way it is harped upon now.

[On June 14 they passed the end of the tracks that had been laid for the Union Pacific Railroad. Later they caught up with "Blowhard."]

[Saturday, June 16.]

Charlie [Caldwell] & [Frank] Harper have had a great deal of fun to day—Haven't laughed so much since we started. They tried to make a bargain for a dog. Charlie offered the man 10 dollars & while he was gone to see his brother about it made off and left the man to deal with Harper as they are in "Partnership" Harper discovering by the man's actions that he was going to take him up told him the dog was too young for their purpose.

Charlie threw a snake on Harper and liked to have frightened him to death. We are encamped on the Platte River 40 miles from Kearney [Fort Kearny].[16] Mosquitoes thick and biting terribly.

16. They have been traveling up the north bank of the North Channel Platte River, which flowed on the northern side of Grand Island.

Sunday, June 17.

Went in bathing. "Blowhard" went by. Did my washing. Took our baggage out to dry. Had a good nap. Wrote two letters.

Monday, June 18.

Did not sleep very well. Was up before 4 o'clock and helped Charlie Rich put out the mules. Broke camp and got under way at half past six. Passed "Grand Island City."[17] It consists of one store and a wind saw mill. Crossed Cotton Wood River [Wood River] ten miles beyond.[18] Roads were good. I worried a gopher out of his hole when we stopped to lunch. Passed Union Ranch. Encamped tonight on Wood River.[19] Pleasant place. Are within about 16 miles of Fort Kearney—Saw some Prairie Dogs in cage at the last house we passed. Feel very tired & sleepy. Got out violin. Played some   Charlie R[ich] sang "What's the old man thinking". Hopkins [Taylor] sang with him and I played, accompanying him with violin. Mr. Buck one of the party, who joined us, going to California, shed tears. He is a good man.

Tuesday, June 19.

Traveled about 5 miles and stopped to load on corn at private house.[20] The lady was from New York state. Arrived at house [Miller Ranch] opposite Fort Kearney. Found "Blowhard" there. Took lunch. Charlie C.[aldwell] went to the fort after letters. Wrote to Zelia. Could not wait for Charlie so started on and encamped 6 miles west of Kearney. Charlie C came back about dusk with good news from home. Could not enjoy them much. A circumstance occurred that gave me many sad reflections. It seemed for the time being that my enjoyment was to be completely marred for the remainder of the journey and perhaps for a long, long period beyond. What these reflections were I need not tell here. They were indelibly stamped upon my memory.[21]

17. They had camped the night before just east of the community of Grand Island. The town was first settled in 1857.

18. The trail crossed Wood River at present Alda, Nebraska, just above its mouth at the North Channel Platte River.

19. They camped on the south bank of Wood River. During the afternoon they passed Wood River Center at present Shelton, Nebraska, which was perhaps Willson's "Union Ranch."

20. The "private house" may have been James E. Boyd's ranch at Nebraska Center, one mile west of present Gibbon, Nebraska.

21. The "circumstance" that shocked and saddened Willson occurred when Tuller and Caldwell crossed the Platte River to Fort Kearny. His close friend Caldwell became drunk at the sutler's store and nearly drowned while recrossing the river. Although Willson did not record any details and dwelt instead on the effect of Caldwell's behavior on their friendship, Frank Rich described the incident in his diary. Rich diary, *Billings (Mont.) Gazette,* September 7, 1941.

[Willson's party continued traveling up the north side of the Platte River.]

Saturday, June 23 =

Started at half past seven. Came to where low sandy bluffs extend to the river. Camped at noon by a frog pond. Three men came in from Wind River while we were at lunch; from appearances would judge them to be old miners. Came as far as the crossing of Skunk Creek and camped to lay over Sunday.

A terrible hole for mosquitoes. Charlie [Caldwell] & I slept out of the tent. Never suffered so in my life. The air was fairly thick with mosquitoes. Never saw the likes before in my life. The mules could not be fed, but would roll and groan nearly all of the night. Had some fun in renting my mosquito net. Finally sold it for five dollars. Cost me one. Can get along without one if the rest of the boys can.

Sunday, June 24.

The mosquitoes drove us out of our camp, and at eleven o'clock found us on our way in search of a place to spend the Sabbath. About seven miles found a beautiful cold spring.[22] The water boiled out of the ground. Went on to the [Platte] river about 2 miles further and camped. It was about 4 o'clock. Went in bathing.

Monday, June 25.

Came to Carrion Creek about 9 oclock in the morning.[23] Watered teams and filled our canteens. Came out to the [North Platte] river—broad level plains. Stopped for lunch. Charlie R.[ich] & [Loren] Tuller went in bathing. The party all felt well. Some fun at noon. Came to a party of [railroad] surveyors in the afternoon. Crossed wide deep creek and camped. A thunder shower came up. My turn on guard

Tuesday, June 26.

Only had two hours sleep last night. Felt tough. Slept in wagon. C. R. [Charlie Rich] didn't like it. Crossed

22. The spring was at the foot of the bluffs on the north side of the road, at the head of the Pawnee Swamps. The Pawnee Swamps, known today as Pawnee Slough, are just west of present Maxwell, Nebraska.

23. J. F. Manning was buried at Carrion Creek in May 1864. Several 1864 and 1866 diarists mentioned his grave. A mile before Carrion Creek the road passed the junction of the North Platte and South Platte rivers and continued up the North Platte.

Black Mud Creek.[24] A party of the surveyors of the
Pacific R.R. were at work. A cool day and traveled fast.
Stopped for lunch on North Bluff Fork—a stream about
six rods wide and two feet deep   In the afternoon
crossed over high sandy bluffs. Had to double teams.
Could see off over the country   Camped for the night
about half past three about a half a mile from the river.
After supper McConnor's train from Omaha passed
returning from Laramie   C.[harlie] R.[ich] and Perry
Earl went over the bluffs hunting. Found nothing. Got
out violin and played some   to bed early. Mosquitoes did
not trouble us so much

    Wednesday, June 27.

    Up at 4 o'clock this morning. Had scarcely finished
breakfast when a party of Indians all mounted,
numbering eighteen or twenty, were observed close upon
us. When within about five rods they dismounted and
their Chief came in. He asked where our "Chief" was. I
pointed to Charlie Rich. Then he walked up to him and
shook hands. He wanted something to eat for his men.
Told him we could not give it to him. "Too many Sioux."
Finally told him would feed him but could not the rest.
He didn't seem pleased with the idea. At last he took
what we gave him, took a small morsel himself and
divided the rest. They hung round until we got ready to
start and seemed quite interested in our work, watching
everything we did very closely. They seemed very
friendly and I did not feel frightened at all.

    We started off at just five minutes to six a very early
start. The Indians all road on ahead but the Chief and
four or five others who kept up with us. [Frank] Harper
wanted to run a race with one of them on his poney.
Finally agreed to do so but C. R. [Charlie Rich] told him
not to. There is no trusting them a moment out of sight
however friendly they may appear. Before leaving camp
the Chief said it was "five sleeps to Laramie"   Said we

24. Abram Voorhees
recorded burying a man
in his train who had died
at the Black Mud Creek
crossing. Voorhees diary,
May 20, 1864.

would come to a big Chief in one sleep, meaning
tomorrow. He told Charlie Rich not to sleep when he
got beyond Laramie. This he said by pointing "Laramie
no sleep" meaning there was danger beyond there. This
did not set well on us, for it signified that he wanted we
should sleep this side. After riding with us about half an
hour they went on ahead and were soon out of sight
Came to more sandy bluffs. Had to double teams to get
through. Got through about 10 oclock. As we came off
from the bluffs to our surprise came up suddenly to see
same Indian party. But they possessed an entirely
different appearance. Their hair was combed smoothly
and faces were painted for the war-path. Their actions
were so much different that we could tell nothing about
them. They said not a word to us nor scarcely to one
another and possessed a sort of savage dignity that was
really terrifying. As we got opposite their camp [which
was] a little way from the road they mounted and rode
on some going before some at our side and the larger
party remaining behind came up in our rear.

We saw two or three of them examine their Revolvers.
They were all well armed besides having Bows and
Arrows. I must confess I was somewhat frightened as
there is no knowing when they attack   As it was most
time to pull out and lunch we quietly reined out of the
road—began unharnessing and at the same time pulling
our guns out of the wagons and putting caps on them (as
we always keep them loaded)   They probably saw our
preparations. They road on—forded the river came down
on the other side and went over bluffs out of sight. They
told us in the morning they were going to Laramie to
receive the presents by treaty being made there, but the
course they took did not substantiate it. Charlie
C[aldwell] says his curiosity for Indians is satisfied.

Came on about 4 miles in the afternoon and camped
by the [North Platte] river. Good feed. Went to bed

early. Good cool night for sleeping no mosquitoes.
Boys felt pretty well but [a] little pokish about Indians.
Some talking before going to sleep and few dry notes.
[Frank] Harper & Charlie C.[aldwell] were full. Harper
said "My God boys I wish I knew how this thing was
coming out."—"Boys I wish the [railroad] cars were
running thru here now I think I should go back to
Canton [New York] as soon as I could travel"—Turning
over in bed with a sudden thought and speaking as one
about droping to sleep, very solemnly and honestly
broke out with "Boys there is this thing about it we
must have less rough talk & blackguarding going on here
for we don't know but we shall be called away some
night!" Charlie C. said, "They don't catch me going
across here again for a thousand dollars though by
gracious! I am paying now a hundred and fifty for the
privilege of going!"[25]

[*During the next two days, Willson commented on the
"troublesome" mosquitoes and concerns about a possible
Indian ambush on the herd.*]

Saturday, June 30.

Broke camp about six o'clock. Didn't like getting up
so early. Was on guard night before last and couldn't
sleep much last night for mosquitoes and felt bad. Boys
had some fun at [Hopkins] Taylor's and my expense over
our lack of ability to make good mule drivers. Roads
rather badly cut up Had to pick our way [Hopkins]
Taylor drove at about 9 o'clock more sand. Met Peck's
train. They had been to Laramie with presents for the
Indians. Came to Wolf Creek about noon and camped to
lay over Sunday. A quarter of a mile of bluffs are before
us over which we shall have to double teams Monday
morning. Went in bathing, felt well. Charlie C.[aldwell]
caught some fish for supper. Played violin. Smoked the
mosquitoes out of the tent and tied it up close. Had a
very good sleep.

25. Charlie Caldwell was
referring to the price of
$150 he paid for his
passage with the Tuller
and Rich Company.

Wednesday, July 4.

Up at sunrise and fired a salute in honor of our Independence   underway at six oclock. Carried Charlies revolver. Rocky bluffs on our right. [Frank] Harper and I went on ahead. Teams took a road to the left and struck the river to water mules. Boys found a cow that the Mormans had left behind, being lame and wouldn't drive. They milked her and left her alone in the wilderness. Got about a pail full of milk—counted on a "time" for dinner. Passed "Cobs Hills" [Cobbs Hills][26] Camped at "Ancient Bluffs" [Ancient Bluff Ruins] for a lunch.[27] Had a Fourth of July celebration. Played "Hail Columbia" & "Yankee Doodle" on violin & also on the fife. Milk punch and canned peaches & milk for dinner. Drank a few toasts & made some <u>responses</u>.

Passed Ancient Bluffs [Ancient Bluff Ruins]   they resemble the ruins of old castles and are great natural curiosities. Passed two graves to day. Awful hot. Teams left the road to avoid the sand and got into the mud. Was taken sick a little. Came to camp by the [North Platte] river about half past 4. Rocky bluffs on our right. On the left of the river a smooth rolling prairie. Was my turn to go on guard   did not feel able so made a bargain with [Frank] Harper to stand for me & I would take his place to morrow evening

Saturday, July 7.

. . . Passed Scott's Bluffs   Camped on the river were visited by a squad of 8 Indians. Were a little frightened at first but they seemed very friendly. The Chief was the handsomest & most honest looking Indian that I have seen. Was on guard again with Baker. Some expected to hear from the Indians but all was quiet.

Sunday, July 8.

. . . A large Indian camp just ahead of us. [Frank] Harper thought it was rather "ticklish place"   Charlie R[ich] bought a quarter of antelope of an Indian who

26. The Cobbs Hills are gravelly bluffs on the north side of the North Platte River that extend from four to twelve miles east of present Broadwater, Nebraska. The north-side trail traversed these bluffs, and this segment was difficult for oxen to negotiate. The bluffs were named the Cobble Hills by the 1847 Mormon pioneer party but were usually named Cobb's Hills in subsequent emigrant guidebooks.

27. The Ancient Bluff Ruins is an eroded sandstone emigrant landmark on the north side of the North Platte River, four miles east of present Broadwater, Nebraska, that was named by English members of the 1847 Mormon pioneer party who thought it resembled ruined castles in England. The Ancient Bluff Ruins was of particular interest to north-side travelers as the first place Chimney Rock, ahead on the opposite side of the river, was visible.

passed. Sweetest meat [I've] ever tasted. Indians have
been visiting us all the afternoon. They say the treaty has
been made.[28] All are "good Sioux" they say now. Two
squaws came into camp. Charlie C[aldwell] wanted some
of their paint. She took it out and painted his face. I and
Baker took a ride on two of their poneys

Monday, July 9.

Up at three oclock in the morning. Passed through an
Indian village. Met an Indian on horseback leading
another which had their only means of conveyance other
than their pack animals and consisted of two long poles
strapped to each side of the horse with one end draging
on the ground. A couple of crossbars were placed from
each pole directly behind the horse upon which a
papoose was strapped and some baggage[29] Camped on
the [North] Platte upon very high ground. Scarcely any
feed. Charlie and I slept by the wagons without a tent.

Tuesday, July 10

Did not get underway till about six o'clock. Charlie
and I were getting impatient for our mail and as we were
only 10 miles from Laramie we started on afoot. I
received 4 letters. Did not get a letter from Miss G.—as I
expected. Waited for the train. Went into camp on the
river about 6 miles above the Fort. My turn on guard

Wednesday, July 11

Never had so hard work keeping awake as last night
Would fall asleep while walking and would stagger like a
drunken man. Charlie R[ich] [Loren] Tuller and Prior went
to the Fort to see about getting tire set and to see the
Commander [Major James Van Voast][30] in regard to the
safety of the route on North side. Found couldn't go farther
short of 20 wagons and 30 men.[31] Concluded to go back to
the ferry cross over to the Fort and go with the first mule
train that came along. I wrote to Lester and took a nap. The
boys came back about dusk. Found that one of the skins
[skeins] to Perrys [Perry Earl's] wagon was broke.[32]

28. Seven Brulé Sioux and
six Oglala Sioux leaders
signed the Fort Laramie
treaty on June 27.

29. This is an excellent
description of a lodge-
pole travois.

30. Major James Van Voast,
Eighteenth Infantry, was
the commanding officer at
Fort Laramie from June 12
to December 7, 1866.
John D. McDermott,
"Military Command at
Fort Laramie," *Annals
of Wyoming*, 38 (April
1966), 18.

31. General John Pope's
General Order No. 27,
February 28, 1866,
specified that a train must
have twenty wagons and
thirty armed men in order
to receive permission
to proceed.

32. An axletree is a
crossbar under the wagon
box that has terminal
spindles on which the
wheels revolve. In the
later emigration years, a
forged steel thimble skein
(literally, a "skin")
encapsulated the spindle.

Thursday, July 12

Charlie R[ich] [Loren] Tuller & [Frank] Harper were up at 3 o'clock and went away with the wheels of Perrys [Perry Earl's] wagon to get them set but failed. They got back about 3 oclock in the afternoon. I and Charlie went in evening. I got out to[o] far in the river and came near drowning. If had not been for a dry root that stuck out from the bank which I caught, I should have gone under. Were back camp about five oclock. Rained some before starting and good deal of wind. Went to the Ferry and camped

Friday, July 13

Up at day light. Crossed the ferry by eight oclock.[33] Went to the Government Blacksmith Shop and got tire set. Bought a skin [skein] for Perrys wagon. I went behind the shop in the shade and wrote two letters one to Lester and another [to] Miss G. In afternoon went on about 6 miles to where our wagons were camped   I came back on [Frank] Harpers poney after the mail. Found three letters for [Loren] Tuller. Came up with Phillips & Co's train for Mountain[s] [Montana] with whom we are to travel with.[34] They are a hard set. Was on "heard" [herd] with Charlie C.[aldwell] He was tired and sleepy when I woke him up to take my place and scolded me for calling him

[Willson's party traveled west from Fort Laramie on the south side of the Platte River to Bridger's Ferry. They took the River Road, the variant route that was favored in the 1860s. The other route, the Hill Road, went over the hills south of the river route. Davis's "terrible rough road" was the segment of the River Road that went through the sandstone hills south of present Guernsey, Wyoming.]

Sunday, July 15.

Thought it was best to travel to day and lay over at the ferry [Bridger's Ferry]. Went within about 5 miles of the Ferry and camped on the [North] River Platte. The

33. They crossed the North Platte River on the ferry because they planned to travel west from Fort Laramie on the south-side road in a train that was strengthened to meet government regulations.

34. This was a freight train of fourteen wagons from Leavenworth, Kansas, belonging to William Phillips and John Freeland. The train left Leavenworth on May 28 and arrived in Virginia City on September 18. *Virginia City Montana Post*, September 22, 1866.

35. Horseshoe Ranch and telegraph station was on the east side of Horseshoe Creek. They passed the ranch and went on to the stream. The road forked at Horseshoe Creek, and Willson's party took the right fork, which went to Bridger's Ferry on the North Platte River.

36. David Jones's name appears occasionally in the Tuller and Rich business ledger. This is when he joined the Rich party.

boys went in swimming. We passed the Horseshoe Ranch to day [at] noon and lunched on Horse Shoe Creek.[35] Met soldiers in forenoon. [David] Jones left Prior to day and is going through with us.[36] Played the violin in eve.

Monday, July 16.

Started at daylight. Went through a small patch of timber. Bad roads. Had to cut poles to cross on. Got to the ferry about 9 oclock A.M. Took until noon to get 24 wagons over the river. It is about 410 miles from this point (Bridger Ferry) to Virginia City. There is a co.[mpany] of soldiers stationed here.[37]

Tuesday, July 17.

My Birthday. Am 25 years of age. It was marked by no particular incident except that I am out on the plains a thousand miles from civilization, and it seems at times as though marked as far from hope or anticipation. But we are all fatigued and "cross" and do not look upon things as they are. Like our worn mules we are almost willing to stop here without "feed" or "water" though it requires but very little exertion to bring us in reach of it. We can hardly look beyond this barren life to the bright fields beyond, which are surely in store for us if we can but keep alive the fires of energy and bright hope. I wrote to Lester. Went to the Capt.['s] Quarters and played violin.

Wednesday, July 18.

Took an early start. Passed the ox train which had crossed the river yesterday, and went on. They had lost some of their stock.[38] Passed through some Rocky highths. Grand scenery. Came to the river about 10 oclock.[39] Watered mules Drove across a ravine[40] and halted for dinner. In the afternoon roads were winding and hilly. Discovered some coal. Rough scenery. Camped near the "Black Hills" about half mile from the [North Platte] river. A shower came up. Eat supper by candle-light.

37. Fort Laramie–area trader Benjamin B. Mills set up a ferry in 1866 at Bridger's Crossing, near present Orin, Wyoming, for Bozeman Trail travelers crossing from the south to the north side of the North Platte River. Although this crossing was traditionally associated with Jim Bridger's name, he was not involved with the 1866 ferry operation. Ferry operator Mills had been a trader and clerk for the Fort Laramie sutler since 1857. By 1860 he had married Sally No Fat, an Oglala woman belonging to Red Cloud's band. While Mills operated the ferry in the 1866 season, he lived there with his Oglala wife and three children. In 1867 he moved back to Fort Laramie where he was employed as a clerk by the sutler. That fall he built a log cabin three miles west of the fort, and a year later he entered the cattle business. Mills died in summer 1871, and his wife and children went to live with her family at Red Cloud Agency.

38. This was Samuel Finley Blythe's train. That morning seven horses and two mules were missing but were later found. Blythe diary, July 18, 1866.

39. They were at the site of present Douglas, Wyoming.

40. The "ravine" is now known as Harvey Gulch, three miles north of Douglas. A deep swale is visible today coming out of the north side of the gulch.

41. They crossed over McKinstry Ridge, a rugged hill five miles north of present Douglas, Wyoming, and came back to the North Platte and camped opposite the later site of Fort Fetterman.

42. They left the North Platte River just east of the mouth of Sage Creek and turned north on the Bozeman Trail.

43. Davis's impression that the road they would take was Bridger's route is correct. Jim Bridger guided General Patrick E. Connor over this new cutoff from the North Platte the previous year. This road joined Bozeman's 1863–1864 route seven miles south of present Buffalo, Wyoming

44. Brown Springs is twenty-six miles north of the trail's departure from the North Platte River. The spring is along Brown Springs Creek, four miles south of the Dry Fork Cheyenne River crossing. The spring and creek are named for Second Lieutenant John Brown, Company E, Eleventh Cavalry. Brown was with a detachment sent from Deer Creek to rescue Fanny Kelly, who was captured by Sioux raiders on July 12, 1864, at the Little Boxelder Creek crossing on the emigrant road on the south side of the North Platte River. Brown was wounded in a skirmish and was brought to the detachment's camp at this spring, where he died on July 20. He was buried at the camp, and three days later his body was disinterred and taken to Deer Creek for burial.

Thursday, July 19.

Took an early start. Traveled over 8 miles. A long winding road. Made one drive and camped on the river near a cold spring. [41] Went in swimming in the [North] Platte for the last time as we leave it tomorrow about three miles from here. Feed is first rate. Our mules are doing well but Phillips & Freelands are about "played [out]." Slept and read some in the afternoon. Charlie C[aldwell] and I on guard a good place to watch.

Friday, July 20.

Left camp at day break. Traveled about 3 miles and took our final leave of the Platte.[42] Are traveling on the "Bridger Cut Off" which joins the Bozeman route some distance above here.[43] Roads are generally good. About six miles of sand & hard pulling at first after which they grow better. Made but one drive. Camped near a spring [on Sage Creek]. Saw some game A few of the party killed a half dozen sage hens.

Saturday, July 21.

Started about daylight. Made a dry camp at noon. Got some wood out of an old Government wagon that had broken down and been abandoned. Stoped at Brown's Spring and watered mules.[44] I took [Frank] Harpers mule and rode on ahead. Camped at the Dry Fork of the Cheyenne.

Sunday, July 22.

Thought it was best to travel to day [on Sunday]. I rode with [Loren] Tuller part of the way. Tuller made the remark that he thought it was rather strange we had not seen Indians. I had just been thinking about them. Traveled about 9 miles to Humfrevilles Camp.[45] Saw some bear tracks after getting settled for a halt for a few hours to feed and lunch. Some of our party went out to hunt the bear that they imagined they could see in the distance. We watched them from a rocky knoll above the camp to see the bear-fight. It proved to be nothing but a rock in the distance.

Some of the party remained there until the bear-hunters had got nearly back to camp when they came down to lunch.

They had no more than got seated at the meal than a party of Indians dashed upon our heard from the very place we had been watching the "bear-fight" and tried to stampede the stock   But it was fortune that saved us. The returning of the <u>bear hunters</u> were a surprise to them and as they had their arms with them fired upon them instantly. We all got our guns and gave chase. One Indian run against [Loren] Tuller with his poney who was hearding the mules at the time and was afoot without arms, and knocked him flat upon the ground He was not injured however. Several shots were fired & according to all accounts three were dismounted   We captured a quiver of arrows as a trophy. They scattered as rapidly as their ponies could carry them.

Went on to Wind Creek [Antelope Creek], 7 miles, and camped about dark.[46] We used a little more caution in traveling that afternoon. Keeping the wagons well closed up and mounted guards in advance, rear and at our flanks

Monday, July 23.

Discovered a large party of Indians at day break. Had it not been for this discovery at the time it was, which we just[ly] credit to Charlie Rich they would undoubtedly have captured our whole stock as we had got them all correled and were about to turn them out for water. We only had to fire a few guns at them when the red Devils were put to flight. One got a little cornered and passed by the correll as fast as his poney could carry him, but several of the boys got a shot at him though they could not <u>fetch</u> him. We laid over all day so as to give our animals strength for the drive tomorrow which is 20 miles.[47] Close watch of [for] Indians

Tuesday, July 24.

Charlie Rich discovered an ambush this morning of about a half dozen Indians who were undoubtedly lying

45. Humfreville Camp, named for Captain J. Lee Humfreville with General Connor's command in 1865, was on a branch of the Cheyenne River now called Stinking Water Creek. But Willson's train probably traveled more than nine miles and was camped at Sand Spring, which is surrounded by rocky bluffs that better fit his description of the camping spot.

46. They camped on Antelope Creek, then called Wind River. Today a small branch of Antelope Creek to the north is called Wind Creek.

47. Most emigrants were apparently aware of the twenty-mile dry stretch ahead, between Antelope Creek and Dry Fork Powder River.

in wait for our stock when we took them to water   A few shots however frightened them away. Broke camp between seven and eight o'clock. Scouts were sent out on all sides to give the alarm in case the Indians made their appearance   Saw a notice where a train ahead of us had lost two men.[48] One of our scouts killed two Antelope. A spur of the rocky mountains [Bighorn Mountains] was seen in advance covered with snow. The whole country wore a sublime aspect. No halt was made for feed but drove till dark and camped on the Dry Fork of the Powder River. Feed and water scarce

Wednesday, July 25.

Lying still to give the mules a chance to rest. Charlie R[ich] and I went a long way for water to fill the canteens. Had antelope for breakfast. Is the sweetest meat I ever tasted. I was on picket the forenoon. Pulled out in the afternoon and went about 7 miles. Saw the remains of a wagon that had been attacked and plundered by the Indians[49] Traveled most of the time through a deep cañon, frightful place   Camped on good level ground and first rate place to repel an attack by Indians.

Thursday, July 26.

Had to dig for water; found enough to water all the mules. Phillips lost one of his mules this morning. Died from lung fever. Got under way about eleven oclock. Passed the grave of Cheny [Mansel Cheney] killed by the Indians the 22nd inst.[ant] [this month][50] Traveled nearly half the way through the same deep and awful dusty cañon   Killed a few sage hens. Came out upon the open country, and made Fort Reno about five oclock. Camped near the Fort. Here [hear] awful stories about the Indians [who] have been murdering and plundering trains in good earnest. They are on the "warpath" and are determined to keep the whites from the upper country   The greatest portion of the force [soldiers] have gone up about 55 miles from here where they intend to move this Post[51]

48. On July 22 Indians killed emigrant Mansel Cheney, who was separated from his party, and another man who was guarding stock. Perry Burgess, Cheney's nephew, recorded the details of the incidents. Susan Badger Doyle, *Journeys to the Land of Gold: Emigrant Diaries from the Bozeman Trail, 1863–1866*, 2 vols. (Helena: Montana Historical Society Press, 2000), 2:563–64.

49. The Indians took or destroyed all of the items in the plundered wagon, including Perry Burgess's "watch, clothing, keepsakes, [and] a small collection of curious petrifications." Ibid., 563.

50. This was the grave of Perry Burgess's Uncle Mansel Cheney. Burgess describes burying him on July 23, eight miles from Fort Reno. Ibid., 564.

51. The army's original intention was to abandon Fort Reno and rebuild it farther along the trail. However, in early July the plans were changed. Fort Reno was ordered to remain active, and Fort Phil Kearny was established farther north.

Friday, July 27.

We are to lay over here for repairs and until emigration enough comes up to make it safe traveling. Had sage hen for diner. The "bull train" came up to day.[52] They were attacked by Indians the day that we were first attacked [July 22] and lost two men [Moore and Carr]. We are camped on Powder River   The Dr whom [Loren] Tuller knew in the army paid us a visit [from the fort]. Gave us some interesting incidents of that country

Saturday, July 28.

The Indians came down upon our heard in forenoon but the hearders managed to drive them down by the river and save them while we with our guns ran to support them and they fled but drove off 9 yoke of cattle. A party [of] soldiers and our boys mounted mules & horses and went after them. They regained the stock. They had shot arrows in nearly all of the cattle but none were very seriously injured. Charlie Rich & I went out with our guns to "scout"

Sunday, July 29.

Was over at the Captain's Office writing letters[53] while there a Government mule train came in with over fifty wagons. Several trains behind. They keep coming in from day to day. The train in which our friends Barton & Dearborn were in came up. Barton & Dearborn's brother were killed in a fight with the Indians with six others of their party.[54] They were a sad looking set. 8 were <u>killed</u> & two wounded out of their whole party

Charlie Rich & I were down near the river as [C. L.] Dearborn with Charlie C.[aldwell] came up. At sight of us he burst into tears. He shook our hands warmly but could not speak. He came to our tent with us and as we got him a lunch he told us their story. It was truly affecting and a sad one indeed. [Charles] Barton was most barbarously murdered. He was found with 20

52. This was probably the E. and B. Morse train, a freight train run by the E. and B. Morse freighting firm in Montana.

53. Captain Joseph L. Proctor, Eighteenth Infantry, was commanding officer at Fort Reno in July 1866. The post return for July lists Proctor as present at the post but sick.

54. The *Denver Daily Rocky Mountain News*, August 21, 1866, identified nine victims of the attack on July 24: William H. Dearborn, Hiram H. Campbell, Charles H. Barton, Zach Husted, John Little, Stephen Carson, Nelson [Nathan] Floyd, William Bothwell, and John Sloss (who was wounded in another attack). The surviving Dearborn brother was C. L. Dearborn, who is listed in the 1870 Montana Territory census, Jefferson County, White Hall, p. 1, with his wife Fidelia, sons Henry, 6, and William, 1. Presumably William, born in Montana, was named after his deceased uncle.

arrows piercing his breast and was cut open with the knife left sticking in his side. His whiskers were scalped from his chin, and scalps were taken from the top of his head and from behind each ear. Was stabbed with a knife in several places around the eyes, and otherwise horribly mutilated. He leaves a wife and three children. His body and that of young Husted[55] (from another train) were in such condition when found that they buried them where they fell—between Brown's Spring and the Dry Fork of Cheyenne to the right of the road upon some bluffs across the creek. The others were taken to the road and buried.

Poor Barton! He was a good man and we wronged him in giving him the name that we did. He is the man whom we traveled with upon the fore part of our journey and called him "Blowhard" Many men have deserved that name where he has not in the least. It was his free easy and open manner and his familiarity of conversing of his own affairs and inquiring into others which is so characteristic of all the Western people, and which we at that time did not understand, that led us to speak of him in the terms that we did. He sleeps the cold sleep of death, and his bones lie in mournful solitude upon the broad desolation of the wild prairie. What an overwhelming thought for those who mourn him! The terribly grand and sublime character of his resting place is like the wreck of mans immortal hope upon the trackless waters of oblivion.

In all the trains that have come up to the present time there have been 10 killed and 5 wounded. [Nathan] Floyd had his head cut off.[56] How many have been killed who were in advance of us we do not know. The Capt of the post [Captain Joseph L. Proctor] has had 33 killed reported to him. The mules got frightened and broke out of the correl last night about one oclock and we chased them for an hour before we got them in again   They broke two wagons

55. Zach Husted was eighteen years old when he was killed. He was one of six children of James and Drusilla Husted. His father was a prosperous farmer in Southland Township, Iowa. 1860 Iowa census, Muscatine County, Southland Township, p. 506.

56. The sensational report of Nathan Floyd's death was widely published in western newspapers, including the *Virginia City Montana Post*, September 15, 1866. Born in Ireland, Floyd arrived in Montana Territory in 1863 from mines in Colorado. In 1866 he went to Leavenworth, Kansas, and purchased merchandise to bring back to Virginia City. He was thirty-eight years old at the time of his death. *Virginia City Montana Post*, September 22, 1866; 1860 Kansas Territory census, Arapahoe County, Nevada Gulch.

Monday, July 30.

Rained nearly all the forenoon. Wrote a letter home and finished one for Lester. Was pleasant in the afternoon. A man was buried who died at the Fort from the effects of wounds received at the hands of the Indians[57]

Tuesday, July 31.

Had intended to roll out about noon to day but on account of rise in the [Powder] River the train on the other side could not cross. Charlie Rich was elected captain of all the train. There are about 200 wagons and 275 or 300 men.[58] Are to make four separate correls. About 3 P.M. there were three loose mules came in from above. Some argue that the Gov[ernment] train expected down has been attacked and the mules stampeded. Many dark forebodings arise as to our future. That the Indians intend to stop emigration through this country is evident. Whether they will succeed or not blood alone will tell. Those who have lost friends by the depredations of the Indians are stricken with awe. Some are disheartened others are filled with vengeance. They are sad times for us all but we hope for the best yet.

Wednesday, Aug 1.

River went down so that we were able to cross the trains and roll out about 3 P.M. Some hesitancy about starting. A majority were in favor of pushing on however and we were soon on the way. "Trust in God and keep our powder dry" is our only safe motto. Made a dry camp about 10 miles out. Had bread and milk for supper. There are two droves of cows with us.

Thursday, Aug 2.

Broke camp about sunrise. I and Perry [Earl] were on guard last night. Dutchman thought I was an Indian and came near shooting me. [Charles] Dearborn lost his mare. Gov. train took the lead. Passed through the grandest scenery that we have met on the trip. Came to "Crazy Womans Fork" about noon. The name is appropriate for the place   A

57. Samuel Finley Blythe identifies him as a man by the name of Sloss, who was wounded on July 22. Blythe diary, July 30, 1866. This was the John Sloss listed in the *Denver Daily Rocky Mountain News*, August 21, 1866.

58. Samuel Finley Blythe was also in the train, and he recorded 210 wagons and 300 men. Blythe diary, August 1, 1866.

59. This detachment on its way to Fort Reno was Company F, Eighteenth Infantry, under the command of Lieutenant Henry H. Link. In the train were Captain Henry Haymond, Captain Frederick W. Phisterer, and Lieutenant Isaac D'Isay, who were returning to the East for recruiting duty. Frederick Phisterer, "My Days in the Army," p. 107, Larew-Phisterer Family Papers, U.S. Army Military History Institute Archives, Carlisle Barracks, Pennsylvania.

60. Lieutenant George Templeton's command was attacked on July 20 at Crazy Woman Creek, and Lieutenant Napoleon Daniels and Corporal Terrence Callery were killed. On July 24 six men were attacked near Hugh Kirkendall's freight train, six miles south of Clear Creek. Wagon master Thomas Dillon was killed in that engagement.

61. Captain Frederick Phisterer recorded in his diary that when he met the train at Crazy Woman Creek, they reported Indians had killed fifteen men. Phisterer, "My Days in the Army," p. 107.

winding zig=zag road leading for nearly two miles down from the high prairie into a ragged valley, crosses a stream of water 4 rods wide ~~and~~ still more winding ~~than the road~~ and running through many precipitous places, that were highly romantic indeed. To the west rise snow=capped mountains, grand & majestic against the sky. From their base broad smooth vallies incline, nestling between rugged bluffs and high rolling prairies that stretch away into the blue east and the surrounding distance. Met the Gov. train from Fort Philip Kearney expected down some days ago, and encamped with us at this place.[59] They do not report the Indians as bad as we expected though they have had one fight with them and some trains attacked[60]

I went through the whole train and made a report of killed and wounded and gave [it] to the Officer for publication.[61] Two trains are waiting at the fort for the Govt train that is with us. They are going up to establish another fort [Fort C. F. Smith]. He says an escort is going up with the other trains. We shall probably have the benefit of it. This officer says they are going through to Fort Laramie to stop any further emigration coming through this route until some measures are taken to ensure safety

Friday, Aug 3ᵈ

Went in bathing in the river. Quite a <u>scare</u> in camp. A Jack Rabbit got among the mules and the hearders commenced firing at it. The whole camp was aroused and got out their guns thinking the Indians were upon us. Started out about two oclock. Straightened out upon the valley along the river and waited for the Government train to pass and go ahead More beautiful scenery. We're nearing the Mountains [Bighorn Mountains] Made a dry camp. Rained as we were going into camp.

Saturday, Aug 4.

Made an early start "Bull trains" in advance Stoped and wattered at a muddy pool [the Wallows]. Cool driving. Feed growing much better. Still approaching nearer to the mountains. Passed into some beautiful vallies at their base. Made Clear Creek about noon. A beautiful stream with stony bottom. Is the first clear stream of any size we have seen since leaving the <u>Niagara</u> [in] N.Y.[62] It made one think of home & the beautiful steams that watter the hills & vallies of our own native State [New York]. One thing very strange and wonderful was the bluffs that partially surrounded our camping place in this little valley. They were all of a perfect highth and formed against the sky an even outline. They looked as though they had been thrown up carefully with a spade and great pains had been taken to form them alike; the tops being shoveled off a perfect level and all of the same exact highth. Was on heard guard in the afternoon Went in bathing

Sunday, Aug 5.

Dont think it advisable to lay over any more than is absolutely necessary in this dangerous country but to get through as soon as possible   Made an early start Government train ahead. Went down an awful steep hill. Crossed Rocky Creek [Rock Creek] (another clear creek). Passed Smith's Lake [Lake De Smet]   Camped for lunch   Water in the lake was salt.[63] Govt. train went on to the Fort [Phil Kearny]   Started on about one oclock. Watered the mules by a small pond. Came within two miles and a half of the Fort and were stoped by soldiers. Were not allowed to camp nearer the Fort on account of taking feed from Govt trains[64]

Monday, Aug 6.

In camp all day recruiting. I made a report of number of men (their names and residence) of wagons stock guns pistols, and ammunition in the train for the Commander of the Post [Captain Tenodor Ten Eyck]. Charlie Rich desired to be relieved as Superintendent of trains and Mr. Whorner [E. R. Horner] was chosen in his place. Hiatt & McC left Halderman [D. B. Haldeman][65]

62. Willson's party visited Niagara Falls on their way to Chicago.

63. The water in Lake De Smet was saline in the Bozeman Trail era. In the twentieth century dams and water diverted into it changed it into a much larger freshwater lake.

64. Captain Tenodor Ten Eyck, commanding Fort Phil Kearny at the time, recorded the arrival of the trains that day in his journal: "Two Govt trains of 52 wagons came in at noon   About 190 citizen wagons came in within two miles of the Fort & encamped." Tenodor Ten Eyck, Diary, August 5, 1866, MS Collection 82, Special Collections Library, University of Arizona, Tucson.

65. D. B. Haldeman was an independent freighter whose name appears in the Tuller and Rich ledger. Willson usually wrote his name as Halderman.

& went to work in the Bull train   Halderman supplied their places easily

Tuesday, Aug 7.

Wrote Lester a letter last night which Charlie R.[ich] is to get mailed [at the fort] to day. We have got one of Bridgers old guides [James J. Brannan] employed to go with us to the Big Horn.[66] He has been in the country and in California & Oregon for 12 years. He has six soldiers with him and they are to act as scouts and guide for us. The scout will mess and sleep with our party. Rolled out of camp this morning about 8 oclock. The bluffs are growing larger and more mountainous. Arrived at the top of one just out of camp from which we could see below us for nearly two miles, the valley in which lay the Fort [Phil Kearny]. The Fort could not be seen until we had descended nearly half way. It lies in a beautiful spot between two cristle [crystal] streams the First Piney Fork & Second Piney Fork [Little Piney and Piney Creeks]. Upon the other side, opposite, the bluffs [Lodge Trail Ridge] ascend as high as those we had just passed over though more precipitous. The valley where lies the Fort, is perfectly walled in on every side by these same high rolling bluffs, except to the west rise the Big Horn Mountains, snow=capped and, more than ever, grand & beautiful in the light of the golden morning.

As we passed the Fort some distance we came to a halt for nearly an hour & a half on account of the difficulty of the trains in advance, in crossing the stream [Piney Creek] and ascending the bluffs beyond [Lodge Trail Ridge]. As we lay there the brass band at the Fort commenced playing.[67] Such sounds in such a scene! It gave me many strange feelings which I cannot describe. There was something in the wild sweet strains that filled and floated through the deep reechoing valley that spoke of home; yet so far distant and in so wild a place that it partook of the nature of the scenes around it. It was like

66. On August 7 Captain Ten Eyck sent James J. Brannan and four men, with orders to arrest deserters, to accompany the emigrant train. Brannan had been hired at Fort Laramie by Colonel Carrington to be one of Jim Bridger's assistant guides for the Eighteenth Infantry. Brannan had been one of the guides under Bridger with General Connor's expedition in 1865, and it was assumed that he was familiar with the Tongue River country. Brannan was killed by Indians between Fort C. F. Smith and Fort Benton on October 19, 1866, and was buried in the Fort C. F. Smith cemetery.

67. Colonel Carrington brought the twenty-five-piece Eighteenth Infantry Regimental Band with the infantry troops to Fort Phil Kearny. The bandmaster was Samuel Curry, who died two months later in the post hospital of pneumonia.

looking through the "glass of time" into the dim Past,
viewing with kindled emotions the forms & scenes that
once enshrined and hallowed it, and yet the wild
adventuresome Present all the while floating before
diming & blinding the vision.

And it is more than this. The heart is overflowed and
cannot compass its emotions. Fresh strains burst forth
and fresher scenes of home and "what has been," and yet
there is that something in the strange echoes and "dying
fall" that does not breathe of home. Nothing but the
resounding vallies and the mountain air can bring forth
such whisperings. Oh! scenes of other days! Oh time and
distance! How far they seem! How unfeeling cold!
Yonder stands the same grand old mountains, the same
uninhabitable wildes around us. And oh music! thy
sweet breathings have too much of these in them to woo
me wholly into thy absorbing meshes of the past, yet
thou hast awakened within me an unaccountable feeling
that overflows my soul. I cannot compass it, nor give it
utterance. Dim recollections, fond but painful in their
obscurity, coupled with present events, come floating
over the senses, through thy gentle harmony, thrilling
every emotion, and pouring upon the heart, such a
pressure, that it dams up the current, thought.

The teams in advance had got out of the way & we
rolled on, crossed the creek [Piney Creek] and began
ascending the bluffs. One wagon broke down. For three
or four hours we traveled over a winding road, now up,
now down, now halting for the long trains in advance to
get on, yet all the while making a gradual ascent. At last
we came to the top of the highest [Lodge Trail Ridge]
and what a wonderful view was spread before us. The
whole country dropped off for three hundred feet below.
It looked like a rough plain, rolling & rocky, or the
mighty up-heaval of some volcanic eruption, and
extended far away into the distant blue. The tops of the

great bluffs & rocky pinacals, as we looked down upon them seemed to be nearly all of an equal highth, forming a perfect level from summit to summit as far as the eye could reach, except to the far right, they gradually formed into rough rocky steeps irregular & ragged and crowned here and there with the red soil that characterizes the gold fields of California. That gold will someday be discovered in large quantities through this region and among the mountains those that are acquainted with the country here affirm very strongly.

The descent of the wagons into this lower region was obtained with great difficulty.[68] Only one [wagon] could descend at a time. The wheels were double locked and the wagons would slide nearly the whole distance to the bottom. Our road now led off to the left, nearer the base of the mountains and was not so rolling as the other portion of the country. The road was more level and we got over the ground more rappidly and got into camp by a small clear stream about 5 oclock, having been over 12 hours on the road and making the distance of only 5 miles.

Wednesday, Aug 8.

Were up at an early hour. Saw the first rays of the sun just before sunrise as they touched the mountain sides The changing tints of purple, green & gold, that reflected upon them as it rose were of the grandest splendor. We saw them through a very fine field glass belonging to the guide [Brannan]. Every little glen & shrub could be distinctly seen. The large trees that grew in the ravines between the ridges looked as though they had been set out in rows as an orchard so perfectly even were they. I was on heard=guard all the morning. Soldiers passed us from the Fort mounted. A wagon had to be fixed & [we] did not get underway until about 9 or 10 oclock. The route was rather interesting—run between many high buttes that served as look outs for the scouts in guarding against the Indians. A dog chased a Jack Rabbit past the

68. They dropped down to Fetterman Ridge, traveled along its narrow ridge, and descended off its end.

trains. Ever since the Indian troubles I ride on the wagons and carry my gun so as to be in readiness. All "extra" men do the same, that they may engage the Indians while the drivers are correlling the trains. Met soldiers returning. Report Indians ahead.

Arrived at Peno Creek [Prairie Dog Creek] about noon, crossed and drove alongside. A nice little valley. Roads more level. Sharp bluffs on the right, rolling on left. Kept sharp lookout for Indians. About 3 oclock P.M. saw a large party on the hights to the left. Went into camp soon. They came down within a half mile of camp. They raised a flag of truce and our guide, [James] Brannan, went out to meet them. One came in advance had taken off his we[a]pons & called as far as he could make us hear "Arrapahoe, good." They were the Arrapahoe tribe and seemed friendly. They wanted to come into camp but the guide would not let them. There had been a treaty made with some of their tribe about a year ago but as there is no dependance to be placed in an Indian it would not do to let them in. The guide told them that the Sioux had killed 40 of our men and that the white man was mad. He gave them a few pounds of tobacco and they went away seeming satisfied. They knew the guide when they first came in and called him the "Road=finder" They have a name for every white man they see & never see him but once but they remember him.

Thursday, Aug 9.

Was on guard last night with Perry Earl. Wolves howled hideously. Took an early start. Still traveling in the valley by Peno Creek [Prairie Dog Creek] Saw two buffalo on the left. 4 or 5 of the boys went after them but did not fetch them. Camped for lunch about noon. In afternoon took one of our guides "Cut Offs," crossed Peno Creek [Prairie Dog Creek], and camped by Goose Creek 2 miles & a half beyond.[69] The country here is

69. When Brannan was with Connor's expedition in 1865, they continued on down Prairie Dog Creek to the Tongue River. But James Sawyers, following a few days behind Connor, left Prairie Dog Creek at this point, went west over the divide to Goose Creek, and crossed it at present Sheridan, Wyoming. This is the "cutoff" that Davis is referring to.

beautiful. Some of the loveliest vallies and streams I ever
saw. About a hundred buffalo off towards the
mountains. Boys went out & killed one.

Friday, Aug 10.

Had buffalo for breakfast. Rained some in the
morning. Charlie R.[ich] and [William] Phillips had a
"set=too" Both a little out of sorts. One or two others
got into disputes. We laughed it off by laying it to the
buffalo meet [meat]. The country still growing more
picturesque and romantic in appearance. I never set my
eyes on lovelier scenery. As our guide [Brannan] says:
"This is God's country." Feed in abundance clear, cool
mountain streams running every where, coming as it
were directly from the snow=banks on the summits. It is
certainly destined to become one of the greatest
stock=raising countries in the United States. Saw more
buffalo on the right. Crossed South Fork Tongue River
[Wolf Creek]. Camped on Middle Fork Tongue River
[Tongue River] about a mile [two miles] beyond. This is
a large cold stream and is so pure that the waters are blue
reminding one of the Hudson & St. Law.[rence], only on
a smaller scale. A train came up just before sundown of
52 wagons. Boys went fishing and caught a large
quantity. They were Sucker Pike, Sammon [salmon] &
trout. Played violin in evening.

Saturday, Aug 11.

The guide [James Brannan] left us this morning to go
on to Big Horn. Will meet us again between there day
after tomorrow. He left us one of his men. The Emigrant
train went on with the train that came in last night and left
us. Our train behind the "Bulls" [ox train] to day. Saw two
or three carcasses of buffalo killed by the trains ahead of
us. Saw several antelope. Halted near a small stream [Twin
Creek] for [noon] diner The other trains had killed 6
buffalo. A grave of a man killed by Indians near by was
nearly dug open by the wolves.[70] Capt. [E. R.] Horner

70. This was the grave of
George Pease, also
mentioned by diarists
William K. Thomas and
Perry Burgess four days
earlier. Doyle, *Journeys to
the Land of Gold*, 2:543, 566.

covered it again. Very hilly in afternoon. Camped at Fork
[of] Little Horn River [Pass Creek]. Went over to the
"travelling Managins" & bought some milk.

Sunday, Aug 12.

Had to fix the road in crossing the stream Our train
ahead. Got under way before sunrise & without
breakfast. Went to shoot a sage hen. Passed over bluffs,
came out on an open valley. Saw grisly bear track
crossing the road. Charlie R[ich] & John Freeland
followed them over the Bluffs came on him & fired
three shots but did not "fetch him." Horses were afraid
& could not follow. Camped across Trout Creek [Little
Bighorn River] about 8 A.M. for breakfast. The trains
that went ahead were camped here to lay over to day.

These cool streams that every where watter the
country are very refreshing to man & beast during the
excessive hot weather that we experience in this climate.
Wild game is becoming more & more abundant. The hills
ahead are perfectly covered with buffalo. A large drove
of antelope passed. Stock have their comforts here as
well as man There is a little brown bird here, called
buffalo birds that light in flocks upon the mules &
horses and pick off the flies & gnats that bother them.
And they seem to understand the favors thus rendered
with a great deal of appreciation for they feed away very
unconcernedly with scarcely a switch of their tails, and
with perfect confidence that birdie will take care of Mr.
Fly. They are very tame and we could get near enough to
them to almost reach them with our hands.

In the afternoon Charlie R[ich] & myself [David]
Jones & the [Eighteenth Infantry] Seargent went ahead of
the trains to kill a buffalo. Seargent shot one through the
heart killing him instantly It was the first time in my life
that I had got near enough to see how one looked. I rode
back to the train which was a mile distant and got a wheat
[whet] stone and an ax. We cut him up in short order &

loaded down the train with fresh meet. Charlie C[aldwell] & I went ahead the remainder of the afternoon hunting them down. It was a great day for us inasmuch as our great curiosity for buffalo was satisfied. The hills were literally covered with them. Charlie killed one.

I went off from the road nearly a mile and came suddenly on to a large heard behind some high bluffs. When I made my appearance they all snorted and started on a run. One large fellow turned round and faced me until all the rest got by him when he put after them probably performing his services as "rear guard" to the heard. It was a grand sight to see them running over the prairie, snorting at every step & leaping over the bluffs and ravines as they passed. Got into camp rather late & we were pretty tired & lame. Camped by Little Horn River [Lodge Grass Creek].

Monday, Aug 13.

Did not get underway till late in the morning. Had one of Phillips & Freelands wagons to fix which was broken the evening before coming into camp. Fine bright morning. The changing aspect of the country as we move slowly along still keeps up its deep interest. The mountains to the left are gradually sinking into sharp bluffs and rolling hills. Made a short drive and camped on North Fork Little Horn [Rotten Grass Creek]. Bad place to cross. Laid over in the afternoon. Our guide [James] Brannan came in from Big Horn. Reported everything safe on the road. The Indians had run off all the stock [belonging] to one train camped at the Big Horn [Cyrenius Beers's train], and the owner had gone to Virginia City to buy more.[71] The Emigrant train left behind came up in the evening.

Tuesday, Aug 14.

Some sharp practice in seeing who should get the road first. Our mules got beat by the "Bulls." All got concentrated at the top of the hill. Some teams got

71. Cyrenius Beers's heavily loaded freight train was raided by Indians at the Bighorn River crossing on July 18 and 19. As the train was preparing to ferry across the river, the Indians drove off all but a few of their mules in two different raids. The freighters ferried the wagons across the river, formed a corral with the wagon beds, and built fortifications. Beers detailed ten men to remain and guard the wagons, and the rest went to Montana to obtain new teams. The men stayed in the wagon corral for a month, until the new teams arrived. Samuel Finley Blythe also mentioned the stranded Beers train. Blythe diary, August 15, 1866.

"cut=off" from their trains. A good deal of sport. The
Bulls were licked up as fast as possible. "Get up Berry"
"Go long Bright" "Whoa Brady!" "Gee off Beauty"
"Whoa, haw, Brim!" "Go long Blue!" "Get up Skinner"
"Whoa, haw, Gee, Toney" were a few of the <u>expressions</u>
that could be distinctly <u>understood</u> amid the confusion
& the cracking of whips of a hundred drivers all yelling
at the top of their voices. At last got straightened out
and went on.

Made a drive of ten miles to Wind Creek [Soap
Creek] and camped for diner. From the laziness of the
men or the insufficiency of Jim (the wagon master) our
train got behind the whole in making the afternoons
start. Our train (that is Phillips & Freelands) is the most
shamefully managed I think of any train that was ever on
the plains. There are some first rate men in it. John
Freeland the Capt. is a smart man and a good man and is
capable of running the train if the proprietors would give
him full authority. But they wont, and John does not feel
like taking another man's property into his own hands
(though he has got full power to do so if he likes) for fear
that he might be the cause of some disaster & they
become dissatisfied. [William] Phillips is the <u>meanest</u>
man I ever knew. He shall leave the train the first
opportunity & have said so from the start. But we got
along better than most men would, as Charlie Rich can
manage Phillips generally to suit himself as he does
nearly all men who come in contact with him.

Some difficulty in getting up the hill in making
afternoon start. Made about three miles and came to a
bad place in crossing a ravine. Had to wait for the ox
trains to cross. Was nearly dark when we got our train
across. Drove upon the next hill and camped. Charlie
Rich [William] Phillips George & Dick had mounted
horses at noon and rode on to the Fort at Big Horn [Fort
C. F. Smith]. Did not get back ~~that night~~

Wednesday, Aug 15.

The boys got in from the Fort [C. F. Smith] just before daylight They had rode all night with the exception of about two hours when they stoped at the Bull train 5 miles ahead of us and got a little sleep & fed their horses. Charlie R.[ich] had made arrangements to cross our trains at the Ferry as soon as we came up and join Kirkendolfts [Hugh Kirkendall's] train, which had laid at the Ford some five days and had crossed that day. Old [Jim] Bridger is with this train and is "running" it[72] and he told Charlie [Rich] that he would make short drives and let us catch up with him. So Charlie has withdrawn our three wagons from Phillips & Freelands train and so has Dick & George their <u>one</u> (they are the fellows and are fine boys who own the guns & ammunition.) They (Phillips & Freeland) intend to keep up with us if they can, but they can not do it. Their mules are too well "played" & that is one reason, above all others, why we leave them. We can make two days drive to their one.

We pulled out and came on. There was no stopping now for other wagons to get on ahead of us, nor no waiting for those that were stuck & straggled behind us. We passed all the wagons ahead, nearly two hundred in all, and camped for diner on a little clear stream [War Man Creek] about three miles of [from] the Fort. In the afternoon drove on to the Fort.[73] The Emigrant train that was considerable ahead of us yesterday had been here since morning and had crossed all but about 15 wagons. They would cross these early in the morning and give us the next chance. Was on guard.

Thursday, Aug 16th.

The Bull trains with Phillips and Freelands came up [at] 4 oclock this morning Some strife in seeing who should cross first. Caused a great deal of talking & some feeling. 9 of Phillips & Freelands men left them. They are

72. Colonel Carrington instructed Jim Bridger to examine the entire route to Virginia City and to obtain information from the Crows about the other tribes in the area.

73. Willson's train took the cutoff to Fort C. F. Smith opened by James Sawyers in 1865. The cutoff turned off the emigrant route on the Soap Creek divide, dropped down to War Man Creek, and went directly to the ferry crossing six miles above the emigrant ford at Spotted Rabbit Crossing.

in a fix. Charlie R[ich] hired [his nephew] Frank Rich [out] to them under the condition that no one should boss him but Capt. John [Freeland] who is a great friend to Charlie [Rich]   Halderman [D. B. Haldeman], (who owns 5 wagons in Phillips & F's train) has engaged to have his freight lightened and come on with us. He has hired other teams to take on part of his load so that he can keep up with us. He says he knows who his friends are. He is a good man and is a college graduate, and admitted to the bar. Has very good talents but is not much of a business man. He is rather helpless on such a trip as this but as Charlie R[ich] has advised and helped him a great deal and he thinks there was never such a man. He is a Southern man and never did any work in his life. He says mental cultivation is a very good thing but it ain't worth a red [cent] in this country!

As soon as [William] Phillips found he was going to withdraw his wagons he played mean with him by not letting him cross when his turn came, but commenced putting his own teams across. Halderman [D. B. Haldeman] got completely discouraged and did not know what to do, tears came in his eyes when he spoke of it and he said "they have told me I was a "d—d fool" so much that I begin to believe it." I've promised to lay over till to morrow noon and help him get across.

The ferry is nothing but a large flat boat very roughly built and they row it across   The current takes it down stream and they draw it [back] up with the mules. They charge five dollars for each wagon. The Big Horn is a river nearly as large as the Platte. It is about as muddy, more so at this time than it was ever known. For this reason they think there is some mining going on a short ways above here. There have been a great many from Virginia City leaving for parts in some portion of this country.[74] There have been rich specimens taken out very near here.

74. Several prospecting parties from the settlements in Montana ranged throughout this region during the summer of 1866. The largest was Jeff Standifer's expedition of more than 170 prospectors.

Was on heard=guard [herd-guard] all the afternoon.
went in bathing with Perry [Earl]. Dark rainy night.
Indians had been seen during the day and we were
fearful of an attack when we lay down to sleep.

Friday, Aug 17.

The Emigrants broke camp in the morning. We are
going to travel with them but could not start this
morning on account of waiting for Halderman [D. B.
Haldeman]. Phillips & Freelands men after a great deal
of co[a]xing promised to come back to him. So Frank
Rich will still remain with us   Glad of it for we want all
the boys to go through with us that started.[75] Got
underway about two oclock in the afternoon. Tried
awful hard to catch the Emigrants. Drove until half=past
ten in evening and saw nothing of them. Mules were
nearly "played out" and could not go any further. Was
about half=past 11 before got to bed.

Saturday, Aug 18.

Got underway by day light. Went about a mile and
found the trains camped—were cooking their breakfasts.
Halderman [D. B. Haldeman] took off 2500 pounds of
freight which the Emigrants took on for him. Turned out
our stock for feed and cooked breakfast for ourselves
The Emigrants went on. We expected to catch them at
night. Charlie Rich & I went out on picket. Bad roads.
Many bad places in crossing ravines. Had to assist
Halderman a great deal and it detained us very much.
Are in a volcanic region or what they call the "Bad
Lands."[76] There is plenty good water but not much feed.
Found the train in camp about five oclock. Played the
violin and Charlie Rich sung.

Sunday, Aug 19.

Still in the volcanic regions. The scenery is very rough
and singular but uncommonly interesting. There has
been to all appearances at some period of the world's
existence an awful eruption here, probably from an

75. Frank Rich, Charlie
Rich's nephew, was one
of the nine original
"boys" who started from
Canton, New York.

76. The badlands in this
region are not volcanic in
origin. Rather, they are
sedimentary rocks of
Triassic and Jurassic
sandstone and shale.

earthquake. The whole country looks as if it had been a
vast river of burning lava and cooling upon the surface
the subterranean fires would raise up vast acres and
bursting forth again, would ooze out black cinders &
huge rocks piled one upon another. The country
resembles the waves of the ocean when raging fiercest.
The "table lands," covered with grass and quite fertile
would rise up to a great highth like "long swells" and
pitching suddenly off down great steeps, the barren
rocks and rolling piles of lava were like the dashing
breakers that rage and foam so in the rising storm. It was
all terribly grand to look upon. What vast treasures, in
gold iron coal & other minerals the earth has here
unfolded from the secrets of her bossom time will very
soon tell. The hand of civilization is fast grappling the
possessions of the savage barbarian and ere long his
name and nation will be obliterated from off the face of
the earth

We camped at noon for diner upon a small creek that
was filled with be[a]ver dams.[77] In the afternoon we came
out of the "Bad Lands" upon a beautiful country once
more.[78] Some table lands away to the right but mostly
rolling prairie with high bluffs and somewhat
mountainous to the left. Saw several trains ahead of us.
Probably Kirkendolph's [Hugh Kirkendall's] is one.
[Charles] Dearborns wagon tiped over going down steep
hill with wife & child inside. No one injured but damaged
the wagon some. Many bad ravines to cross. Drove a long
way for water. Did not get in camp till sometime after
dark Found Kirkendolphs [Hugh Kirkendall's] train here
and [Jim] Bridger with it. Good cool spring.[79] A party of
prospectors here from Virginia City

Monday, Aug 20.

Found on looking about us at daylight that we were
lying in a beautiful valley walled in by bluffs &
mountains Laid over the forenoon to rest the stock and

77. They probably nooned
at either Beauvais Creek
or East Pryor Creek.

78. In the afternoon they
passed through Devil's
Gap. Devil's Gap is a
modern local name (that
does not appear on maps)
for the narrow gap in the
eroded Cretaceous
sandstone and shale
badlands, twenty-eight
miles west of the Bighorn
River ferry on the cutoff
route opened by James
Sawyers in August 1866.
Devil's Gap was
mistakenly known to the
emigrants as Pryor Gap,
but the actual Pryor Gap
is about fifteen miles
southwest of Devil's Gap
and closer to the Pryor
Mountains. The emigrant
road through Devil's Gap
was a narrow wagon
track winding through
barren bluffs, while the
modern road skirts
around the gap one-half
mile to the south.

79. The spring was two
miles east of the Pryor
Creek crossing. Jim
Bridger named it Ice
Water Spring in his
survey of the trail.

give Dearborn an opportunity to fix his wagon. Got
started about two oclock. Crossed a small stream [Pryor
Creek], ascended into a rolling country. The hills were
covered with large rocks that looked as though they had
been dropped down from above like hail.[80] Came to
camp about dusk. A crowd came up from the other
trains to hear the violin. Three or four players among
them, passed the violin around and had quite a nice time.
Was on guard

Tuesday, August 21.

Got underway before day light so as to get ahead of
Kirkendolphs [Hugh Kirkendall's]. They have a large
train and mules pretty well played. Make slow time, and
don't care about being behind them. Beautiful scenery.
Main chain of the Rocky mountains in the distance. Are
crowned with snow. I was very sleepy. Came near falling
off of [Loren] Tullers wagon. Got into the "Buggy" and
slept. Buffalo ahead. Wharton hunting them. Crossed
Clarks Fork of the Yellow Stone is quite a large river.
Camped here. Bridger took diner with us. He is going to
establish a Fort at this point sometime[81] Came through
a pleasant valley in afternoon. Saw [a] deer. Charlie
C[aldwell] tried to shoot him. Crossed the Rocky Fork
of the Yellow Stone [Rock Creek]. Clear stream heavy
timber. Traveled along side [of] the stream for nearly two
miles & camped. Charlie C.[aldwell] went upon the
bluffs to the right and killed a buffalo calf. Did not get
any of the meet—to[o] far back to go after him. Charlie
C[aldwell] saw another buffalo across the creek and got
excited and went after him. Came near drowning in
crossing.

Wednesday, Aug 22

Kirkendolph's [Hugh Kirkendall's] train came up as
we were eating breakfast. They had taken an early start
on purpose to beat us. They crossed just above where we
camped. Had some difficulty in crossing We got ready

80. The hills just west
of Pryor Creek are
covered with large
scattered boulders.
Willson's description is
remarkably accurate.

81. At this point, on the
west side of the Clarks
Fork, Sawyers's Bozeman
Trail cutoff intersected
Bridger's 1864 route
coming north from the
Bighorn Basin. Bridger, a
consummate entrepreneur,
recognized the strategic
location of this crossroads
for a trading post.

as soon as we could, took the old road & crossed the creek some distance in advance and left Kirkendolph [Kirkendall] far in the rear. Saw an Indian grave in morning. Charlie C[aldwell] & [David] Jones were in advance hunting antelope. Were traveling up the Rocky Fork [Red Lodge Creek] all day. [Crossed and] Camped on the North side at night. Charlie & Jones brought in a great buck antelope. A couple of trains passed us and camped just ahead in order to have "<u>the lead</u>" during tomorrows travel

Thursday, Aug 23

Up before 3 o'clock got breakfast and were underway just at break of day. Beat the other trains and got in ahead. Soon left the Rocky Fork [Red Lodge Creek] & came out upon a rolling prairie. I went ahead and rode the mule. Got a shot at an antelope with revolver. Was about 50 yeards distant. Hunted for sage hen. Camped for noon on small creek [Beaver Creek]. Emigrant train ~~broke up~~ split. Rutan and Sherman went ahead to camp on Rosebud Creek. Too steep hill to climb until after I ate. Had made a long drive as it was and we thought it would pay better to stop.

In afternoon ascended the hill and gradually came to greater highths. At last came to a "jumping off" place. A beautiful valley [Rosebud Valley] below some three hundred feet perpendicular highth. Rosebud Creek in the distance. Had to double lock both wheels in descending.[82] Sherman & Rutan were camped on the first fork [East Rosebud Creek]. Had broke a wagon and were obliged to lay over. We went on to second fork [West Rosebud Creek] and camped for the night. Charlie R[ich] discovered a grizly bear. Charlie C[aldwell] caught trout. Played violin til in evening

Friday, Aug 24.

Crossed the Creek and ascended high hill. Many stones in the road. Went ahead and picked them out. Hard work.

82. This was the steep descent to Rosebud Valley. Samuel Finley Blythe recorded that a wagon broke while coming down the hill. Blythe diary, August 23, 1866.

Many up hill places and deep gulches. Could not ride in wagons. Came to very steep hill [Sandborn Hill]. The "Buggy" team spun part way down with Hopkins [Taylor]. Came near having a smash up.[83] Fine smooth bottom for nearly a mile. Crossed a rocky creek [Stillwater River], and camped for diner   had a fine meal of trout. George & Dick left us in the afternoon and went ahead with other trains. Rough stony roads. Camped about sundown by a small stream [Cow Creek]. Within half days drive to Yellow Stone. Wrote letters to send by Rutan to mail who is going to Virginia City on ahead of trains. Was tired out. Charlie C[aldwell] stood guard for me.

Saturday, Aug 25.

Good roads for some ways. Saw a drove of several hundred elk. Roads begin to grow stoney. Had to "pick out" [use pickaxes]. Descended a steep hill into Yellow Stone Valley.[84] Abundance of timber. Pine and Cotton Wood. Drove up the river for about two miles and camped. Had a horrid headache

Sunday, Aug 26.

Rolled out about 8 oclock. Rained last night in the night and routed us out of our beds. Crawled under the wagons and slept till morning got pretty wet. Two trains in advance. Did not feel well. Rode with Charlie R[ich] in the buggy most of the time. Had quite an interesting talk with him   Passed the grave of [William] Thomas & son [Charley] with another man [Joseph Schultz] killed by Indians on the 23rd [24th].[85] Several Indians seen to day by other parties. Have seen their signs. Crossed two creeks. Killed two antelope   Camped for lunch about 2 oclock. Found George & Dick here with two other trains. Drove on about 8 miles and camped for the night. Are feeling a little anxiety about Indians

Monday, Aug 27.

Still traveling up the Yellow Stone. Arrived at the ferry [Bozeman's ferry] about 10 oclock this morning.

83. The descent of Sandborn Hill to the Stillwater River Valley, six miles west of present Absarokee, Montana, was also steep.

84. The road came off the point of the bluff on the east side of Bridger Creek, a mile from the Yellowstone River.

85. William K. Thomas, his eight-year-old son Charley, and his driver Joseph Schultz were traveling from Illinois. Thinking they were safe from Indians, they went ahead of the large train they had been with. On July 24 on the bank of the Yellowstone River, Indians killed the three of them. Another group of emigrants came upon their bodies later the same day and buried them. Finding Thomas's diary in his pocket, they took it to his brother in Montana. The diary is in Doyle, *Journeys to the Land of Gold*, 2:533–46.

Laying over. Dont know whether to cross the ferry or go above & ford. They charge 10 dollars for crossing the ferry. None of the trains would cross. Many went to look for a good place to ford. They came down on the price for ferrying. Shall probably cross to morrow morning. Charlie C.[aldwell] lost his pocket book with over three hundred dollars

Tuesday, Aug 28.

Up early this morning and got breakfast before daylight. Pulled out as soon as possible in order to get to the ferry. Ferry man had come down to five dollars on his price and the trains had all decided to cross. The "first come first served" is the rule they go [by] and there was only one train ahead of us. Had to wait until about ten oclock before crossing   While waiting a couple of fights arose. [Jim] Bridger came. Soon after Halderman [D. B. Haldeman] & [Andy] Wharton.[86] Glad to see them. We had left their trains behind several days back. Got across the river all straight by noon. Will wait for the Emigrants.

86. Samuel Finley Blythe was in Andy Wharton's train.

Saw a tree where the bark was peeled off and the names & dates of trains & individuals at the time of passing were written all over it.[87] From among the number I saw the following: "A. T. Huickleys, Chicago train of one wagon, one man, and one yoke of "dead beasts" passed here Aug 10, all well. Loaded mostly with <u>Quartz Mills</u>." The man certainly must have had <u>pluck</u> and a good deal of fool=hardy "<u>luck</u>" if he has come alone in that way the whole route. In another place I saw this, "Jennie Sanderson. Bound for Virginia City in the Happie land of Caneon." Underneath this some brick of a young fellow has written, "Jennie you are a bully Gall (signed) J. H. Finly"

87. Nellie Fletcher noted that the names were written in pencil. Fletcher diary, July 19, 1867.

[Jim] Bridger & Halderman [D. B. Haldeman] took dinner with us. Roap to the ferry boat broke and no more trains could cross. [Loren] Tuller & Charlie R.[ich]

were on the other side when it broke assisting the Emigrants. Charlie R. came across on Haldermans mare at the ford above [the ferry]. Tuller remained over. Was on guard

Wednesday, Aug. 29.

Up early and moved out about three miles to feed. [Loren] Tuller came up about 10. Got breakfast. Charlie C.[aldwell] and [David] Jones caught a nice string of trout. Made but one drive to day. Crossed a warm creek [Hunters Creek]. [Hunters] Hot springs about two miles north. Went hunting   Saw nothing. Drove about 12 miles and camped on the [Yellowstone] river. Fine grassy bottom. Are traveling with Whitney's train.

Thursday, Aug 30.

Up at three oclock and rolled out at sunrise. Leave the river and go over mountainous country. "Hard" roads. Crossed Seal [Shields] River   Camped for dinner. Commenced to rain just before going into camp. Drove on, but soon began to rain very hard. Went two miles and camped on the [Yellowstone] river. Charlie Caldwell and [David] Jones caught a large string of trout.

Friday, Aug 31.

Pleasant but cold this morning. Mountains covered with snow. Two trains came up—old chums—Started about half past eleven. Drove about 11 or 12 miles. Left the Yellow Stone. Delightful country. Picked out my "ranch" & future home. Camped on small creek. Met party of prospectors.

Saturday, Sept 1 =

Had breakfast at daylight and "pulled out" going into the mountains. Very hard roads. Boys stopped & picked gooseberries. Boots hurt my feet.[88] I went ahead with Charlie Rich with one boot off and in my stocking. Limped along by Charlies side who was giving me a sketch of his life. Some Romance & some Love. Very interesting. Went over a very large hill and camped for

88. In a published reminiscence Willson recalled that on the day they went through Bozeman Pass, his boots rubbed blisters on his feet, so he took them off and walked in his stockings. *Bozeman (Mont.) Republican-Courier*, August 13, 1913.

noon near a spring, one of the sources of the Gallatin
River, and consequently one of the "heads" to the
Missouri. The first spring is a very small one where the
water boils out of the ground and forms a stream about 4
inches wide. Below, other little springs are formed which
mingle their waters—little tiny rills at first—& joining,
form but a short distance below, quite a little brook. On
a little farther it has grown to a creek of about 5 or 6 feet
in width. Then winding among the mountains it makes
its way into the valley and forms the Gallatin River.

Emigrant train passed us. Went on in the afternoon;
soon came to the summit of a hill [Bozeman Pass] from
which we could see stretching far away before us the
Gallatin Valley. Beautiful Valley. All took off our hats
and swung them. It was about five miles in descending to
the valley and very rough road. Soon struck the valley
from behind a bluff. The first thing we saw that showed
signs of a settlement & gave us the smile of civilization
was a ~~rude~~ fence! At this we cheered vociferously! On a
little farther and saw a ranch! Another cheer! More
ranches, more cheers! At last a wheat field! Still another
cheer! A patch of potatoes and still another cheer! And
once for all a cheer for the whole country and our safe
arrival! The care and anxiety which were so upon us in
our continual watching and looking [out] for Indians,
were here completely lifted from us and we felt like new
creatures. Camped in the valley about three miles from
Bozeman City

Sunday, Sept 2.

Drove out about 9 oclock and made Bozeman City. It
is a small town of about half dozen buildings. Lay over
to shoe mules & fix lock chain. Got some work for
[Frank] Harper

Monday, Sept 3 =

A cold rainy day. A few wagons pulled out in the
morning. We remained in camp. Was on guard last night

Tuesday, Sept 4.

Pleasant & cold this morning. Got diner at 11 oclock & harnessed up. Three antelope came up near camp. Boys fired several shots at them but without success. Drove down to Penwells, about 10 miles to camp. Fine country. Large fields of grain ready to harvest. We shall probably live here until Charlie R[ich] goes to Helena and finds out something about the country, our future prospects and what is to become of us. [Oscar] Penwell is the man whom we got acquainted with on the boat coming up the Missouri River to Omaha last May. Is a fine fellow and were glad to see him. Had started from Omaha about a week before us and arrived here 5 weeks ago. Was just two days ahead of the Indians (that is when their depredations broke out) & consequently was not delayed on account of them. Went into the house this evening & had a visit. Played violin   Begin to feel as though we had got home. [Oscar] Penwell is farming on big scale. Has two brothers [Merritt and John] in partnership.[89] They own over 6 hundred achers [acres]. Will raise about 15 or 20 thousand dollars worth of crops this year. Were poor boys when they started.

Wednesday, Sept 5.

Up at daylight and got breakfast. Charlie R[ich] and Perry [Earl] went to Bozeman with our wagon to meet Halderman [D. B. Haldeman] to see about the freight we bought for him & that which we had charge of brought by Emigrants. Also to settle with him. They returned & Halderman with them, about dark. [Frank] Harper is binding grain at three dollars a day. Frank got work in the afternoon. Went in bathing and did my washing.

Thursday, Sept 6.

Charlie R[ich] Halderman [D. B. Haldeman] Perry [Earl] and Charlie C[aldwell] started at 12 oclock for Helena. It is about a hundred miles and will be gone 7 or 8 days. There is some talk of our staying here this winter &

89. In 1864 brothers Oscar, Merritt, and John Penwell located a farm on the East Gallatin River about twelve miles from Bozeman. Tom Haines, *Flouring Mills of Montana Territory* (Missoula: Friends of the University of Montana Library, 1984), 19. Willson met Oscar Penwell on the steamboat from St. Joe to Omaha before departing overland.

puting up a shanty to live in. Goods will sell better here than in Helena at present. We may take up a ranch near here if we can find a good one. Haldermans teams came up in the afternoon and camped about a half a mile from here. [David] Jones went to work for [Oscar] Penwell.

Our mess of 9 good jolly boys is now dwindled down to only 4.[90] A lonesome time this evening   Charlie C.[aldwell] will not come back again if he can find any employment in Helena or elsewhere. We have been together through all the perils & hardships of the journey across the plains, and these associations coupled with our past in our school boy-hood has rendered our parting of such a nature that is too oppressive for utterance. My reflections lead me into many winding trains & I wander up and down the pleasant vallies of the past plucking the sweet and tender flowers of hope & boyish anticipations that always blossomed there, till every time I lift my eyes to this hard scene before me the shrill blasts of the present snatch them from me & twirl them aloft, out of sight and out of mind. We have been boys together, and mingled our boyish dreams. All this is done away now and we stand against the stiff realities of manhood, naked and alone!

The way looks hard and toilsome, cold and unfeeling; and my wandering thoughts fall back again into the soothing channels of the past. Other thoughts crowd in upon me that awake my soul! "As flyes the inconstant sun over Larmons grassy plain, so pass the tales of old along my soul by night." It was just four months ago that I spent my last night at home. The very hour, the very atmosphere, and a lonely time it was. There were those present I may never see again! Oh, how the presence of the old Home breathes upon my heart to night! Parents, brothers, sisters and the long line of dear associations through the dim years past and gone forever, crowd upon my thoughts and press me heavily! No

90. The original nine traveling companions were Charlie Rich, Loren W. Tuller, Frank Rich, Hopkins Taylor, Perry Earl, Charlie Caldwell, Frank Harper, John Hershaw, and Davis Willson. Five had gone to Helena, leaving Willson, Tuller, Taylor, and Hershaw in the camp at Bozeman. Charlie Rich, Earl, and Harper soon returned to Bozeman, but Caldwell and Frank Rich did not.

wonder I am sad to night. I see them, hear their voices—
hear them still; and the two great pictures, that loom up
so vividly before me now—the Tender Past & the Stern
Present—form a strange comparison that alike, both
warms & chills & chills & warms again, as I turn my
wandering gaze from one upon the other.

Samuel Finley Blythe

Diary, 1866

SAMUEL FINLEY BLYTHE turned onto the Bozeman Trail on the same day as—in fact, only a few hours behind—Davis Willson. Willson mentioned passing Blythe's train two days earlier, and both had camped the night before they turned onto the Bozeman Trail on the North Platte River at the popular camping ground opposite the site where Fort Fetterman would be established the next summer. On July 20 both trains began traveling directly into the path of the waiting Indian war parties. There were striking similarities between Sam Blythe's and Davis Willson's trains. They were both small, three or four wagons, and both were incorporated into larger trains for safety. Blythe, who was the same age as Willson, was also traveling with a group of close friends.

Like Willson's train, Blythe's party was careful and took extra precautions so that, when the Indians did attempt a raid, they suffered no casualties. With conflicts occurring all around them, these two trains got through relatively unaffected. The train ahead of Willson's had two men killed and one mortally wounded on the Dry Fork Powder River; the train between them had two killed on the Dry Fork Cheyenne River; and the train following Blythe's had nine men killed two miles beyond Brown Springs—all in two days. Perhaps Blythe's and Willson's good fortune was because they were watchful and cautious. Perhaps they were just lucky.

In contrast to the New York boys in Willson's party, Blythe and his four traveling companions were all from Ohio. They were all Civil War veterans, seemingly at loose ends, and the goldfields in Montana beckoned as a great adventure. The young veterans fell into a familiar pattern. William Lockwood, who had been Blythe's infantry company captain, became the party's captain on their journey west.

SOURCE DOCUMENTS: Samuel Finley Blythe, Diary/Reminiscence, 1866, original, MS 3, Oregon Historical Society, Portland. Reproduced as Samuel Finley Blythe, *Saga of the Prairies*, comp. George Finley Marlor and Thelma Irene Marlor (La Mesa, Calif., 1982).

Samuel F. Blythe.

NEG. NO. 000947, OREGON HISTORICAL SOCIETY, PORTLAND

Samuel Finley Blythe was born in Fairfield, Adams County, Pennsylvania, on February 14, 1842.[1] He was the fourth of seven children of David and Julia Ann Hoover Blythe. David Blythe was a tanner. He died when Sam was seven years old. In 1856, when Sam was fourteen, he left home and worked for the next two years as a printer's apprentice at a newspaper in Chambersburg, Pennsylvania. In 1858 he went to visit his mother in Eaton, Ohio, where she was living with her other children Barbara Elizabeth, twenty; Rosalinda, eighteen; and twins Julian and Junian, thirteen.[2] Sam worked as a typesetter for the *Eaton (Ohio) Democrat* for a few months and then traveled around Ohio and Indiana, working for various newspaper printers. He returned to Eaton in fall 1860 and worked on the *Eaton (Ohio) Register* for nearly a year.

In September 1861 Blythe enlisted in the Twenty-second Ohio Volunteer Infantry. He served for three years in Company E and was mustered out with his company in November 1864.[3] He then enlisted in Company I, Second U.S. Volunteers, and received his final discharge in February 1866. He returned to Eaton, but he could not find work as a typesetter since women were doing all the typesetting in the printing offices.

Feeling that there was nothing for them in Eaton, Blythe and Dan Ridenour, a boyhood friend who had served with him in the Twenty-second Infantry, decided to go West. Their plan was to go as far as public transportation would take them and then hire out to drive oxen across the plains to Colorado. They left Eaton on April 17 and went by train to St. Louis and from there by steamboat to St. Joseph, Missouri. They did not find positions as drivers in overland wagon trains, so Blythe found work as a compositor at the *St. Joseph Gazette* and joined the typographer's union. Within a few days, Ridenour got homesick and returned to Eaton, and Blythe never saw him again.

Around the first of May, four friends Blythe had known during the Civil War came to St. Joe. One of them was William Lockwood, the captain of his Twenty-second Ohio Infantry company. The men were on their way to Montana and invited Blythe to go with them. Blythe at first declined, thinking he had found a good job in St. Joe, but his friends

---

1. Biographical articles on Samuel Finley Blythe appear in Fred Lockley, *History of the Columbia River Valley* (Chicago: S. J. Clarke Publishing Co., 1928), 295–300; and Frank E. Hodkin and J. J. Galvin, *Pen Pictures of Representative Men of Oregon* (Portland: Farmer and Dairyman Publishing House, 1882), 193–94.

2. Julia Blythe, widow, age forty, and her children, including Sam, are listed in the 1860 Ohio census, Preble County, Washington Township, Eaton, 66.

3. *Official Roster of the Soldiers of the State of Ohio in the War of the Rebellion, 1861–1866*, 12 vols. (Akron, Cincinnati, and Norwalk, Ohio, 1886–1895), 3:54.

were persistent, and his resistance slowly disappeared. He quit his job on May 19 and joined his friends, who had one wagon and ox team ready to go. Blythe paid Lockwood his entire savings, seventy-five dollars, for his share in the company. He later learned that they had been so anxious for him to join them because they were short of the amount they needed to buy their outfit.

The Lockwood party crossed the Missouri River the same day and were on their way. They traveled on the Pony Express, Fort Leavenworth, and Independence–St. Joe Roads to Fort Kearny, where they intersected the south-side route of the Platte River Road. Blythe later described the group's awkward efforts, during the early part of their trip, to learn to drive their ox team. He recalled, "Captain Lockwood was a good infantry officer, but he didn't know any more about driving oxen than the rest of us, which was nothing at all. All five of us walked beside the oxen and herded them along." That night they left the unbroken oxen in their yoke, tied to a tree.[4] After several days of struggling, the men and animals began getting along better.

About ten days out they overtook a freighting party going to Virginia City, Montana. D. F. Percival, his partner McArthur, and an unnamed black driver were in a wagon carrying nine thousand pounds of merchandise for their store in Virginia City. After some negotiating, Blythe's party agreed to take part of Percival's load in their wagon to Virginia City for twenty cents a pound. Percival also loaned them one of his three yokes of oxen, and from then on, two ox teams pulled each of the two heavily loaded wagons. Percival also let his black driver drive for them until they learned how to manage their two teams. The arrangement was satisfactory to both parties, and Blythe, overjoyed at the prospect of easy access to Percival's grocery supplies, wrote, "we had struck it rich."

From Fort Kearny they traveled up the south side of the Platte River, joining two more wagons bound for Montana after crossing the South Platte. The four wagons continued north and passed Fort Laramie two days after Davis Willson's party, which had crossed over from the north side of the Platte. From there they stayed behind Willson on the south-side route to Bridger's Ferry, crossing one day later than his party. Both Willson and Blythe turned onto the Bozeman Trail on July 20, but Willson's party traveled a few miles farther before camping and gradually pulled ahead over the next few days.

At Brown Springs Creek a freight train from Omaha caught up with Blythe's train. Four miles farther, at the Dry Fork of the Cheyenne, both

---

4. Lockley, *Columbia River Valley*, 298.

trains came up with a freight train belonging to the E. and B. Morse firm in Montana. Two men in the Morse train had been killed when Indians tried to stampede their herd. The next day the three trains stopped for noon at Humfreville Camp, on a branch of Stinking Water Creek. After the three trains had corralled separately and let the cattle loose to graze, a party of Indians attempted to stampede one of the herds. The freighters shot at and drove off the Indians, and the three trains hurriedly reformed into one large defensive corral. Then about a hundred Indians appeared menacingly on the hills, but the corral was too formidable to attack, so the Indians circled the enclosure but kept out of range of the emigrants' gunfire. In the evening the Indians left, going off in the direction where the next day they struck the Floyd and Barton trains.

From the Dry Fork Cheyenne River to Fort Reno, the three trains traveled together for safety. Andy Wharton was the captain of the combined train. At Sand Creek they found a note telling of the Indian attack on Davis Willson's train. Two days later they passed the grave of diarist Perry Burgess's uncle Mansel Cheney as they neared Fort Reno. They arrived at the fort on July 27, two days after Davis Willson. While at the fort, Blythe learned of the raids along the trail. A few days later his party joined the combined train of more than two hundred wagons and three hundred men (in which Davis Willson was also traveling), and they left for Fort Phil Kearny, arriving there August 5. They camped near the fort, met the soldiers, and reorganized the train, leaving two days later. They experienced no further Indian problems, although some hunters came across a party of Arapahos, and refusing to believe them when they said they were "good Arapahoe," the hunters fired at them and scared them away.

After they reached the Gallatin Valley, they heard that the mines were overrun with too many men, so Blythe, Henry Kline, and William Lockwood filed on three adjoining quarter-section homesteads on the Gallatin River. They built a cabin that they shared until the following spring. Blythe found a job cutting wheat, and he worked for a nearby rancher through the fall. During the winter the three men survived on game and odd jobs, and in March 1867, Blythe was the first to leave their ranch. He went to Virginia City and worked for a year as a typesetter for the *Virginia City Montana Post*, the leading paper in the territory. He returned to Eaton in spring 1868 to visit his mother, traveling by steamboat from Fort Benton.

Blythe returned to Montana in October 1868, this time traveling by railroad to the end of the line at Green River, Wyoming, and then by stagecoach. The next spring he went to California, where he worked on several newspapers. In 1870 he went to Portland, Oregon, to work on Ben Holladay's recently established *Portland (Oreg.) Bulletin*. He worked on the *Bulletin* for five years. On July 30, 1873, Blythe married Emma Jane Nation in Portland. In 1875 he and a number of other printers started the *Portland (Oreg.) Daily Bee*. After eleven months he sold his interest in the paper, and in 1877 he bought a farm on the Hood River.

Sam and Emma moved to their homestead—which they named Twin Oaks Farm—in March 1878. Living at Twin Oaks for the rest of their lives, they raised their two children, Edward N. and Clara, there. Blythe concentrated on farming at Twin Oaks for several years, but in 1894 he purchased the *Hood River (Oreg.) Glacier* and ran it for ten years. He continued farming until he retired, and then he and Emma lived on the homestead and leased the land. When Sam and Emma celebrated their fiftieth wedding anniversary on July 30, 1923, the *Portland (Oreg.) Oregonian* published photographs taken when they were married and contemporary ones in a highly complimentary article.[5] In both photographs, Blythe has a long, full beard.

Blythe's grandson George Finley Marlor had fond memories of his grandfather Sam, whom he said stood six feet tall. Blythe often amused his grandchildren with such acts as juggling or balancing a corn stalk on his nose. He also delighted them with stories about his past, reading to them at bedtime, and playing games with them. After a long and full life, Blythe died in May 1928 at the age of eighty-six.

The other men in Blythe's train also eventually left Montana. Henry Kline worked in the mines for a while, and then he went back to Eaton, married a local girl, and moved to Peru, Indiana, where he was a building contractor. He died in 1924. William Lockwood went to Arizona in late 1867, became a sheep rancher, and was killed by cattlemen while herding his sheep. Robert Denny stayed in the territory, mostly unemployed, until severe rheumatism forced him to return east, to Dayton, Ohio, where he died in the Soldiers' Home in the 1890s. Pliney Crume went back to his home in Indiana and died within a few years.

Blythe's diary is in the Manuscripts Department of the Oregon Historical Society in Portland. It is a small, leather-bound pocket diary. He wrote in pencil, sometimes neatly but occasionally erratically, as if he were rushed. Nevertheless, his handwriting is for the most part quite legible. Blythe also wrote a reminiscence in 1925 titled "Recollections of a Long Life." His grandson George Finley Marlor transcribed both the diary and

---

5. *Portland (Oreg.) Oregonian*, August 5, 1923.

the reminiscence in 1982, and he and his wife Thelma printed a compilation of Sam's diary, family letters, and his "Recollections of a Long Life," in *Saga of the Prairies*. They distributed copies to several libraries.

The portion of the diary included in this collection begins with Blythe's decision to travel to Montana with his acquaintances from Ohio and ends with his arrival in the Gallatin Valley. Only a few passages from his "Recollections of a Long Life" are included, since most of them add little to the diary. Those passages that are relevant are inserted in italics. William Lockwood kept a journal for part of the trip, ending it at the Bighorn River, and Marlor inserted it into the text of *Saga of the Prairies*. Most of Lockwood's diary entries also add little to Blythe's narrative, but where appropriate I have included them in footnotes.

Blythe's diary, like Davis Willson's, adds much to our understanding of what the trail experience was like for young single men traveling with close friends. It, too, reveals the exuberance of youth, the stress in uncertain and difficult times, and the bonding that often occurred during the overland journey. Not as long as Willson's diary, nor as filled with nonstop jocularity, Blythe's diary is nevertheless equally exciting, entertaining, and memorable.

SAMUEL FINLEY BLYTHE DIARY AND REMINISCENCE

DIARY OF SAMUEL F BLYTHE, EATON, O.[HIO],
COMMENCING APRIL 17, 1866.

6. All four men were acquaintances of Blythe from Ohio. William Lockwood and Robert Denny had served with him in Company E, Twenty-second Ohio Infantry Regiment; Henry Kline had served in the Seventy-fifth Ohio Infantry Regiment; and Pliney Crume had served in an Indiana regiment.

7. The party crossed the Missouri River on the steam ferry between St. Joseph, Missouri, and Elwood, Kansas, on the west bank.

8. In his reminiscence, Blythe wrote that the two young oxen had probably never been yoked up to work before. In other words, an unbroken team had been sold to them as "well broke." According to William Lockwood, they were named Buck and Bright. Blythe, *Saga of the Prairies*, 6.

9. Lockwood noted in his diary that evening that if anyone had come along and offered them three dollars apiece for the outfit, they would have sold out, since they all had "the blues" and just wanted to go home. Blythe, *Saga of the Prairies*, 7.

May 18.—Made up my mind to go with [William E.] Lockwood, [Henry] Kline, [Pliney] Crume & [Robert] Denny, to the mountains who are going with a team of their own.[6]

May 19—Quit work in the Union office [Daily Union Printing Office, St. Joseph, Missouri]. Our party had our team, rations and everything ready. We crossed the Big Muddy [Missouri River] about 4 P.M. and pitched our first camp on the Kansas side of the river.[7] About sundown, a storm came up, and for about two hours blew a regular hurricane. The thunder & lightening was terrific. We all piled into the wagon where we staid during the hardest part of the rain. Our wagon cover turned the water first rate. We took our first meal in the wagon, during the rain.

Sunday, May 20—Our first nights experience was pretty rough. Three of us slept inside the wagon and two on the outside. The subscriber reclined on the top of two barrels of hardtack. We got up with the sun, and after breakfast Lockwood and Crume went over to St. Joe after the mail. They returned about 11 1/2 o'clock, when we hitched up and started on our way intending to go seven miles to where we could get grass for our cattle. Our cattle are green and we had considerable trouble with them to keep them on the road.[8] We halted on Peter's creek, where we arrived about 3 o'clock, and went into camp for the night.[9] We had dinner and supper together. Four miles from the river we passed through the town of Wathena which seems to be quite a business little place. Our road

from the river, the first four miles lay over low bottom
land.—after passing the town [Wathena] the country was
hilly and the road quite rough.[10]

[In the] *morning we managed to get the oxen hooked
up to the wagon and started. We had proceeded but a
little way when we came to a high grade thrown up
across a ravine, probably a quarter of a mile* [in length].
*The oxen would try to turn to the right or left from the
trail and it required the constant vigilance of all five of us
to keep them on the trail. We negotiated that dangerous
piece of trail in safety, but when we got out on the open
prairie the oxen got a start of us, veered to the left and
ran about a half a mile from the trail before we could
round them up and get them back. This occurred several
times during the day.*

We went into camp on the prairie just as the night
was coming on and it commenced to rain. We had made
five miles that day towards our goal and had run
probably 25 miles in rounding up the oxen. As we turned
off the trail to go into camp, Kline and I were walking
behind the wagon. I remarked to Kline, "Well Henry,
how do you like it as far as you've got?" "Sam," he said,
while his countenance assumed a woe-be-gone
expression, "all I've got in this world is in this outfit. But
I have a great notion to turn back and make my way to
Eaton as best I can." "Nonsense," said I. "You want to
brace up, why, we've made 5 miles the first day out; and
now we have only 1495 further to go." Kline could see
no humor in my remark. All of the party were tired,
disgusted and homesick.

May 21—Left our camp about an hour after sunrise
and traveled about 4 miles, when we stopped to graze the
cattle, and take dinner. Denny was lucky enough to catch
a *big snapping* turtle, and we had some splendid soup
and dumplings made by Lockwood. Myself and Crume
went to the branch and caught a few fish. *I went to a*

10. From the ferry
landing at Elwood, the
road went west across
timbered bottomland to
Wathena, at the base of
the bluffs.

11. Daniel Francis Percival, known as Frank, married Blythe's sister Barbara Elizabeth in 1873.

12. The *Denver Daily Rocky Mountain News*, June 25, 1866, reported on Andy Wharton's train, which Blythe was traveling in: "June 15—Conductor Whorton, 26 ox wagons, 33 men, 32 revolvers, 6 guns; bound for Montana."

13. See 92 n. 12 for details of General Winfield Scott's death. The Fenian revolutionary movement for Irish independence was also a topic of much interest in summer 1866. In June a former Union army officer and eight hundred Fenians attempted an invasion of Canada from New York. They crossed the Niagara River and captured Fort Erie, opposite Buffalo. They were quickly cut off by U.S. troops and retreated, and seven hundred men were arrested.

14. Legh R. Freeman was the editor of the *Kearney (Nebr.) Herald*. At the end of May, Freeman turned the newspaper over to his brother Frederick and went to Fort Laramie to report on the Indian treaty council with the Sioux and Cheyennes. From there he traveled the Bozeman Trail to Montana with two wagons of goods. He set up a trading business on the Yellowstone River for a few months, first at Bozeman's ferry and then at Mill Creek. He left Montana Territory in spring 1867. Freeman later became widely known in the West as the editor of the *Frontier Index.*

ranch about two miles away and paid a woman my last 25 cents for a dozen eggs. We had a dinner fit for a king.

[*Blythe's party traveled west on the Pony Express Road to the Big Blue River at Marysville, Kansas.*]

May 30—Made 14 miles to=day.

Starting along in the afternoon we came to where a heavily laden wagon was stuck in a mud hole. The owners of the wagon were two men named D. F. Percival[11] *and* McArthur. They had 9,000 pounds of freight on their wagon, six yoke of cattle and a negro driver. We let them take our two yoke of cattle to hitch on to their team and the negro driver, who was a crackerjack at his profession, soon had the wagon free of the mud hole.

Mr. Percival then proposed to our party that we take about 2,000 pounds of his freight for which he would pay 20 cents a pound for it hauled to Bozeman, Montana, give us a yoke of cattle to put in our lead and the negro to drive for us until we learned how. We had struck it rich and accepted the proposition at once. The big freight wagon was loaded with tobacco, sugar, bacon flour, overalls, boots and shoes, etc. Things were coming our way. No more doing without tobacco and sugar while Percival's stores held out. By this time we had found these articles very necessary to make life worth living.

[*The next day, May 31, they crossed the Big Blue River at Marysville, Kansas. Ten miles northwest of Marysville they intersected the Independence Road, and from there they traveled on the combined Independence–St. Joe Road to Fort Kearny.*]

June 15.—We rolled out at 4 1/2 o'clock, made about 5 miles and camped for noon within three miles of Fort Kearney. In the afternoon we rolled on to Kearney City.[12] At the Fort we all got mail, & here we first learned of the death of General [Winfield] Scott, and also the Fenian War.[13] Kearney City is a small place of about 200 inhabitants. Most of the buildings are built of prairie sod, which is the case with most of the ranches along the road. Kearney City supports one newspaper [*Kearney (Nebr.) Herald*]—a small sheet—semi=weekly.[14] From St. Joe to Kearney—280 miles

June 16—This morning we fell in with a large train of 25 wagons which is going to Denver. We will go as far as Cottonwood Springs with them. One of their teams broke a tongue which delayed us about two hours, and we only made 10 miles

June 17.—We had an early start, and rolled 10 miles by 9 o'clock. This afternoon we had some fine sport with an antelope, which was seen not far from the road. About 15 of the men from the train got out their guns and each man fired from one to seven shots, but not one of them were able to hit it. The antelope seem quite tame, and wouldn't run but a short distance when shot at   We made 20 miles to=day

June 18.—20 miles to=day   Our road from Kearney follows along the south bank of the Platte. Platte Valley is from 10 to 25 miles wide   A large Mormon train of 150 wagons passed us to=day en route for the Missouri river for a load of pilgrims to [take back to] Salt Lake City.

June 19. 20 miles to=day.

June 20.—20 miles to=day and camped within 5 miles of Cottonwood Springs[15]

June 21—Soon after we started this morning we passed a prairie dog village, which was something new to most of us, it being the first we had seen on the road. We passed through Cottonwood and carrelled for noon about 3 miles from the place   Fort McPherson is the name of the Fort at Cottonwood[16]   We made about 18 miles to=day   Distance from Fort Kearney to Cottonwood 90 miles.

June 22—We made about 18 miles to=day and camped at Jack Morrow's Ranche[17]

June 23—We crossed O'Fallon's Bluffs,[18] and found

15. In the late 1850s Charles McDonald built a road ranch that later served as a Pony Express, mail, and stage station at Cottonwood Springs, on the east side of Cottonwood Creek, southeast of present Maxwell, Nebraska. In fall 1863 Fort Cottonwood (renamed Fort McPherson) was established a quarter mile west.

16. Fort Cottonwood was established in 1863 on the west side of the Cottonwood Creek crossing. The name of the post was changed to Fort McPherson in January 1866.

17. Jack Morrow's Ranch was one of the best-known road ranches on the Platte road. It was sometimes called Junction House or Junction Ranch because it was located just below the confluence of the North and South Platte rivers, about five miles southeast of present North Platte, Nebraska. Morrow's imposing house was two and a half stories and sixty feet long.

18. O'Fallon's Bluff is situated 130 miles west of Fort Kearny and three miles southeast of present Sutherland, Nebraska. The bluff was probably named for early Indian agent Benjamin O'Fallon or his equally prominent fur-trading brother John. O'Fallon's Bluff is a low sandstone ridge that comes down to the south bank of the South Platte River, forcing the road to swing to the left or south and detour over the bluff. O'Fallon's Bluffs (generally spelled as a plural) Pony Express and stage station and occasional military post was just east of the bluff, at the point where the upland detour began.

19. Blythe is expressing a typical emigrant impression of the Plains tribes that camped along the overland roads. These bands had become dependent on government handouts as well as begging from travelers, a direct consequence of American expansion.

20. The total population of the Northern Sioux tribes and their allies in the Powder River Basin in 1866 consisted of approximately eighteen thousand people. The actual number of warriors was approximately one-sixth of the population, or about three thousand.

21. The Sioux, Cheyennes, and Arapahos were often allied, but the alliances at any particular time were complex and depended on the circumstances.

22. The Brulés were camping near James Bordeaux's ranch, eight miles east of Fort Laramie, after their leaders had signed the Fort Laramie treaty on June 27.

23. This soldier could be any one of three Eleventh Ohio Cavalry privates named Chambers who were stationed at or near Fort Laramie in July 1866: George W. Chambers, Company E; Ezra B. Chambers, Company G; or John M. Chambers, Company I. *Official Roster of the Soldiers of . . . Ohio*, 11:561, 568, 574.

24. They camped near Register Cliff, ten miles west of Fort Laramie, on the River Road. From

the road pretty bad on account of the sand   We carrelled for noon near an Indian encampment of 55 lodges, of the Sioux tribe. Several of them visited our camp for the purpose of begging and to trade skins for something to eat. They were a poorly dressed, dirty looking set of people, and being the first savage ones that I had ever seen, they created rather a poor impression.[19] We passed close by their camp in the after=noon. This band belong[s] to the Great Sioux Nation which are said to number 18,000 warriors.[20] The Sioux, Arrapahoes, and Cheyennes are friends, and make war together on neighboring tribes and the whites.[21] 18 miles

[Blythe's party crossed the South Platte River at Julesburg and continued on the road to Fort Laramie. Blythe wrote about climbing to the top of Courthouse Rock, swimming in the North Platte River, and a particularly bad meal when their evening mush was tainted with alkali in the cows' milk.]

July 11—Camped within 8 miles of Fort Laramie. Passed several bands of Indians of the [Brulé] Sioux tribe[22]

July 12—Passed Fort Laramie 3 miles, where we lay over the rest of the day. Met with Chambers, of the 11th O.V.C. [Ohio Volunteer Cavalry][23]   Julesburg to Laramie 180 miles.

July 13.—Drove about 5 miles, and camped where we will leave the Platte River for the next 40 miles.[24]

July 14—Made 12 miles by ten o'clock, and camped for noon on Bitter Cottonwood Creek [Cottonwood Creek][25] where we found good water but no grass for our cattle. Our road to=day lay over the Black Hills. Most of it pretty rough[26]—some places quite sandy. At this place Kit Carson and a party of white men had a fight with a party of Indians in which 700 Indians were slain.[27] We found good springs here. In the afternoon we pulled out and made about 3 miles and camped near a good spring [Little Cottonwood Creek]. The grass was poor and we herded our cattle about a mile from camp. Just before sundown our herders discovered a couple of Indians lurking in a canyon near the herd. The herders immediately sent word to camp. We expected a raid on our cattle and made preparations to receive them. About 9 o'clock the Indians attacked the herders by shooting arrows at them The herders immediately returned the fire, and as soon as we heard their firing, ten men mounted horses and mules, rode out to the herd and drove them into the carrel, where we kept them all night We stationed guards and kept a good watch during the rest of the night but the Indians had left and made no further demonstrations Our cattle were all safe and no one hurt, but all pretty badly scared.

July 15—We turned our cattle out soon after daylight, and let them eat about 2 hours, and in the mountains we had breakfast. We then yoked up and made about 6 miles and camped for noon on the Platte.[28] Rolled out in the afternoon and rolled 4 miles to Twin Springs, where we camped for the night.[29]

July 16—Took an early start, and rolled 9 miles in the morning We crossed Horse Shoe Creek 3 miles from last nights camp Camped on the Platte. In the afternoon had 9 miles to go to the crossing [at Bridger's Ferry]. Started about 3 o'clock, made about 5 miles, when a heavy rain came on, & we had to carrel for the night.

July 17—Drove to the river—4 miles—& crossed all our teams by noon.[30] The ferry=boat was small and took but one wagon at a load This ferry is called Loaliente's [La Bonte's] Crossing, or Bridger's Ferry.[31] Paid $3.00 ferriage Pulled out about 3 o'clock and made 6 miles

July 18—This morning 7 horses and 2 mules were missing, which delayed us about 3 hours before they were found. Camped at the foot of Big Hill [McKinstry Ridge] this evening, 18 miles from the Ferry.

July 19—Two oxen died last night—one belonging to

here the trail left the river and went northwest over the hills before coming back to the North Platte a few miles from Bridger's Ferry.

25. Cottonwood Creek was often called Bitter Cottonwood Creek by the emigrants because of the groves of bitter cottonwood trees there.

26. They crossed the soft sandstone ridge south of present Guernsey, Wyoming, where thousands of iron wagon tires have worn deep grooves in the rock.

27. This is one of those completely unfounded stories that emigrants encountered along the trail. John C. Frémont chose Kit Carson to guide his western expeditions in the early 1840s, and popularized accounts of his exploits propelled him into national prominence. However, Carson had never been in an engagement along the Oregon-California Trail in which seven hundred Indians were killed. His last major campaign, which ended in 1864, was in New Mexico against the Apaches and Navajos. Carson retired and settled in southern Colorado in 1866.

28. They went east from the road and camped for their noon stop on the bank of the North Platte in the vicinity of Bulls Bend, a well-known emigrant campground in a bend of the river.

29. The Twin Springs, sometimes known as Red Springs, were five miles

[Frank] Percival and the other to [Andy] Wharton, Captain of the train. The general opinion is that they ate some poison weed, which caused their death   We crossed Big Hill [McKinstry Ridge]—11 miles across, and camped on the [North] Platte, where we lay over the rest of the day.[32]

July 20—Another ox, belonging to [Andy] Wharton, and a cow belonging to Boyle, died this morning from the effect of eating this poison weed   Three others were pretty sick, but by being doctored in time were saved. One of the oxen, January, was sick, and we dosed him with vinegar and lard and this evening he is all right again.[33] About 3 miles from camp we struck the "Cut Off" the new route to Virginia City [the Bozeman Trail] Here we leave the Platte and the Old California road, at the mouth of Sage Creek, which we traveled along for 16 miles. This creek is apparently dry, the water sinking in the sand & rising again at different places. Water can be found anywhere along its bed by digging a few inches beneath the surface. Grass is very poor along this creek. We made about 14 miles to=day

July 21—Rolled 5 miles to the last camp on Sage Creek, where we found pretty good grass. Here we laid over the rest of the day.[34] Two more oxen sick

July 22—Made an early start,—for we had 12 miles to go without water—to Brown's Spring. Got there at 12 o'clock & found water scarce, but camped. Two more cattle died at this place. An emigrant train camped along side of us [the Omaha train]. About 2 o'clock, a horseman came into camp and reported that the Indians had stampeded the cattle belonging to a train 4 miles ahead of us [the Montana train], on the Dry Fork of the Cheyenne River   We immediately yoked up & went ahead to the train, keeping a sharp lookout on the way. Arrived there we found 2 men killed, 2 oxen killed and several badly wounded, 3 of which died during the night. The Indians had left without taking any of the cattle. The

south of present Glendo, Wyoming. The springs were a favored emigrant camp-ground. Today the site of the springs is on private land. They have been plugged by the landowner and no longer exist.

30. Davis Willson's train crossed at Bridger's Ferry the day before. Willson diary, July 16, 1866.

31. An old ford known as La Bonte's Crossing was an alternate place to cross the North Platte River, a few miles upstream from Bridger's Ferry. Its exact location is not known today. The ferry operator at Bridger's Ferry was Benjamin B. Mills.

32. They camped at the popular emigrant camp-ground opposite the site of Fort Fetterman. Davis Willson was nearby in the same campground that night.

33. Administering vinegar and lard were standard emigrant treatments for alkali poisoning. Strong vinegar neutralized the alkali, while the lard was an anti-inflammatory agent. Whether the ox suffered from alkali or plant poisoning, the treatment evidently aided his recovery.

34. William Lockwood recorded in his diary that in the evening they were joined by two more trains, which they "named respectfully the Omaha train and the Montana train." Blythe, Saga of the Prairies, 25. The Montana train was probably the freight train

three trains formed one carrel, and herded our cattle altogether. We found water scarce, and had to ditch for it for our cattle. We found no water fit for cooking or drinking. The two men killed were buried by moonlight. The funeral services were conducted by a minister belonging to our train. The unfortunate men's names were Moore and Carr—both from Illinois.[35]

July 23.—Rolled 9 miles to Humfrevilles Camp, where we found the next water.[36]—Plenty of grass & water for our stock, but hardly fit for our own use. The three trains made separate carrels here. Soon after we watered the cattle and turned them out to graze a squad of Indians made a dash on one of the herds, but the herders were on the alert, and gave them a volley, which soon routed them. One of the Indians was seen to fall from his pony, and was helped on again by the others   They killed one ox and maimed several others, with their arrows.

We then formed the three trains into one carrel and the cattle in one herd, and stationed a strong guard around the cattle   Soon after the Indians reappeared in more force, over 100 of them, and circled around us on the hills, but they wouldn't venture within gunshot. They seen we were too well prepared for them. Towards evening they left us going back in the direction that we came, I think with the intention of attacking a train which is about one day behind us[37]   The three trains here organized into one, and the Capt of our train, Andy Wharton, was made Captain of the whole   Our train now numbers 63 wagons and 109 men

July 24—Drove about 5 miles and camped on what we took to be Wind Creek [Sand Creek], according to our table of distance[38]   We found water here, but it was not very plenty, grass good. We lay over the rest of the day. As the next drive is 20 miles without water. We found a notice stuck up here which told that a train had been attacked here on the 22[d][39]

carrying goods for E. and B. Morse, a Montana freighting firm.

35. The deceased men were L. C. Carr from Carlinville, Illinois, and George W. Moore from Georgetown, D.C.; *Denver Daily Rocky Mountain News*, August 21, 1866.

36. Their mileage indicates they were at a branch of Stinking Water Creek, a fork of the Cheyenne River.

37. The next day, July 24, Indians attacked a group of men who were separated from the train traveling behind Blythe's, between Brown Springs and the Dry Fork of the Cheyenne. Nathan Floyd, Charles Barton, and seven other men were killed. See note for Davis Willson diary, July 29, 1866.

38. They were probably at Sand Creek, about five miles south of Antelope Creek. Antelope Creek was then called Wind Creek.

39. Someone in Davis Willson's train, which was attacked here at their noon stop on July 22, left the note.

July 25—Had our water casks all filled and ready to make the 20 miles to=day. We rolled about 6 miles when we came to a creek [Antelope Creek] where we found water plentier than at what we took to be Wind Creek,[40] so we lay till noon and made over 6 miles in afternoon. To=day we got the first view of the Snowy Range of the Rocky Mountains [the Bighorn Mountains]   No sign of Indians to=day or yesterday   We made a dry camp to=night. Our two yoke of cattle fared better than others, as we hauled 20 gallons [of water] for their use

July 26—Rolled 14 miles and camped on Dry Creek [Dry Fork Powder River]. Water and grass poor and scarce, and the stock suffered a good deal   Sent three scouts ahead to look for water—found none   but [saw] plenty of fresh Indian signs. Had to ditch for water for the stock

July 27.—Started early as we had 17 miles to go without water, to Fort Reno on Powder River. Arrived on Powder River, opposite the fort, about 3 o'clock. Our road lay along the bed of Dry Creek [Dry Fork of the Powder]. The day was hot, hardly a breath of air stirring,—the dust and sand was heavy, and the cattle suffered severely. We seen the grave of a man [Mansel Cheney] that was killed by Indians on the 22[d]   At Reno we learned that there had been a general attack all along the road on the 22[d]   A train that came in ahead of us lost 2 men and [had] one badly wounded.[41] A squad of 20 soldiers, on their way to New Fort Reno [Fort Phil Kearny], were attacked on Crazy Woman's Fork, and one Lieutenant and one private killed.[42] French Joe [French Pete], an Indian trader, who was on the road up near New Fort Reno [Fort Phil Kearny], was attacked, and himself and four others killed.[43] He had been a trader among the Indians for the last 40 years. Each of the white men had Squaws. They didn't kill the Squaws, but told them they had commenced a war of

40. They were on today's Antelope Creek, near the site of the ambush attempts on Davis Willson's train on July 23 and 24.

41. This was Perry Burgess's train. Doyle, *Journeys to the Land of Gold*, 2:563–64.

42. Lieutenant Napoleon Daniels and Corporal Terrence Callery, Eighteenth Infantry, were killed on July 20 at Crazy Woman Creek.

43. Peter Cazeau, known as French Pete, his partner Henry Arrison, and their three employees were killed July 17 on Prairie Dog Creek, six miles north of Fort Phil Kearny.

extermination, and that all the whites on the road had to die. They also attacked the fort here, and stampeded a lot of stock. Our train will lay over here a few days to rest our stock, reset tires and prepare ourselves for a march of 300 miles to Virginia City. 165 miles from Fort Laramie to Fort Reno.

July 28.—A squad of 14 Indians made a dash on a herd of cattle on the other side of the river, and stampeded 12 head. They were followed by 20 Cavalrymen from the fort, and the cattle retaken, without anyone hurt. Wrote home

July 29—A government train of 56 wagons, on their way to New Fort Reno [Fort Phil Kearny], came in to=day. They brought the news that an emigrant and freight train had been attacked at Brown's Spring. Their captain [Nathan Floyd] had rode ahead of the train to look for water, when he was shot by the red skins. Hearing the firing at the train, 13 men armed themselves with Spencer rifles, and went to his assistance. They were seen surrounded by Indians, 8 of them killed & the other five got back to camp more or less wounded. The next day this government train came up, when 45 men went back out to get the dead. They found the Captain (Floyd, from Leavenworth) with his head cut off, and his body stuck full of arrows. The other 8 men were also found with their bodies stuck full of arrows. Only one man was scalped They found a wounded Indian who begged for his life, but one of the men killed him by putting a bullet through his head[44]

This afternoon the emigrant train [Barton's and Floyd's trains] came in, who reported Harner's [Horner's] train, camped on Dry Creek, & that they will be in in the morning. This emigrant train lost 5 men, and three of them belonged to one wagon. I was on herd to=day, & carrel guard at night. Soon after dark it commenced raining, and by 9 o'clock a severe thunder storm prevailed.

44. Davis Willson describes the engagement that took place between Brown Springs and the Dry Fork Cheyenne River on July 24 in detail on July 29. Thomas Creigh noted the graves of the four victims on August 16 when he passed by them.

The rain came down in torrents, while the vivid flashes of
lightning, and the rapid peals of thunder which
immediately followed, were both grand and terrible
While the storm was raging its fiercest, our herders were
attacked by the Indians   The herd was a short distance
from camp, and as soon as the alarm was given, a party of
men went to reinforce the herders, but the Indians had
left, and no one hurt. Six mounted Indians, and about that
many on foot were seen by the herders.

As the party was returning to camp from the herd, a
dog belonging to one of the wagons, sprang out &
attacked one of the men. The man drew his revolver, and
shot the dog—wounding him. The owner of the dog
became pretty wrathy, and wanted to shoot the man that
shot his dog. Soon the muss became general—some sided
with the owner and others with the man that done the
shooting, and for a while all thoughts of danger from
Indians were banished, and there bid fair to be a general
<u>dog fight</u> among ourselves. Finally the Captain of the
train gave orders for every man to go to his quarters and
the crowd was dispersed

July 30—Harner's [E. R. Horner's] train came in this
morning   A man by the name of [John] Sloss, who was
wounded by the Indians on the 22^d, and who belonged
to the ox train that came in here a few days before us,
died in the hospital at the fort to=day. He owned two
teams, and he left them in charge of his hired hand. We
leave here to=morrow   It is 23 miles to the next water, in
Crazy Woman's Fork.

July 31—All the trains at the fort, eight in number,
organized to form different trains, and Captain ———
[Charlie Rich], Captain of one of the mule trains, was
appointed to command the whole.[45] We were yoked up and
ready to start at 10 o'clock, when it was found that the river
had been swollen so by the late rains, that it was too high to
ford. We then unyoked, and remained in our old camp

45. Davis Willson, in one
of these trains, recorded
that Charlie Rich was
appointed captain of the
whole train. Willson diary,
July 31, 1866.

Another Indian scare in the afternoon. 16 Indians seen.

August 1, 1866.—Made another start to=day, and this time succeeded in crossing the river. Our whole train now numbered 210 wagons and over 300 men.[46] We started at 1 o'clock, and made 10 miles by sundown. The whole train formed in four carrels, all joining each other. The cattle suffered considerable on account of water, as the Powder River water was so thick with mud that the cattle would not drink.

Aug 2—We arrived on Crazy Woman's Fork at 1 1/2 o'clock, and it was after 5 before we got into carrel on the north bank of the river The train advanced cautiously to=day, as we expected an Indian attack. We had out an advance guard, a rear guard, and flankers on each side of the train Four of us on foot, and three others on horseback formed the rear guard The day was hot, the road dusty, and the cattle suffered extremely When we arrived on Crazy Woman's Fork, we found a government train camped there guarded by a company of soldiers. They are on their way from the new fort [Fort Phil Kearny] to [Fort] Reno. 20 miles to the next water—Clear Creek

Aug 3.—Started at 10 o'clock, and rolled 8 miles. Made a dry camp. This afternoon was cool, and about sundown commenced raining.

Aug 4—Started at 6 o'clock, and rolled to Rock Creek [Clear Creek] by 1 P.M. a distance of 17 miles. Rock Creek [Clear Creek] is a fine stream, clear as crystal, and rapid current. Here our cattle got plenty of good water and grass. We are on the northeast side, near the foot of Big Horn Mountain, whose snowy summit looks to be not more than 5 miles off.[47]

Aug 5—Made an early start, and camped near Smiths Lake [Lake De Smet] at noon,—a distance of 10 miles. About 2 miles from camp we crossed another fine mountain stream [Rock Creek] which is about half the

46. William Lockwood listed the trains that had combined in the order they traveled: "'Milk and Honey' train which was ours, in front, [followed by] 'Montana,' 'Horners,' 'Emigrant,' 'Mule,' 'Omaha,' and 'Government.'" Blythe, *Saga of the Prairies*, 31.

47. The peak is probably Cloud Peak, which was twenty-five miles directly west. Countless diarists were deceived by the phenomenon of atmospheric deception. The clarity of the High Plains atmosphere, combined with a lack of intervening objects between the observer and distant objects to aid perspective, had the effect of magnification at horizon distance. This phenomenon often affected visitors to landmarks along the Platte, such as Chimney Rock—who learned that what appeared to be two miles was actually ten— as well as hunters who routinely missed their targets.

48. In the twentieth
century dams and water
diverted into it changed
Lake De Smet into a
larger freshwater lake.

size of what we took to be Rock Creek. So I think this
last creek must be Rock, and the other Clear Creek. The
water of Smith's Lake [Lake De Smet] is clear and nice
looking, but it is salty, and not fit for [the] stock.[48] This
afternoon we drove about 2 miles to within 3 miles of
Fort Phil Kearney, where we carrelled on a small stream
[Shell Creek]. Plenty of grass. Fort Phil Kearney is a new
established fort, and is the headquarters of the 18th. U.S.
Infantry   We will lay over here to=morrow

Aug 6—Our train reorganized and Captain Harner
[Horner] was put in command. The Government train,
56 wagons, leave us here, and they will start for the States
in a few days. Several parties of hunters went out from
our camp, and two antelope and lots of small game were
brought in. I was on herd to=day

Aug 7.—Made an early start and rolled 8 miles by 5
P.M. This day's drive was decidedly the roughest we have
had since leaving the Missouri River. We crossed Piney
River, near the fort, which is a rapid stream and cold as
ice. The bed of the river is covered with big, round
boulders, which were hard on the wagons. The next 5
miles of road was up and down high hills, or rather
mountains [Lodge Trail Ridge]. On these hills 7 wagons
were broken down. We camped on Reno Creek [Prairie
Dog Creek], the same spot where French Pete [Pete
Cazeau] and his four men were murdered by the Indians.
Their graves were there, but the wolves had partly dug
up and eaten their bodies.

Aug 8—By 11 o'clock the broken wagons were all
repaired, and we rolled out. Several soldiers and a
mountain guide [James Brannan], who are going with us
as far as Big Horn River rode ahead, and when about 4
miles from camp they returned with the information that
there were Indians ahead, and that they expected an
attack. At first it was thought best to carrel, but after a
consultation held by the different Captains, they decided

to go on two miles further, where, the guide [James Brannan] reported, there was a good camping ground.

When we arrived at the camp about 30 Indians were seen on a high hill with a white flag waving   Our guide made a sign, which they understood, for them to come in. Soon three of them were seen coming down the hill, when our guide and three others started out to meet them. When they got within speaking distance they reported themselves to be Arrapahoes. The three Indians then laid down their arms, unstrung their bows, and came up to our men to have a talk and smoke with them. They reported that there was sixty lodges of them 4 miles back from the road, and that they were on their way to the fort [Fort Laramie] to make a treaty of peace—that the Sioux and Cheyennes had gone south to make war on the South Platte.[49] The guide knew one of the Indians and has been acquainted with him for the last five years. He says he is one of the meanest men on the road. The guide was instructed by the Captain to notify the Indians that they wouldn't be allowed to come near our camp. They soon after left and all disappeared over the hill. The Captain had hard work to restrain some of the men of the train from firing on the Indians when they rode up. All sensible men ascertained the Captain, and were in favor of finding out first whether they were hostile. Crume to=day found a needle book, containing a gold pen, 25 c[en]ts in currency, and a lot of Indian beads and jewelry.

Aug 9—Rolled 7 miles and camped on Goose Creek. A good many buffalo were seen just before going into camp, and about 15 mounted men and a good many on foot, went out hunting   The mounted men brought in one buffalo. Five of the mounted party and two that were on foot, run across about a dozen Indians. The Indians rode up to our men and said "good Arraphoe" but our men thought that was about "played out," and they fired on the Indians   One Indian fell from his

49. The Northern Arapahos did not go to Fort Laramie that summer, and the Sioux and Cheyennes were camped not far away on the Tongue River.

saddle, but jumped and ran on foot. Our men returned to camp, the Indians following. Crume was with the party on foot

Aug 10—Rolled 17 miles to Tongue River   Roads hilly—grass and water good and plenty. Crossed the Montana [Territory] line.⁵⁰

50. At the Tongue River they were still about twelve miles from the Montana line.

Aug 11.—The emigrants of our train pulled out with a train that came up with us yesterday. Made 11 miles this forenoon, and camped on a small mountain stream [Twin Creek]. This afternoon rolled 5 miles & camped on Fork Little Horn [Pass Creek]   To=day 6 buffalo were killed by our train, and we had plenty of fresh meat.

Aug 12—Rolled 6 miles, and camped on Trout Creek [Little Bighorn River] for noon. This is a large mountain stream, and full of fish   This afternoon we rolled 10 miles to Little Horn River [Lodge Grass Creek]. A good many herds of buffalo were seen to=day.

Aug 13—Camped on North Fork Little Horn [Rotten Grass Creek]. Broke a wagon, and lay over here the rest of the day. I am on herd   Met a government train from Big Horn River. They report a good prospect for gold near Big Horn. The grass and water, ever since we left Reno, has been good, and plenty of it   Buffalo and all kinds of game in abundance.

Aug 14—This morning the different trains all tried to be the first to pull out, so as to be the first at the ferry. All the trains were in motion by sun rise, and our train was next to the last one to get started. We rolled 10 miles by noon, & camped again on Mud Creek [Soap Creek], which is a fine stream and deserves a better name. In the afternoon we rolled about 7 miles & camped again on Mud Creek [Soap Creek].

Aug 15—Rolled about 4 miles and carrelled on Big Horn river, 5 miles below the ferry, where we lay in camp all day. The river is too high to ford at present, and a mule train which has been carrelled here for the last two weeks[51] have built a boat and were charging $10 per wagon ferriage.

Our lead oxen has gone entirely blind in the last 24 hours,—and one of our wheelers blind in one eye. It seems to be a disease which is spreading among our herd.

Two companies of regulars [Eighteenth Infantry] arrived here on the 12th from Phil Kearney and they set the price [for the ferry] at $5 per wagon.[52] 50 wagons can be crossed in one day. The train that has been carreled here lost their mules by the Indians, and they are now awaiting the arrival of mules from Virginia City, which they sent for. Plenty of fish in the Big Horn, and we had a fine mess this evening. Several old miners in our train done some prospecting to=day, and found the "color," but not in sufficient quantities to pay.

Aug 16.—One train made a "<u>flank movement</u>" on the others, and were the first to the ferry. We yoked up at 12 o'clock and let the cattle stand in the yoke until the train close to us commenced to drive in their stock, when all we had to do was take on our cattle and pull out. Our train got over all safe by 4 P.M. We all worked beautifully and put in a hard day's work.

Aug 17.—Rolled out about 9 o'clock and made 9 miles to the first creek [Muddy Creek], where we ~~watered and~~ came up with the emigrant train encamped. We stopped long enough to get our dinner when we rolled 6 miles further and camped on a creek [East Buster Creek] with the emigrant train. The roads were very rough to=day and it was dark when we got into carrel. A mule train came up with us.

Aug 18—We only made about 5 miles to=day on account of the bad roads The road we are now on is a new cut off from the old road,[53] and ours is the second outfit that has traveled it We came up with Kirkendal's [Hugh Kirkendall's] train to=day which left Big Horn three days before us.

51. These were the ten teamsters on the west side of the river guarding the Cyrenius Beers freight train that was stranded after most of their mules were taken by Indians on July 18 and 19. Davis Willson also mentioned the stranded train. Davis diary, August 13, 1866.

52. After Fort C. F. Smith was established August 12 near the ferry, the post sutler, A. C. Leighton, took over the ferry. Leighton may have been conforming to military regulations concerning its operation.

53. They were traveling on James Sawyers's cutoff from the Bighorn River directly west to Clarks Fork that he opened at the beginning of August. This route was "new" in contrast to the earlier Bozeman route that all trains before Sawyers had taken.

Aug 19.—Rolled 6 miles before noon and in the afternoon made 15 miles, and camped by a fine Sulpher Spring [Ice Water Spring]. Passed through Pryor's Gap [Devil's Gap].[54]

Aug 20—Started about 12 o'clock and made 6 miles. Crossed Pryor River.[55]

Aug. 21—This forenoon rolled 12 miles and camped for noon on Clarke's Fork [Clarks Fork] of the Yellowstone. Andy Wharton, Captain of our train, killed a fine buffalo heifer. Buffalo, deer, and antelope are quite numerous   We saw two large herds of buffalo to=day. This afternoon we made about 7 miles, and camped on Cross Creek [Rock Creek].

Aug 22—We traveled up Rocky Fork [Red Lodge Creek] about 10 miles [and] camped for noon   This afternoon rolled about 6 miles   when one of our wagons upset and broke a wheel. Camped on Rocky Fork [Red Lodge Creek]. I am on herd

Aug 23—Rolled 10 miles by noon—camped near a fine spring. Pericval & McArthur's wagon broke down. They bought a wagon of Wharton and abandoned theirs. This afternoon we rolled about 5 miles & camped on Big Rose Bud Creek [East Rosebud Creek]. One of Wharton's wagons broke down while coming down a steep hill.[56] The roads to=day have been quite rough

Aug 24—Lay in camp all day repairing wagons Lockwood, Crume and I went fishing and caught a mess of trout.

In our big train we had vehicles drawn by horses, mule trains and ox trains. Horses and mules couldn't eat grass as fast as the cattle and didn't get enough to eat, so we had to lay over a day occasionally to allow them to catch up. When we went into camp quite a tent city would spring up. In an emigrant train from the state of Iowa, the women were all dressed in bloomers.[57]

54. They nooned at East Pryor Creek, passed through Devil's Gap, and camped in the evening at Ice Water Spring, two miles east of the Pryor Creek crossing.

55. They crossed Pryor Creek two miles from their previous camp and probably camped on Macheta Creek in the evening.

56. This was the steep descent to Rosebud Valley. Davis Willson graphically described descending the hillside. Willson diary, August 23, 1866.

57. The Bloomer costume, or Bloomers, were a knee-length skirt worn over long loose trousers that were gathered at the ankles. Elizabeth Smith Miller introduced the style in 1850 and popularized by Amelia Jenks Bloomer, editor of the feminist magazine *The Lily*. Bloomers declined in popularity in the late 1850s but had a revival in the mid-1860s.

Aug 25—Took an early start and followed after Kirkendal[l]'s train, which [Jim] Bridger is piloting around the bad roads. Bridger has been along with Kirkendal[l] since he left Big Horn River. Our train has been traveling with them, and as Bridger is an old mountaineer well acquainted with the country, he has furnished us with a good deal of useful information. We kept on down the valley of the Rosebud about 5 miles and found a ford just above the junction of the two Rose Buds [Rosebud Creek and Stillwater River].[58] The stream was very rocky and swift and quite dangerous to cross, but we all got over safe. We then traveled up the right bank [south side] of North Rose Bud [Stillwater River] and crossed it about 7 miles above its junction with the other [Rosebud Creek].[59] This stream is as large, if not larger, than the other, but we had no difficulty in crossing it. We camped on the north bank [of Stillwater River] about 1 o'clock. Made about 11 miles and forded two large creeks [Rosebud Creek and Stillwater River] which should be called rivers. By coming this route we escaped several large hills which are on the main road.[60] This afternoon we made about 8 miles and rolled long after dark before we encamped. 19 miles to=day

Our trail followed the south bank of the Rose Bud [Stillwater River]. The water was so clear and inviting that I was anxious to take a swim in the river. So one morning I started ahead of the train to have my swim before the train rolled along. I was overtaken by Jim Bridger riding his mule. Bridger being a government scout it was his duty to go in advance of the train and look out for Indians and Indian signs. He always rode a mule and was armed to the teeth. He called to me and asked where I was going. I told him I was going to take a swim in the Rose Bud. "You want to be mighty careful, young fellow," he said. "Ingins are mighty unsartin, you don't know when one of the red rascals might be hiding

58. Guided by Jim Bridger, the trains took a new route in this area. They went down the east side of East Rosebud Creek, past the junction with West Rosebud Creek, and continued down the east side of Rosebud Creek. They crossed Rosebud Creek above the junction with the Stillwater River, just north of present Absarokee, Montana, then went up the south side of the Stillwater River seven miles.

59. They crossed the Stillwater River at the established emigrant ford seven miles above its mouth.

60. This new route avoided the treacherous Sandborn Hill.

behind a bush and pop you over. Better stay close to the train." I didn't take his advice. I was bent on having a swim. I stripped and plunged into the stream. The water was fearfully cold. All at once Jim Bridger's advice impressed me as being sound. I hurridly put on my clothing and got back to the train.

Aug 26.—This morning Lockwood, Crume, Johnson and myself went ahead of the train to fish in the Yellowstone, which we thought was about 6 miles ahead, but we found it to be along 12 before we got there. We stopped a couple of hours on a small stream before we got to the river and it was about one hour before sun set when we got there. We fished about three quarters of an hour, and caught 20 fish, which would weigh about 25 pounds By that time the train came along and we went on to camp. We camped near the graves of three men that were killed here on the 24th inst.[ant] [this month] by Indians. They had been traveling alone with one wagon, and had no arms. [William] Thomas, the man that owned the team was a religious man and said he put his trust in the Lord, and didn't think he needed any arms. His son and a hired man were the other two. Thomas had 14 arrows put through him. He had $3,000 in greenbacks which was taken   A party which came along the next day found these men and buried them.

Aug 27.—Traveled up the Yellowstone Made 21 miles & camped within 6 miles of the ferry. Forded La Grasse, or Boulder River, the roughest stream we have crossed

Aug 28—Rolled to the ferry [Bozeman's ferry], where we found several trains waiting their turn to cross This is a safe ferry, and they had been charging as high as $10, in gold, per wagon, but the river is falling and they now charge $4 in greenbacks. The rope broke this afternoon, and they were not able to fix it to=day. Lockwood was on the boat when the rope broke, and will have to stay on the other side to=night.

Aug 29—The several trains laying on the east side of the river concluded to ford the river, as it has fallen 6 inches in the last 24 hours. About 250 wagons forded to=day and all got over safe with the exception of one wagon belonging to Tootle & Leach   The cattle became unmanageable, the wagon was upset and one yoke of oxen were drowned

Aug 30—Left the Yellowstone, crossed a high ridge and came back on the Yellowstone 16 miles from the ferry   It commenced to rain soon after we camped and kept it up all afternoon and the biggest part of the night. Turned cold during the evening and we could see it snowing on the mountains above us   McArthur & Percival broke their wagon. Bought a pair of boots of McA[rthur] & Percival

Aug 31—To=day was quite cool and overcast, were warm all day with comfort   We rolled about 6 miles this forenoon over a rough road. Crossed Sheals [Shields] River & camped on the Yellowstone. Made about 8 miles this afternoon. Lockwood shot a Jack Rabbit and we had rabbit pot pie for supper. We have had all the fish we could eat since we came to the Yellowstone. 14 miles to=day

Sept 1—More snow fell on the mountains during last night. To=day was cooler than yesterday. We left the Yellowstone to=day & traveled up a small stream [Billman Creek] about 10 miles by noon   This afternoon crossed the dividing ridge [Bozeman Pass] between Yellowstone and the Gallatin   The roads were rough. Day cool. About 17 miles to=day

Sept 2.—We made about 10 miles to=day, and arrived in Gallatin Valley   We are now within the sounds of civilization once more   Went into camp at Bozeman Town, a trading post at the junction of the Helena and Virginia City roads—115 miles to Helena, and 70 miles to Virginia. We hear all kinds of discouraging reports from Virginia, Helena and the mines. The country is said to be overrun with men out of employment. We think our best show now is to locate in this valley, take up a ranch and go to farming. The farmers are all busy harvesting their wheat, which is a sure crop in this valley. One man, this fall, raised 117 bushels of fall wheat on two acres of ground. This valley is pretty well settled, mostly along the streams. There is a good deal of vacant land yet to be taken up.

Thomas Alfred Creigh

DIARY, 1866

THOMAS ALFRED CREIGH was in one of the last trains to travel over the Bozeman Trail in 1866. Because he was a professional freighter, his experience differed significantly from those of the previous travelers. Creigh was in charge of one of two divisions of a freight train carrying a quartz mill to the mines in Montana.[1] As division supervisor he had the considerable responsibilities of overseeing the transportation of the machinery as well as managing the teamsters. This was no easy task in that hectic post-war season. Consequently, his diary goes beyond recording the traveling experience and often delves into personnel and other business matters.

Creigh's train also differed from the other freight trains traveling over the Bozeman Trail in 1866. The other freighters transported relatively portable supplies and equipment to the mining camps, but his ox train was loaded with eighty-one tons of heavy mining machinery that could have been more easily transported by steamboat. In the same season that Creigh brought the quartz mill over the riskiest overland route, thirty-one steamers reached Fort Benton and unloaded 4,441 tons of freight. A year later, in September 1867, the weekly *Helena (Mont.) Herald* reported that there were thirty-two quartz mills in the territory.[2] Most of these undoubtedly came by steamboat.

SOURCE DOCUMENT: Thomas Alfred Creigh, "From Nebraska City to Montana, 1866: The Diary of Thomas Alfred Creigh," ed. James C. Olson, *Nebraska History*, 29 (September 1948), 208–37.

1. The quartz mill that Creigh transported was extremely unusual. Virtually all the other known mills in the Montana mines were stamp mills. This mill was a Chili or Chilian roller mill, which crushed gold-bearing ore much finer than a stamp mill did. Two large iron wheels (rollers) ground and crushed the ore in huge pans. The resulting pulp was amalgamated in revolving amalgamating barrels, rather than in the amalgamating pans used by stamp mills.

2. Henry Pickering Walker, *The Wagonmasters: High Plains Freighting from the Earliest Days of the Santa Fe Trail to 1880* (Norman: University of Oklahoma Press, 1966), 212–13.

Union City, Montana Territory. Thomas Creigh's freight train brought the machinery for the Christenot Mill, the large building, center left.

PENCIL SKETCH BY A. E. MATHEWS, 1868. MONTANA HISTORICAL SOCIETY MUSEUM, HELENA

Since Creigh was traveling late in the season, the rivers were often low enough to ford more easily. The only Indian difficulties his train experienced were annoyingly frequent and sometimes successful attempts to capture their stock. Nevertheless his train did encounter problems, most of which resulted from the heavy machinery loaded on several wagons. The mill pans and boilers caused the most problems.[3] They were constantly falling off wagons or causing them to tip over, making it extremely difficult to negotiate the roads with the heavily loaded wagons.

Thomas Alfred Creigh was born at Mercersburg, Franklin County, Pennsylvania, on October 6, 1840. He was the son of Thomas, a minister, and Jane M. Creigh.[4] He was the fourth of six children: John, James,

---

3. The pans were large iron saucers in which the rollers crushed the ore. The four pans, which were five feet in diameter and eighteen inches high, made a clumsy load. The boilers, used to generate the steam to operate the mill, were also extremely top-heavy to transport.

4. Pastor of the Presbyterian Church in Mercersburg, Reverend Thomas Creigh, D.D., kept a diary throughout his adult life. Thomas's diary keeping followed his father's example. Excerpts from Reverend Creigh's wartime diary, 1862–65, in which he mentions his son Thomas's activities, are available on the Internet. See J. D. Edmiston Turner "Civil War

Joseph, Thomas, Eleanor, and Jennie.[5] He attended Franklin and Marshall College and clerked in a drugstore prior to 1862. When President Abraham Lincoln issued a call for men to enlist in the Union Army for nine months, Creigh helped recruit a regiment in Mercersburg and was mustered into the 126th Pennsylvania Infantry in August 1862. He served until June 1863, participating in the battles at Fredericksburg and Chancellorsville.

Following his discharge Creigh went to Omaha, then the capital of Nebraska Territory, where he was employed as a clerk in the commissary department of the Union Army until the end of the war. His chief duty was to assist the Pawnee Indian agent and take a census of the Pawnee Indian tribe at the Pawnee agency near Genoa, Nebraska.[6]

Creigh returned to Pennsylvania in summer 1865 and began working as managing clerk for the Montana Gold and Silver Mining Company that had been formed by some of his acquaintances and neighbors. The company had prospects and mining claims in Montana, and he was assigned to supervise part of the wagon train that was to take milling machinery to the company's mines. The heavy machinery and special wagons with wide iron tires were transported down the Ohio River by steamboat to St. Louis and from there to Nebraska City, Nebraska Territory.[7]

Creigh traveled by railroad to St. Joseph, Missouri, and by steamboat to Nebraska City, where he met the others in his traveling party who had come with the machinery on the steamboat *Nile*. There they loaded the machinery onto wagons and formed the train. The mining company's representative, B. F. Christenot, traveled separately and arrived in Virginia City in mid-summer 1866, well ahead of the train.[8] The

---

Days in Mercersburg as Related in the Diary of Rev. Thomas Creigh" (paper read before the Kittochtinny Historical Society, Feb. 29, 1940, Chambersburg, Pennsylvania), http://valley.vcdh.virginia.edu/KHS/creigh.html (accessed November 19, 2003).

5. The family is listed in the 1860 Pennsylvania census, Franklin County, Mercersburg.

6. In 1865, 2,800 Pawnees were enumerated on the agency's annuity roll. George E. Hyde, *The Pawnee Indians* (1951; repr., Norman: University of Oklahoma Press, 1974), 365.

7. Biographical information is from a family publication, Thomas C. Creigh, ed. and comp., *Hitting the Trail: 200 Years of the Creigh Family, from the Old Tin Box* (Highland Park, Ill., 1946), 41–72, copy at Nebraska State Historical Society, Lincoln; and William E. Lass, *From the Missouri to the Great Salt Lake: An Account of Overland Freighting* (Lincoln: Nebraska State Historical Society, 1972), 228.

8. Benjamin Frederick Christenot, generally known as B. F. or Frank, was the mill's founder. He was thirty-six in 1866. Although he was married, he traveled alone to Montana. His wife Janie M. is recorded in legal documents in April 1866, but no further record of her is known. His marriage to Janie must have ended sometime in 1866 or 1867 as Christenot married Azubah Smith, a single woman traveling in Creigh's train, in Montana in 1867.

party in the train also included B. F. Christenot's parents Frederick and Margaret; his brother Charles Frederick, thirty-two; Charles's wife Martha, twenty; and Martha's daughter by a previous marriage, Alice Wilton, three.[9] Creigh recorded that two single women, Miss Christenot and Miss Smith, were in the party. One of the larger trains in the 1866 season, the Christenot train consisted of fifty-two wagons pulled by 235 yoke of oxen. The wagon master was Joe Richards. The train was organized into two divisions that Creigh called "wings." In addition to his clerical duties, Creigh was in charge of the second division.

Creigh's second wing of the Christenot train left Nebraska City on June 23. Unlike diarist Perry Burgess whose train went over the older, longer Oxbow Trail, Creigh's train took the more direct Nebraska City Cutoff to Fort Kearny preferred by freighters in the 1860s.[10] The Nebraska City Cutoff was opened in spring 1860 at the instigation of Alexander Majors of the predominant freighting firm Russell, Majors and Waddell. Majors hired the Nebraska City city engineer August F. Harvey to survey and mark a direct route to Fort Kearny. From Nebraska City to Olathe (later known as Saltillo) on Salt Creek, Harvey followed an established local trail. Beyond Salt Creek, the cutoff was marked by a single furrow made by a mule-drawn breaking plow that followed behind his surveyors. Wagons coming along soon afterward straddled the furrow, and by the end of the travel season, the road was clearly defined. The resulting cutoff saved about twenty miles over the older Oxbow Trail and was a better road for wagons. Through 1866 it was heavily used by freighters from Nebraska City, but then as the Union Pacific Railroad progessed west from Omaha, the cutoff's use declined rapidly.

The Nebraska City Cutoff was also popularly known as the Steam Wagon Road. In 1862 prominent Minnesotan and former fur trader, Indian agent, and politician, "General" Joseph R. Brown, brought his "steam wagon" by steamboat to Nebraska City. Brown planned to use the wood-burning, steam-powered engine to pull freight wagons across the treeless plains to Denver. The steam wagon started west from Nebraska City on July 12, 1862, pulling a string of freight wagons. Seven or eight miles out of town, it broke down, and Brown abandoned it. In 1866 his associates tried unsuccessfully to repair it and

---

9. Extensive material on mining machinery, the Montana Gold and Silver Mining Company, the Christenot mill, and the Christenot family was provided by Nick Shrauger, Bozeman, Montana, great-great-grandson of Charles F. Christenot.

10. Sources for the route of the Nebraska City Cutoff are Lass, *From the Missouri*; and Stanley B. Kimball, *Discovering Mormon Trails: New York to California, 1831–1868* (Salt Lake City: Deseret Book Co., 1979).

then hauled it back three miles, where it stood for many years. Eventually it was taken to an iron works and dismantled. Although it failed in its purpose, the spectacular steam wagon was the first self-propelled vehicle used west of the Missouri River.

From Fort Kearny, the Christenot train continued on the south-side Platte road, crossing the South Platte at Julesburg. They crossed the divide to the North Platte River and arrived at Fort Laramie on August 3. They joined another train at the fort, and after they were inspected, they were allowed to go on. They probably forded the North Platte River at Bridger's Ferry, although Creigh did not record where they crossed. When they reached the turnoff at the mouth of Sage Creek, Creigh's train was one of the last of the season to turn onto the Bozeman Trail. The train passed the three Bozeman Trail forts with little notice. In contrast to the earlier trains, the army barely paid attention to them. They were like other emigrant trains, however, in that—when they came to the buffalo herds in the Tongue River valley—the men could not resist hunting. But they spent less time at it than the emigrants, and they killed only one buffalo. Similarly, while the wagons were being taken across on the Bighorn ferry, Creigh prospected for gold and was pleased to find "some good signs." They continued moving steadily and relatively rapidly over the road. When they reached Bozeman's ferry on the Yellowstone River, they found that it had been abandoned "on account of Indians."

Creigh arrived in Virginia City on October 1 and helped unload the machinery at Christenot's mill near Summit in upper Alder Gulch. He remained in Montana, working as the managing clerk at the mill. In 1869 he moved to Brownville, Nebraska, where he and a partner started a drug store. In 1873 he married Mary McClelland Irvin, who was from his hometown of Mercersburg. They lived in Lincoln for two years, where Creigh served in the office of the state auditor. In 1875 they moved to Omaha, and he became associated with the C. F. Goodman wholesale drug firm until 1883 and then entered the real estate business. He lived in Omaha for the remainder of his life, actively involving himself in civic affairs in the city and statewide. He died May 16, 1909.[11]

Creigh seems to have had future readers in mind when he wrote his diary, for he was unusually detailed in his descriptions. He elaborately described his wagon and its contents, down to a three-foot flag that was attached to the front bow and waved overhead. He had fixed up

---

11. J. Sterling Morton and Albert Watkins, *History of Nebraska* (Lincoln, Nebr.: n.p., 1913), 3:436.

the inside of his wagon with bedding and bags laid over the machinery in the bottom, so that it was comfortable to ride in. It was also well stocked with reading material, and Creigh called it the "Reading Room."

Creigh's diary provides significant commentary on the social dynamics of a freight train rather than an emigrant train. His was a typical 1860s freighting outfit comprising a diverse group of men. Many of the teamsters were veterans of the Union or Confederate armies. Some were foreign born, recently arrived in the United States. Although the train was well organized, the men were often difficult to control. Thomas wrote about problems with rebellious and scheming teamsters and about how these problems were resolved. He must have been somewhat of a diplomat, since he seems to have been respected by the men with whom he worked.

Creigh's diary clearly reveals his personality traits. He was a voracious reader, naming the titles of the books, magazines, and newspapers he was continually reading. When he could find newspapers at the forts, he was extremely interested in reading the latest news. He also had strong opinions. He expressed vehement anti-Mormon views and made deprecating comments about the western soldiers. He thought not only that the soldiers were more trouble than they were worth, but also that they were not doing their jobs. At one point, frustrated by the delays the soldiers caused his train, he angrily wrote, "<u>Emigrants have to protect U.S. troops.</u>"

Creigh's original diary is in the possession of his descendants, who loaned it to historian James C. Olson in 1948. Olson transcribed the diary and placed a copy in the Nebraska State Historical Society archives. It appears to be an accurate transcription. Olson published a lightly edited version of the diary in *Nebraska History*, which is the source document for the diary that follows. Thomas Creigh's diary is a fascinating document with which to end this collection. It superbly expresses the essence of a successful Bozeman Trail experience: hard work, caution, cooperation, and confidence.

THOMAS ALFRED CREIGH DIARY

[Creigh left his home in Mercersburg, Pennsylvania, on May 17 and traveled by railroad, by way of Indianapolis and St. Louis, to St. Joseph, Missouri. At St. Joseph he picked up the wagons, which had been transported by steamboat, and traveled overland from St. Joseph to Nebraska City. The mill machinery had been shipped in April from Pittsburgh on the steamboat Nile *and arrived in Nebraska City on June 14. He supervised loading the machinery onto the wagons during the next few days. Half of the train started from Nebraska City on June 20, and Creigh started out with the second half three days later.]*

[June] 23—Breakfasted at 3 A.M. Pulled out [with] second wing of train at 7 A.M. Considerable trouble in crossing slough—a number of [wagon] tongues broken— First part of train started a new corral 7 miles from Neb. City at 2 P.M.[12] balance of train came up during afternoon and evening. Windy & Hot. Mess consists of [J.] Cook, Simpson, Vandergriff, Small & Myself—We have in our train four ladies—Mrs [Margaret] Christenot Sr.[13] Mrs. [Martha] Christenot Jr.[14] Miss [Amelia] Christenot[15] & Miss Smith.[16] The train consists of 235 Yoke of cattle, 52 wagons divided into two wings. Joe Richards, Wagonmaster Bowman and Sam C. Moore Assist. There is 81 tons of Machinery including 2 Boilers—5 wagons of Provisions & 5 private wagons of [B. F.] Christenot.[17] May God spare our lives and take us to our destination (Virginia City Montana Ter) in safety. How many anxious hearts are now turned towards this train, and many fervent prayers in our behalf. May we all meet again.

[June] 24—Sunday—Beautiful Morn—up at 5 am. We are now beyond civilization, where Sunday is unknown

12. The camp was at or near the terminus of the steam wagon's overland attempt and also the juncture where the Oxbow Trail branched off from the Nebraska City Cutoff.

13. Mrs. Christenot Sr. was Frederick Christenot's wife Margaret.

14. Mrs. Christenot Jr. was Charles F. Christenot's wife Martha. Charles had married Martha Craig Wilton, a Civil War widow, on May 9, 1866, in Illinois. Traveling with them was Martha's three-year-old daughter Alice Wilton. Martha was pregnant for nearly the entire journey, as she gave birth to the first of nine children by Charles on March 28, 1867. Following Charles's death in 1886, Martha married his brother B. F. Christenot, whom she divorced three years later.

15. Miss Christenot is probably Miss Amelia Christenot, who was registered at the International Hotel in Virginia City in October 1867 along with other Christenot family members.

16. Miss Smith is undoubtedly Azubah Smith, a relative of the Christenots. Azubah Smith married B. F. Christenot on October 16, 1867, in Virginia City. *Virginia City Montana Post*, October 19, 1867.

17. The *Virginia City Montana Post*, October 6, 1866, reported that a train of 52 wagons arrived in Summit City on October 2 and that Joseph Richards was in charge of the train bringing two quartz mills and machinery for Frank Christ[e]not.

18. From their camp they began traveling on the Nebraska City Cutoff. A few miles from camp they crossed North Fork Little Nemaha River just south of present Dunbar, nine miles from Nebraska City, and went on a couple of miles and stopped for noon camp.

19. In the afternoon they probably traveled about five miles and camped at Brownell Creek, two miles east of present Syracuse.

20. Creigh had been a clerk at the Pawnee reservation on the Loup River. The Indian agency at Genoa where he lived was not far from his present location.

21. Although chips (dried dung) commonly referred to buffalo chips, cattle chips were more available to the travelers in the 1860s.

except in the name, when it will be observed in this country. Having none of the privileges of the day here we travel on the day, believing it but little if any worse than laying in a camp, when most likely card playing &c would be the order of the day. Broke camp at 8 A.M.[18] Crossed the little Nemaha River [North Fork Little Nemaha River] at 11 AM—Halted at 1 PM. Started at 4 P.M. drove till 8 P.M.—10 miles.[19] Heard from front wing of our train—10 miles in advance of us.

[Creigh's train traveled on the Nebraska City Cutoff to the Platte River, where it intersected the older Oxbow Trail just west of present Doniphan, Nebraska. The junction was forty miles east of Fort Kearny. In addition to recording daily activities and miles traveled, he noted he was reading Harper's Magazine, *Erastus Beadle's* Home Monthly, *and Victor Hugo's* Toilers of the Sea. *He also added such comments as "Suffering with toothache" and "Spent the afternoon whilst traveling, learning to play cribbage."]*

July 4th Wednesday. Clear—To day we <u>celebrate</u> the 91st anniversary of Am.[erican] Ind.[ependence]   How? Crossing the great Am.[erican] Plains in a "bull" [ox] train. One year ago I spent this day at the "Pawnee Indian Reservation" 120 miles from Omaha.[20] Today 160 miles from Neb. City. Three years I have missed celebrating this day in the good old Penna. style. We broke corall at 4 AM, driving till 9 AM. Spent an hour in washing clothes, my first experience in that line of business, <u>succeeded well</u>. Dined with the Misses Smith & Christenot, & Mr. F. Morrill in company with [J.] Cook, [Joe] Richards, Bowman, & [Sam] Moore on oyster stew, Peaches, Tomatoes, Pudding &c—after[ward] assisted in breaking a dozen Scotch Ale, a present from Lathrop of St. Joe, to J. Cook conditionaly to be broken on this day. Long live Lathrop. Broke corall at 4 P.M. drove till 7 P.M. To day the battle flags of all Penna. Reg[imen]ts are to be presented to the state at Phila, long will we remember the old 120 P. V. Infty [120th Pennsylvania Volunteer Infantry]. may her flags occupy a conspicuous place. Spent the day whilst traveling in wagon reading Hugo's "Toilers of the Sea." Began to day a regular mess of our own. No wood through this country, using "chips" to cook.[21] Roads on through the Platte River bottoms— level and sandy. Went to camp of right wing in evening with Cook & Morrill, entertained with songs &c.

July 5th 1866 Thursday—Clear—Broke corall at 4:30 AM drove till 9 A.M. passing through Valley City,[22] bought and issued clothing to men. Camped on bank of Platte. Broke corall at 2:45 P.M. halted at 5:30 two miles from Fort Kearney   Went to Fort in evening to the Post office, received two letters one from Sister Ellie, the other from Lizzie C.[ook] Fort K.[earny] contains only about a dozen soldiers commanded by Brig. Genl Wessel [Henry W. Wessells] of U.S.A.[23] Found my old acquaintances all gone. Lieuts. Mitchell and Evarts [Evans] having left yesterday.[24]

[During the next few days, Creigh recorded having wild ducks for supper one evening and playing eucher with the women in the train on another.]

Tuesday July 10. Clear—Cloudy only in morning. Broke corall at 4:30 AM. Passed the Mormon "Mule Train" for the third time since leaving Neb. City, Passed Granger Ranch at 7 AM. Camped at 8.30 AM. Had a bushel of ice to day, a perfect godsend to us in this country of poor water. The pasture has been poor for three days, eaten off by grasshoppers of which there is myriads. Walked during most of morning drive with the ladies. Broke corall at 3 P.M.

Have become acquainted with most of teamsters, nearly all are green hands in this business—they represent all parts of the country, from Maine & Michigan, to Texas, also embrace all classes. Among them are Nave [Navy] Captains, Lieuts. & privates, from both

22. A settlement of several buildings grew up at the junction of the Independence–St. Joe Road and the trails from Nebraska City nine miles east of Fort Kearny, variously known as Junction Station, Valley City, Valley Station, Hinshaw's Ranche, Hook's Station, and Dogtown. The name Dogtown came from a vast prairie dog town there.

23. The garrison at Fort Kearny was nearly depleted in summer 1866 from expired enlistments and the departure in late May of Colonel Henry B. Carrington's Eighteenth Infantry troops for Bozeman Trail duty. Furthermore, the transcontinental railroad was approaching Fort Kearny in 1866, rendering its military function obsolete. During his inspection of the fort in early May, General William T. Sherman commented that it would soon be abandoned, although it was not closed until 1871. Lieutenant Colonel (brevet Brigadier General) Henry W. Wessells, Eighteenth Infantry, was the commanding officer of Fort Kearny June to October 1866. D. Ray Wilson, *Fort Kearny on the Platte* (Dundee, Ill.: Crossroads Communications, 1980), 150, 161, 167–68, 199.

24. Creigh is most likely referring to Lieutenants Gavin Mitchell and Michael Evans, who had served one year with the Omaha Scouts on the Bozeman Trail and were mustered out July 16, 1866. Wilson, *Fort Kearny*, 159.

25. This photographer's identity is not known, but one of the best known emigrant trail artists and photographers, William Henry Jackson, was working for a freighting outfit in a train that was only a few days behind Creigh's. William Henry Jackson, *The Diaries of William Henry Jackson, Frontier Photographer: To California and Return, 1866–67; and with the Hayden Surveys to the Central Rockies, 1873; and to the Utes and Cliff Dwellings, 1874*, ed. LeRoy R. Hafen and Ann W. Hafen (Glendale, Calif.: Arthur H. Clark Co., 1959).

26. Earlier Creigh noted Beadle's monthly magazine, but here "Beadles" refers to the extremely successful Dime Novels published by Erastus Beadle. Beadle published his first dime paperback in 1860; portable and inexpensive, the novels sold extremely well during the Civil War.

27. A mosquito bar is another name for a mosquito net, netting that keeps out or "bars" mosquitoes.

28. John Kendall Gilman and his younger brother Jeremiah C. "Jud" Gilman established a road ranch and stage station in 1859 nearly eighty miles west of Fort Kearny. The ranch was seven miles due west of present Gothenburg, Nebraska. In 1931 the main two-story log building was dismantled and reassembled into a one-story log cabin in the Gothenburg town park.

the Northern and Southern armies during the late war. We also have a soldier of the English Army, who was wounded twice at the fall of Delhi, India. We have mechanics of all kinds. Clerks, telegraph operators, an artist & Photographer, but unfortunately without the crayon or paper or camera.[25] How we would like to have some sketches for future reference, when this country will be spanned with Rail Roads and this long wagon journey done away with forever. Then perhaps we could look upon them with more pleasure than we do now.

Every thing is progressing quickly and we are making extraordinary time for the first two weeks of the trip. As I travel along today writing as the wagon moves a short description of our wagon may not be uninteresting hereafter. We are hauled along by four yoke of cattle. Fastened in the front bow of wagon and waving over us is the "Stars and Stripes" about 3 ft. long. on the bottom of our wagon is heavy machinery filled up with blankets, tobacco &c for the men—canned fruit—a small keg of whiskey (for our own use) carpet sacks, mess kit &c—the blankets making a comfortable loafing place. This wagon is also termed the "Reading Room" having no small number of "Beadles" & other intersting reading matter.[26] We are not unarmed, for if we look in front of us we see a Spenser [Spencer] rifle—behind us a Henry rifle, on our left, strapped to the bows a Colts Navy & a Remingtons Revolver, above is tied a long knife & scabbard, also pistols in pockets. On looking around we also discover a violin, clothes & hair brushes, mosquitoes bars,[27] pipes, old clothes & boots and a general mixture of every thing that goes to make up <u>quarters</u>, inhabited only by <u>man</u>, Halted at 6.30 P.M. Passed several trains returning from the mountains. Camp 1/2 mile west of Gillmans Ranch.[28]

[Creigh's train continued up the south side of the South Platte River to the ford at Julesburg, passing several road ranches and Fort McPherson.]

July 19th. Thursday. Clear   Broke corall at 8 AM, drove to ford at Julesburg, commenced crossing immediately, crossing 9 teams at a time with from 10 to 12 yoke cattle—bottom sandy, water 4 ft in deepest places, everything worked well so far. The men of Bowmans wing rebelled this morning, refusing to yoke until certain demands (silly ones) were complied with. soon settled. Anticipated last night, trouble, and all reliable men were prepared for anything. Singular how one or two designing men can lead a camp.

Received at Julesburg two letters one from Lizzie [Cook] and one from [sister] Ellie, the former discouraged about her health. May God yet spare her life—a dear friend of mine. A conspiracy formed among a few of our men for a desperate act, but happily for those engaged it was discovered and preparations made to meet them, which they saw and remained quiet.

July 20th—Clear warm crossing balance of train all across safely at 2 P.M. The boilers & all—the boilers were brought over with 26 yoke of cattle & 15 drivers, the other [with] 48 yoke cattle and 21 drivers. Crossing the river has been a grand scene, one seldom witnessed, may I never have to cross it again. A treacherous stream, the bottom (if any) composed of quicksands. Cannot stop a team in a stream, for danger of sinking out of sight. May the rest of our journey be accomplished as speedily & successfully as these 400 miles. The river we looked upon as the worst on our route. that is now over and we are out of Nebraska, across the corner of Col.[orado] Ter[ritory] and now in Dakota Ter.

[From the crossing the train went north up Lodgepole Creek, went across the divide between the North and South Platte rivers, and came to the road on the south side of the North Platte near Courthouse Rock. Creigh walked to Courthouse Rock and tried to climb to the top, but he became so dizzy that he had to come down. As the train

For an informative family history of Gilman's ranch, see Musetta Gilman, *Pump on the Prairie* (Detroit: Harlo Press, 1975).

continued on to Fort Laramie, he described Chimney Rock, Scotts Bluff, Mitchell Pass, and other emigrant landmarks, and he noted that he finished reading another novel.]

Aug. 3rd 1866—Broke corral at 5:30 am. Cattle became mixed with the other herd causing delay. Corraled at 8:30 A.M. near Ft. Laramie remained corraled all day—received letters as follows—Father [Thomas Creigh] July 12th Mother [Jane M. Creigh] 14th [sister] Ellie at Indianapolis 16th enclosing one from from Maggie Beall. Wrote to father a long letter,[29] also P.[ost] M.[aster] Julesburg.

Aug. 4. Saturday. Broke corral at 6 am. Passed over Laramie River and thro' Ft. Laramie for inspection— recd a letter from Coz. [cousin] May, dated 23rd Uncle Alex McC. died 14th near 90 years old, death is a relief to him. Corraled at 10 am west of Fort. A view of the Rocky Mts [Laramie Mountains]—Seen Balt.[imore] Am.[erican] of 16th & 18th late news to us. Would that we could receive them every day. Broke corral at 3 P.M. drove over heavy sand bluffs with great difficulty, doubled on teams—corraled at 9 P.M.[30] Thunder shower in afternoon. Two men left us to day.

Sunday Aug. 5th—Broke corral at 5:30 am. returned to Fort [Laramie] with [Joe] Richards to settle with men that left us—Com'der [Major James Van Voast] decided in our favor[:] "Men leaving a train on the road not entitled to any pay". Came back to camp about 15 miles from Fort at 12 M. The longest horseback ride I have taken for many a day—feel tired after it. A threatened rebellion again amongst the teamsters, the Indian <u>scare</u> has <u>scared</u> most of them, demanding more arms. Broke corral at 2:30 P.M. and drove till 8:30 P.M. passing over hilly road, spurs of the mountains.[31] Poor grass, good water.

Monday Aug. 6th. Broke corral at 4:30 passing over very rough hills, (sand and lime mixed) Corraled at 9 AM in a cottonwood grove, near Platte River, a cool

29. A copy of this letter is included in the back of Creigh, *Hitting the Trail.* Creigh wrote that they would probably have to go by the "old road" because the Indians "are taking everything before them on the 'cutoff' which we hoped to travel." As he was writing, he learned from post commander Major James Van Voast that they would be allowed to proceed on the Bozeman Trail. Van Voast had been waiting for their train so that he could send a train transporting supplies to Fort Reno with them for added strength.

30. They took the Hill Road that went over the hills west of Fort Laramie, which required double-teaming their oxen to pull their heavier loads through the sand.

31. They went through the hills south of present Guernsey, Wyoming, today known for the deep ruts in the sandstone.

pleasant place for men to camp after being for weeks without seeing a tree—but grass scarce. Cattle looking thin. Broke corral at 2:30 P.M. drove till 6 passing over Horse Shoe Creek and corraled on bank [of Horseshoe Creek] and at forks of road, the left leading to Salt Lake via Ft. Halleck [Fort Bridger]   hand board says 425 m[ile]'s to Virginia City.[32]

[The train drove to the North Platte and traveled along the south bank to Bridger's Ferry. They forded the river rather than crossing on the ferry. It may be that the ferry was no longer operating, or Creigh's train may not have wanted to wait in line.]

Aug. 9—Anniversary (one of my happiest days—but alas all is over in this mode)   Remained in corral all day by order of Military Authorities, waiting on gov't train to come up.[33] <u>Emigrants have to protect U.S. Troops</u>.

Aug. 10—Remained in corral, still waiting, all day. Tiresome work, hope they will soon come.

Aug. 11th—Saturday—Broke corral at 5 AM   drove 10 miles for grass. Camped in a valley near [North Platte] river.[34] Our road to day hilly but good. Here we must wait again on the government train—three days already lost. Would that there was no military force in this country. Our delays cost more ten times than their protection, for it amounts to nothing. There is to day 90 wagons of us camped in this little valley 4 miles square about, Reading "John Halifax—Gentleman", by Mrs. Murdock—good.[35]

[The train remained in corral the next day, and while they traveled on the following day Creigh read Jane Eyre.*]*

[Aug. 14—Tuesday]   Broke corrall at 5:30 a.m. drove 8 miles over winding roads high hills and deep ravines [McKinstry Ridge] and corralled at 10 am in sight of last nights corrall. Some singular formations of rock. And much [illegible word] sheet isinglass [mica].[36] Broke corrall at 3 P.M. a return to our old and regular drives.

32. The south-side road forked on the west side of the Horseshoe Creek crossing, where a sign indicated the distance to Virginia City via the Bozeman Trail. The main road, or left fork, stayed on the south side of the North Platte River to the crossing at present Casper, Wyoming, and then went to Salt Lake City via Fort Bridger. Creigh is mistaken that the left fork went by Fort Halleck, which was on the Overland Trail to the south that went through Bridger Pass. The right fork, which Creigh took, went to the North Platte crossing at Bridger's Ferry.

33. They were waiting for the army supply train that Major Van Voast ordered to travel with Creigh's train.

34. They camped on the east side of the North Platte River at present Douglas, Wyoming.

35. Dinah Maria Mulock Craik, *John Halifax, Gentleman* (1856).

36. Theodore Bailey noted isinglass by the roadside farther north, on the Bozeman Trail. Bailey diary, June 19, 1866.

May we now pass speedily on without any obstructions. Not very well today—headache—corralled at 5:30 P.M. near [North] Platte River where the Old Mormon and California road leaves us.[37] This was the old original road to Utah & Cal. but more lately not used [to go to Montana] on account of its being too long. We here leave the Platt River which we have followed for 600 miles and go due north.[38]

37. They camped on the north bank of the North Platte River at the turnoff to the Bozeman Trail, two miles west of the site of Fort Fetterman on the opposite side of the river.

Aug. 15—Wednesday   Broke corral at 5 AM passing over rolling prairies, with some heavy sands   corraled on Sage Creek (15 miles) at 12:30 P.M. Alkali water and no grass here. Broke corral at 5 P.M. drove till 7 P.M. no water, little grass—23 miles to day.

38. They left the North Platte River and turned onto the Bozeman Trail east of the mouth of Sage Creek.

Aug. 16th Thursday—Broke at 4:30 AM   passing over a rolling prairie. we were suddenly coraled at 8:30 by the return of Joe Richards (wagon master) who had run into a small party of Indians (Cheyenne) [Sioux] whilst ahead of train 4 miles looking for water—Said Indians chasing him 3 miles, within sight of our train. Having corralled all trains, we waited an attack for two hours nearly, but as no demonstration was made, except the appearance of 5 or 6 on a bluff opposite, we again started our wing of train in the advance—drove 3 miles to water and corraled. Passed on our road four graves, marked with names &c killed by Indians July 24th[39]   Many signs of a battle having been fought there. A paper picked up says "A train of 36 wagons 40 men some women and children corraled by Indians two days["] This is our first sign of hostile Indians, may we have no further trouble than to day. The gov't train which has led us so far, fell in rear of us after this small scare.

39. These were the graves of four of the men killed in the attack on Nathan Floyd's and Charles Barton's trains between Brown Springs and the Dry Fork of the Cheyenne on July 24. Davis Willson and Samuel Finley Blythe described the engagement in their July 29 entries.

Broke corral at 5 P.M. Our wing & train in advance except the mule train. Another scare this evening. When we had corraled a messenger arrived saying Martins train (in rear) was attacked and scattered all over the country—and fighting. Soon however it appeared that they had seen five Indians at a distance but had made no demonstration. All excitement during night but no reappearance of any Indians.

Aug. 17—Broke corral at 5 am camped at Humphrivill [Humfreville] camp at 8:30. Water & grass tolerably good. Broke corral at 2:30 P.M. crossed Middle Fork Cheyenne River [Sand Creek], heavy quicksands corraled at 5 P.M. travelling only 3 miles—Another uncalled for Indian scare owing to Bowmans exciteability. Thunder Storm in afternoon with some hail, causing us to corral on road for half hour. The rain has filled all the streams with water a great blessing to our cattle, they having suffered for want of it.

August 18th Saturday. Broke corral at 4:30 AM crossed North Cheyenne River [Antelope Creek] and corraled at 8. On guard last night from 12 till daylight— Broke corral at 2:30 drove till 6 P.M. and finding some water at Antelope Springs[40] unexpectedly we corraled to water and get supper. Broke corral at 8 P.M. and drove till 10 P.M. The thunder storm of yesterday has been a great blessing to us filling the streams that are usual[ly] dry.

August 19—Broke corral at 4:30 AM drove till 9 AM. Corraled on Dry Creek [Dry Fork Powder River]—a little water in it now. Our road for some days has laid over a rolling prairie. To day we pass the "Three Buttes" [Pumpkin Buttes] and are in sight of the "Snowy Range" [Bighorn Mountains] the top is now covered with snow— a singular appearance for middle August. Made usual drive in afternoon—Wrote a letter to [sister] Ellie—mailed 20th.

Aug. 20. Monday Broke corral at 5 am. my wagon was upset with me in it—near 4000 weight of machinery on top of me—completely fastened under it—but escaped, miraculously without a scratch or bruise. Corraled at 9 A.M. Broke corral at 1 P.M. drove to <u>Fort Reno</u> at 3 P.M. & corraled. Broke corral at 5 P.M. and drove till 9 P.M.—10 miles.

40. The springs, about five miles north of Antelope Creek, were also known as Curtis Springs in military documents.

Aug. 21—1866 Broke corral at 4:15 AM. drove till 8 am about 4 miles, delayed crossing a muddy stream. Broke corral at 1 P.M. Drove till 8 P.M. 14 miles corraled on "Crazy Woman Forks" [Crazy Woman Creek].

Aug. 22 Wednesday Broke corral at 4:30 am. crossed Crazy Woman Forks. Made one bridge and cut out bank of east fork—west fork good crossing— corraled after crossing. Broke corral at 3:15 P.M.—drove till 6:30 P.M.—no water good grass.

Aug. 23. Thursday Broke corral at 5 AM—upset both boiler wagons within half mile of each other—no damage delayed three hours. Corraled at 9:30 am. Broke corral at 2 P.M. drove till 8 P.M.—14 miles passing thro the most fertile valleys we have yet seen—beautiful. good grass & water. Camp on Clear Creek.

Aug. 24—Broke corral at 5 AM crossed Rock Creek and corraled at 7:30 AM continuation of [Clear Creek] valley passed thro yesterday—Broke corral at 1 P.M. corraled at 5 P.M.

Aug. 25 Saturday Broke corral at 4:45 AM corraled at 7:30 AM on 1st Piney Fork [Little Piney Creek], close to "Fort Philip Kearney" Walked to Fort [Phil Kearny] (1 1/2 miles) met Jeff, Megeath & Dr. [Samuel M.] Horton.[41] Train moved across 2nd Piney Fork and corraled at 5 P.M.

Aug. 26 Broke corral at 5 AM drove 5 hours & made 5 miles. Corraled on small creek [Prairie Dog Creek]. Broke corral at 2 P.M. drove till 7 P.M. passed an old volcano, many traces of its work.

[August] 27—Monday—Broke corral at 5 AM drove to Goose Creek and corraled at 9:30 am—We had yesterday the first buffalo of the trip. Broke corral at 1 P.M. drove till 6 P.M. Our train killed a buffalo to day. Road hilly. No water tonight.

[August] 28—Tuesday—Broke corral at 4 AM drove till 9 AM—plenty of buffalo along the road corraled on

41. "Jeff" and "Megeath" are unknown. Dr. Samuel M. Horton was the post surgeon at Fort Phil Kearny. His wife Sallie Knox Dunnica Horton was also at the fort. Father Barry Hagan, "Samuel Miller Horton," in Fort Phil Kearny/Bozeman Trail Association, *Portraits of Fort Phil Kearny: Civilian, Military and Native American* (Banner, Wyo.: Fort Phil Kearny/ Bozeman Trail Association, 1993), 136–41.

N.[orth] F.[ork] Tongue River [Tongue River]. Broke corral at 4 P.M.—Three head of cattle missing. After starting three men went to hunt them—found them surrounded by Indians. Indians drove them to camp, attacked the train—got one mule from [illegible] yard—but was recaptured—a number of shots fired but no damage done. All our trains corraled on road. Halted one hour—awaited further attack—not being made drove three miles and corraled. Indians numbered from 30 to 50—Arrapahoes.[42]

[August] 29—Wednesday—Broke corral at 3:30 AM. Corraled at 8 A.M. on small creek [Twin Creek]. Broke corral at 1 P.M.—drove till 4:30 corraled on small creek [Little Bighorn River].

[August] 30—Thursday Broke corral at 5 A.M. drove till 8 AM crossed S.[outh] F.[ork] Horn River [Lodge Grass Creek] & coraled. We were aroused suddenly last night at 12—by the alarm of Indians—stampeding our stock but all was soon quiet, could not discover the cause of alarm among the cattle. Broke corral at 1 P.M. drove till 6 P.M.

August 31st Rain last night compeled us to remain in camp till 11 AM when we drove till 2:30, coraling on N[orth] F[ork] Little Horn River [Rotten Grass Creek]. Broke corral at 5 P.M. drove till 6:30 P.M. and corraled, night being cloudy—too dark to drive.

September 1st. Rain nearly all night. Awoke this morning to see the mountains all around us white with snow, which fell during the night. The road being slippery with mud on hills cannot make an early start. Broke corral at 9 AM. drove till 11 AM, coraled on Rotten Grass Creek [Soap Creek] Broke corral at 4 PM drove till 7 P.M.—corraled on Rotten Grass Creek [Soap Creek].

September 2nd. Broke corral at 5 AM drove till 8 AM corraled on Big Horn River near ferry & three miles from "Fort C.F. Smith" Not being able to ford

42. Although Creigh identifies the raiders as Arapahos, they were more likely warriors from Red Cloud's camps of mostly Sioux located downstream on the Tongue River.

this river, are compelled to wait & ferry at $5 per wagon.

<u>September 3, Monday</u>. Broke corral at 5 am   drove up to ferry. Commenced ferrying at 10 am   finished Martin's wing of train at 7 P.M.

Sept. 4 Tuesday   Still crossing train—the Left wing will be over to day. Prospecting for gold some good signs on the river—wrote to [sister] Ellie—

Sept. 5—Wednesday. Both boilers landed safe on North side of river at 9:30 am. Broke corral at 12 M [noon] drove till 5 P.M.[43]

Sept. 6th. Broke corral at 5 am   drove till 8:30 am. corraled on small creek [Muddy Creek]. Broke corral at 12:30 P.M. driving about 4 miles over very hilly roads, crossed three creeks [branches of Buster Creek] and corraled at 6 P.M.

Sept. 7th   Broke corral at 5 am   passed over a miserably hilly road and corraled on creek at 12 M. Sam's [Sam Moore's] Boiler upset again this AM—delayed two hours but no damage done   a party of Indians are now (1 o'clock P.M.) passing us on the bluffs 1/2 mile distant— suppose them to be Crows, who are friendly. Corraled at 6 P.M. on creek. Overtook Indians who turn out to be Sioux on the war path, but only numbering twenty, fear our numbers and pretend to be friendly, begging tobacco &c. Their war paint, dress &c show them to be hostile. They are mounted on American horses, which are shod, showing that they have been recently captured, they have also a lot of gov't clothing sabers &c—Would not tell their tribe. Cloudy & rain—Hilly roads. (Passed thro' Pryor's Gap [Devil's Gap] this P.M.)

Saturday—Sept. 8th 1866   Cold & rainy. Indians stole a mule, our best one, from corral last night, by cutting the rope. Remained in corral all day, cold rain, snowing on mountains [Pryor Mountains] a few miles from us.

September 9—Clear & pleasant—Indians attempted to steal mules last night, but failed. Broke corral at 8:45

43. They probably camped near Gold Springs, six miles west of the 1866 ferry crossing. The springs were on the new route that James Sawyers opened in August 1866. The campground at Gold Springs became known as the ox team camp, since it was a day's drive from the Bighorn for ox teams. The faster mule and horse teams would usually go four miles farther after departing the ferry to the mule and horse camp on Muddy Creek.

A.M. drove till 12 M. roads good (excepting one bad hill) but very circuitous good spring for men—Broke corral at 3 P.M. and drove till 6 P.M. corraled on a large creek [Pryor Creek], good grass.

Sept. 10th Broke corral at 5 AM drove up creek [Macheta Creek] 5 miles and corraled on a dry creek at 12 M. making 13 1/2 miles this morning. Broke corral at 3 P.M. drove till 5 P.M. crossing Clark's Fork of Yellowstone River and corraling—small party of Indians met us and <u>escorted</u> us to our camp—on a begging expedition. The Crows are friendly but notorious thieves and beggars.

Sept. 11th Broke corral at 5 AM drove till 9 AM crossing the Clarks North Fork [Rock Creek] at 8 AM Broke corral at 1.30 P.M. drove till 6 P.M. road hilly for a mile—crossed Clarks fork this A.M. at 8—and a creek at 5 P.M.—followed up Clarks North Fork [Rock Creek] till we struck a creek—name unknown [Red Lodge Creek]. Bathed & washed a <u>little</u> cool for bathing.

Sept. 12th. Wednesday. Broke corral at 5 AM drove till 11 AM crossed a large creek [Red Lodge Creek] at 9 AM followed creek all morning. Broke down a "pan wagon" breaking the pan, causing a delay of 1 1/2 hours (Sam's [Sam Moore's] wing of train)[44] Broke corral at 2:30 P.M. drove till 6 P.M. camped on a hill, no water, poor grass—roads all day hilly & sidling. Sams wing upset another wagon this P.M.

September 13th Broke corral at 5.15 AM drove till 9.30 AM over very hilly roads. Camped on a small creek. Broke corral at 1:30 and corraled at 6 P.M. having terribly hilly roads and fording two creeks. Camp on creek [Rosebud Creek].

Sept. 14th. Broke corral at 5 AM traveled up a creek all morning and crossed two small creeks[45] forded large creek at Ropers Ferry[46] and corraled at 9:30 AM—road level & good. Broke corral at 1 P.M. drove till 7 P.M. road hilly & rough—dry camp.

44. The "pan wagon" was the wagon carrying one of the large pans for the Chilian roller mill they were transporting.

45. They went down Rosebud Creek, crossed it above its mouth, and went up the south side of the Stillwater River seven miles to the earlier crossing. This was the new route opened by Jim Bridger on August 25. From the crossing they traveled northwest on Stockade Hill. Blythe diary, August 25, 1866.

46. "Ropers Ferry" was probably either at the Rosebud Creek or Stillwater River crossing. It may have been what was left of a makeshift ferry left by a previous party. No other diarist mentions it.

Sept. 15th 1866   Broke corral at 5 AM   drove till 12
M. and corraled on creek of good water. Road good
except last mile, which is terrible hill, very long &
steep.[47] Broke corral at 5 P.M. drove till 6:30 P.M. crossing
creek [Bridger Creek] and corraling on the long and
anxiously look[ed] for Yellowstone River.

47. This was the steep
descent to the
Yellowstone Valley
off the point of
the bluffs, just east
of the mouth of
Bridger Canyon.

Sept. 16th Sunday   Broke corral at 5 AM   drove till
10 AM our road leading up the river—passed three
graves "Killed by Indians Aug 23 24" [William Thomas
party] Broke corral at 2 P.M. drove till 7 P.M.—crossing
a river [Boulder River] near junction with Yellowstone, a
very rocky and difficult ford. Corraled on west bank—in
corral till 12 o'clock.

Sept. 17th, 1866   Broke corral at 5:30 AM   drove till
4 P.M.—corraling at ford of Yellowstone. Found
evacuated ranch [at John Bozeman's ferry] on account of
Indians.[48] Snowing, raining and very unpleasant day.

48. This was the log
cabin at John Bozeman's
ferry east of present
Springdale.

September 18th 1866. Commenced fording the
Yellowstone at 8:30 AM. Met with a serious accident,
drowned 3 yoke and one steer in one team, unable by
any means to release them, were compelled to stand and
look at the poor brutes drowning. Water too cold for
man to stand it long enough to help them—raining &
snowing all day—finished crossing at 12.30 M. all except
the pan wagon attached to drowned team.

Sept. 19th Snowing & raining in morning. Began to
take out wagon & machinery lost in river—J. C.[ook]
left us this A.M., going ahead, took one wagon with him
to send back provisions from first ranch, we are entirely
out of flour, bacon and everything. A sad sight to sit and
look at our poor cattle (7 head) still fastened to the
wagon in river by their yokes & chains. By the use of a
flat boat, fortunately found at this deserted ferry we are
enabled to unload part of the machinery. Succeded this
evening in bringing to shore the wagons & pan, all safe
except one fore wheel.

Sept. 20 Thursday Clear and very cold & windy—Broke corral at 9 A.M.—passed some hot boiling springs [Hunters Hot Springs]. These springs are about 20 in number in 200 ft. square, all large springs, and strong sulpher. The water at the spring is a boiling heat. There is also a cold spring not over 50 ft from these. Corraled at 12.30 P.M. Broke corral at 2 P.M. and corraled at 7.30 P.M. Roads hilly but good—Corraled on Yellowstone in a beautiful little valley high mountains on every side.

Sept. 21—Friday. Broke corral at 5 AM a high & rough hill [Sheep Mountain] just at camp. This hill is over a mile & half long and very dangerous, having many short curves and but a single track looking down over high precipices. Corraled at 12 M making about 6 miles. Broke corral at 4 P.M. corraled at 6:30 P.M. making about 4 miles, delayed by upseting pan wagon [in] "Sam's" [Sam Moore's] train—both corrals on Yellowstone.

Sept. 22—Left the Yellowstone at 5 AM, crossed two small creeks and Browns Spring about three miles apart—and corraled at small creek at 11 AM—9 miles—Broke corral at 2 P.M. drove till 6 P.M. about 4 m's. Snow storm all P.M.—met provisions wagon sent ahead four days ago.

Sept. 23—Sunday Snowing—Broke corral at 10 AM drove till 12 making two miles. Compelled to halt owing to snow, making the roads almost impassable. For several days we have met many miners who are going to Yellowstone to go east on Mackinaw boats.[49] they report times dull, and everything cheap. Remained corraled all day. Ceased snowing at 2 P.M. but still cloudy & threatening.

Sept. 24th Monday Cold & cloudy—Broke corral at 5 AM drove till 11 AM making about three miles, road vey muddy and hilly had to make new roads, bridges &c—Broke corral at 2:45 P.M. and drove till 6 PM about 3 miles.

49. A fleet of sixteen Mackinaw boats belonging to C. A. Head with 250 miners left the Yellowstone boat launching site south of present Livingston on September 27, bound for St. Joseph, Missouri, arriving there twenty days later. *St. Joseph (Mo.) Herald*, November 8, 1866.

Sept. 25th   Broke corral at 5 AM and ascended a high
& steep mountain   doubled on all teams, drove over the
"divide" [Bozeman Pass] and a miserably stony, hilly,
sidling road   our wing passed over safely and corraled
on creek [Kelly Creek] at 6 PM (4 miles)   Sam's boiler
upset detaining him, at this time he has not reached us.

Sept. 26th   Wednesday   Broke corral at 5 AM   drove
till 10 AM   crossing branch of Gallatin River [East
Gallatin River] and corral. We are now in the [Gallatin]
valley, and once more in civilization   passed thro'
Bosemans City   our corral is beside a <u>wheat</u> field,
shocked & the field fenced. It seems like a new world to
see fences & grain fields. We can see Sam's [Sam Moore's]
wing of train on the top of the "divide" where they upset
yesterday. Don't know what damage was done—Broke
corral at 2 PM   drove till 6 PM.—Corraled on creek.

Sept. 27th 1866   Broke corral at 7.30 am   drove till 1
PM crossing the Gallatin River   good fording, corral on
west bank. met some "masons" [Masons]   Broke corral
at 3 P.M. drove till 6 P.M.—dry camp—We are now in the
midst of Gallatin Valley—a beautiful valley and much of
it under cultivation.

Sept. 28th   Broke corral at 7 AM   drove till 10 AM
corralled on small creek. Broke corral at 1 PM   drove to
Madison River   crossed and corraled.

Sept. 29—Broke corral at 7:30 AM   Sam's [Sam
Moore's] wing overtook us this AM   drove till 10.30 AM
and corraled on small creek [Hot Springs Creek]. Broke
corral at 2 P.M.—upset "pan wagon" and drove till 6 PM
and corraled on small creek. Broke corral—& near
some hot sulpher springs [Norris Hot Springs].[50] We
passed to day some new quartz claims, reported as
paying well.

Sept. 30th. Broke corral at 6 AM   drove till 10 AM.
Broke corral at 3 PM. drove till 6 PM   met [B. F.]
Christenot & [J.] Cook.

50. Norris Hot Springs
are on Hot Springs
Creek, at present Norris,
Montana. Abram
Voorhees also described
these springs. Voorhees
diary, August 8, 1864.

October 1st Broke corral at 6 AM drove to 12 mile house and corraled. J. Cook and myself left train at 12 M and went into Vir[ginia] City spent the day there.

October 2—In Virg. City till 3 P.M. fixing up a'c [accounts] of men [who] came out & met train at the "Lakes".

Oct. 3—Wednesday—Broke corral at 10 am drove up near [Christenot's] mill and corraled half of train. Left the other half back, having to double on all teams.

Oct. 4—Commenced taking machinery down to mill—<u>here we cease</u>.[51]

51. The Christenot mill was in Spring Gulch, one and a half miles east of Summit, in upper Alder Gulch, six miles south of Virginia City. The community at the mill was Union City, so named because all the men living there reportedly voted the straight Union ticket in an election. The Chilian mill replaced a mule-driven Spanish *arastra*, which Christenot had constructed in winter 1864–65.

Further Reading

FOR A COMPREHENSIVE STUDY of the emigrant period of the Bozeman Trail and thirty-three diaries and reminiscences, see Susan Badger Doyle, ed., *Journeys to the Land of Gold: Emigrant Diaries from the Bozeman Trail, 1863–1866*, 2 vols. (Helena: Montana Historical Society Press, 2000). Until the publication of *Journeys*, the standard histories of the Bozeman Trail were Grace Raymond Hebard and E. A. Brininstool, *The Bozeman Trail*, 2 vols. (1922; repr., Lincoln: University of Nebraska Press, 1990); and Dorothy M. Johnson, *The Bloody Bozeman* (1971; repr., Missoula, Mont.: Mountain Press Publishing Co., 1983). Both are based on primary material but focus strongly on the military period of the trail. For an inclusive biographical approach to the trail's history, see Fort Phil Kearny/Bozeman Trail Association, *Portraits of Fort Phil Kearny: Civilian, Military and Native American* (Banner, Wyo.: Fort Phil Kearny/Bozeman Trail Association, 1993).

Compilations of primary Bozeman Trail material include Margaret Brock Hanson, ed., *Powder River Country: The Papers of J. Elmer Brock* (Cheyenne, Wyo.: Frontier Printing, 1981); Montana Historical Society, *Not in Precious Metals Alone: A Manuscript History of Montana* (Helena: Montana Historical Society, 1976); and *The Books and Photos of Elsa Spear* (Sheridan, Wyo.: The Fort Phil Kearny/Bozeman Trail Association, 1987).

Secondary works on the military period of the trail's history include Dee Brown, *The Fetterman Massacre* (1971; repr., Lincoln: University of Nebraska Press, 1973); and Robert A. Murray, *Military Posts in the Powder River Country of Wyoming, 1865–1894* (1968; repr., Buffalo, Wyo.: The Office, 1990). American imperialism, particularly as expressed by the establishment of military posts in Indian-occupied territory, is a major theme in D. W. Meinig, *The Shaping of America: A Geographical Perspective on 500 Years of History*, vol. 2, *Continental America, 1800–1867* (New Haven, Conn.: Yale University Press, 1993).

Published primary military sources include George P. Belden, *The White Chief*, ed. James S. Brisbin (1870; repr., Athens: Ohio University Press, 1974); William Haymond Bisbee, *Through Four American Wars: The Impressions and Experiences of Brigadier General William Henry Bisbee* (Boston: Meador Publishing Co., 1931); J. Lee Humfreville, *Twenty Years among Our Savage Indians* (1897; repr., New York: Hunter, 1903); James D. Lockwood, *Life and Adventures of a Drummer Boy* (Albany, N.Y.: John Skinner, 1893); and Alson B. Ostrander, *An Army Boy of the Sixties* (Yonkers-on-Hudson, N.Y.: World Book Co., 1924).

For accounts by officers' wives on the Bozeman Trail, see Merrill J. Mattes, ed., *Indians, Infants, and Infantry: Andrew and Elizabeth Burt on the Frontier* (1960; repr., Lincoln: University of Nebraska Press, 1989); Frances C. Carrington, *My Army Life and the Phil Kearney Massacre* (1910; repr., Boulder, Colo.: Pruett Publishing Co., 1990); and Margaret I. Carrington, *Absaraka: Home of the Crows* (1868; repr., Lincoln: University of Nebraska Press, 1983).

On the Connor campaign and its relation to the Bozeman Trail, see Doyle, *Journeys to the Land of Gold*, 1:340–45. Standard works on the campaign are Leroy R. Hafen, and Ann W. Hafen, eds., *Powder River Campaigns and Sawyers Expedition of 1865* (Glendale, Calif.: Arthur H. Clark Co., 1961); and Fred Blackburn Rogers, *Soldiers of the Overland* (San Francisco: Grabhorn Press, 1938). For a full discussion of the Sawyers Wagon Road Expedition and diaries by three members of the train, see Doyle, *Journeys to the Land of Gold*, 1:340–419.

On the cultural history of the northern Plains tribes in the region traversed by the Bozeman Trail and their responses to the intruding Americans, see Susan Badger Doyle, "Indian Perspectives of the Bozeman Trail," *Montana The Magazine of Western History*, 40 (Winter 1990), 56–67. For Sioux culture, see James R. Walker, *Lakota Society*, ed. Raymond J. DeMallie (Lincoln: University of Nebraska Press, 1982); and Royal B. Hassrick, *The Sioux: Life and Customs of a Warrior Society* (Norman: University of Oklahoma Press, 1964). Important works on the two major Sioux tribes involved in Bozeman Trail affairs are George E. Hyde, *Red Cloud's Folk: A History of the Oglala Sioux Indians* (Norman: University of Oklahoma Press, 1937, 1975); and George E. Hyde, *Spotted Tail's Folk: A History of the Brulé Sioux* (Norman: University of Oklahoma Press, 1961).

Discussions of intertribal warfare on the northern plains include, Frank Raymond Secoy, *Changing Military Patterns of the Great Plains* (1953; repr., Lincoln: University of Nebraska Press, 1992); John C. Ewers, "Intertribal Warfare as the Precursor of Indian-White Warfare on the

Northern Great Plains," *Western Historical Quarterly,* 6 (October 1975), 397–410; Richard White, "The Winning of the West: The Expansion of the Western Sioux in the Eighteenth and Nineteenth Centuries," *Journal of American History,* 65 (September 1978), 319–43; and Anthony McGinnis, *Counting Coup and Cutting Horses: Intertribal Warfare on the Northern Plains, 1738–1889* (Evergreen, Colo.: Cordillera Press, 1990).

The nomadic pastoralist culture of the Plains Indian tribes is described in H. Clyde Wilson, "An Inquiry into the Nature of Plains Indian Cultural Development," American Anthropologist, 65 (April 1963), 355–69. For organization of tribal society, deterioration of habitat, and decline of bison on the northern plains, see Marshall D. Sahlins, *Tribesmen* (Englewood Cliffs, N.J.: Prentice-Hall, 1968); Elliott West, *The Way to the West: Essays on the Central Plains* (Albuquerque: University of New Mexico Press, 1995); and Charles E. Rankin, ed., *Legacy: New Perspectives on the Battle of the Little Bighorn* (Helena: Montana Historical Society Press, 1996).

Emigrant wagons are described in Michael A. Capps, "Wheels in the West: The Overland Wagon," *Overland Journal,* 8 (1990), 2–11. Comprehensive works on all types of wagons used in the West include Richard Dunlop, *Wheels West, 1590–1900* (Chicago: Rand McNally, 1977); and Nick Eggenhofer, *Wagons, Mules and Men* (New York: Hastings House, 1961). Emigrant draft animals are discussed in Robert L. Munkres, "Wagon Train Animals," *Wyoming Annals,* 65 (Summer/Fall 1993), 15–27. The importance of oxen to nineteenth-century Americans is examined in Verlyn Klinkenborg, "If It Weren't for the Ox, We Wouldn't Be Where We Are," *Smithsonian,* 24 (September 1993), 82–93.

Two informative sources on food and foodways in the emigrant trails era are Joseph R. Conlin, *Bacon, Beans, and Galantines: Food and Foodways on the Western Mining Frontier* (Reno: University of Nevada Press, 1986); and Jacqueline Williams, *Wagon Wheel Kitchens: Food on the Oregon Trail* (Lawrence: University Press of Kansas, 1993).

The landmark study of the first two decades of the Oregon-California trails corridor is John D. Unruh Jr., *The Plains Across: The Overland Emigrants and the Trans-Mississippi West, 1840–60* (Urbana: University of Illinois Press, 1979). More recent scholarly treatments of overland migration in broader contexts include Patricia Nelson Limerick, Clyde A. Milner II, and Charles E. Rankin, eds., *Trails: Toward a New Western History* (Lawrence: University of Kansas Press, 1991); and Richard White, *"It's Your Misfortune and None of My Own": A New History of the American West* (Norman: University of Oklahoma Press, 1991). For articles on all aspects of the western emigrant trails, see the *Overland*

Journal, the quarterly publication of the Oregon-California Trails Association.

For discussions of gendered experience on the emigrant trails, see Howard R. Lamar, "Rites of Passage: Young Men and Their Families in the Overland Trails Experience, 1843–69," in *"Soul-Butter and Hog Wash" and Other Essays on the American West*, ed. Thomas G. Alexander (Provo, Utah: Brigham Young University Press, 1978), 33–67; and John Mack Faragher, *Women and Men on the Overland Trail* (New Haven, Conn.: Yale University Press, 1979).

On the female emigrant experience, see Julie Roy Jeffrey, *Frontier Women: The Trans-Mississippi West, 1840–1880* (New York: Hill and Wang, 1979); Sandra L. Myres, *Westering Women and the Frontier Experience, 1800–1915* (Albuquerque: University of New Mexico Press, 1982); Lillian Schlissel, *Women's Diaries of the Westward Journey* (New York: Schocken Books, 1982); Glenda Riley, *The Female Frontier: A Comparative View of Women on the Prairie and the Plains* (Lawrence: University Press of Kansas, 1988); and Susan Armitage and Elizabeth Jameson, eds., *The Women's West* (Norman: University of Oklahoma Press, 1987).

The complex issues of emigrant social relations and legal behavior are examined in John Phillip Reid, *Law for the Elephant: Property and Social Behavior on the Overland Trail* (San Marino, Calif.: The Huntington Library, 1980), 136–81. An insightful examination of group dynamics in traveling communities is in Robert V. Hine, "Nomadic Communities on the Trail," in *Community on the American Frontier: Separate but Not Alone* (Norman: University of Oklahoma Press, 1980), 49–69.

INDEX